LGBT INCLUSION IN AMERICAN LIFE

LGBTQ POLITICS SERIES
General Editors: Susan Burgess and Heath Fogg Davis

Disrupting Dignity: Rethinking Power and Progress in LGBTQ Lives
Stephen M. Engel and Timothy S. Lyle

With Honor and Integrity: Transgender Military Personnel in Their Own Words
Edited by Máel Embser-Herbert and Bree Fram

LGBT Inclusion in American Life: Pop Culture, Political Imagination, and Civil Rights
Susan Burgess

LGBT Inclusion in American Life

Pop Culture, Political Imagination, and Civil Rights

Susan Burgess

NEW YORK UNIVERSITY PRESS

New York

NEW YORK UNIVERSITY PRESS
New York
www.nyupress.org

References to Internet websites (URLs) were accurate at the time of writing. Neither the author nor New York University Press is responsible for URLs that may have expired or changed since the manuscript was prepared.

Library of Congress Cataloging-in-Publication Data
Names: Burgess, Susan, 1961–   author.
Title: LGBTQ inclusion in American life : pop culture, political imagination, and civil rights / Susan Burgess.
Description: New York : New York University Press, [2023] | Series: LGBTQ politics | Includes bibliographical references and index.
Identifiers: LCCN 2022032722 | ISBN 9781479819720 (hardback) | ISBN 9781479819751 (paperback) | ISBN 9781479819768 (ebook) | ISBN 9781479819775 (ebook other)
Subjects: LCSH: Sexual minorities—United States—History. | Sexual minorities in popular culture—United States. | Sexual minorities—United States—Social conditions | Sexual minorities—United States—Public opinion. | Sexual minorities—Civil rights—United States.
Classification: LCC HQ73.3.U6 B87 2023 | DDC 306.760973—dc23/eng/20220804
LC record available at https://lccn.loc.gov/2022032722

New York University Press books are printed on acid-free paper, and their binding materials are chosen for strength and durability. We strive to use environmentally responsible suppliers and materials to the greatest extent possible in publishing our books.

Manufactured in the United States of America

10 9 8 7 6 5 4 3 2 1

Also available as an ebook

For Kate, with love, in spite of ourselves

To be hopeful in bad times is not just foolishly romantic. It is based on the fact that human history is a history not only of cruelty but also of compassion, sacrifice, courage, kindness. What we choose to emphasize in this complex history will determine our lives. If we see only the worst, it destroys our capacity to do something.
—Howard Zinn

CONTENTS

Introduction

LGBT Rights, Political Time, and Pop Culture

Political ideas change, sometimes beyond our wildest dreams and nightmares. Ideological, doctrinal, and policy shifts that were once hard to imagine have become widely accepted in mainstream American politics. Examples include the abolition of slavery, universal adult suffrage (except felons and undocumented people), minimum wage and maximum hours laws, and easy access to birth control. Time and again, mainstream and radical politics have transformed the parameters of political debate, broadening political imagination and creating new political horizons.

More germane for the topic of this book, the basic terms of the social compact changed for LBGT people in the early twenty-first century.[1] By 2015, mainstream politics had recognized a new rights-bearing political subject, the gay and lesbian citizen, who was free to have consensual adult sex privately without fear of state punishment, to serve openly in the military, and to marry with legal recognition. This was an enormous political and legal transformation. As he read the majority opinion of *Lawrence v. Texas* in 2003, Justice Anthony Kennedy's voice broke and gay and lesbian lawyers present in the courtroom visibly wept, knowing that the ruling would mean that the Constitution protects consenting and private sexual expression between same-sex couples.[2] Seasoned lawyers wept openly again when Kennedy read his opinion in *Obergefell v. Hodges* in 2015, declaring that the Constitution guarantees same-sex couples the fundamental right to marry. In a period of just twelve years, LGBT people had been transformed from dangerous perverts who threatened family and state, to military heroes and respectable married couples and parents.

This book explores how this transformation happened, as well as its import for the future of the LGBTQ movement in mainstream US politics. Using concepts and methods drawn from the fields of American political development, cultural studies, critical race theory, and queer theory, I show that mainstream pop culture has played an important but often overlooked role in shifting notions about privacy, sex and gender norms, and the family, moving from traditional norms to once radical ideas. This interaction between mainstream and radical ideas provides an excellent example of how political conflict is negotiated in culture over time in US political development.

Marriage equality is the most recent and perhaps most visible of the new LGBT rights and liberties. As recently as twenty-five years ago, I thought that the right to marry would be won eventually, but probably not in my lifetime. Most of the scholars and political activists I knew shared this view. Knowing what we know now, we can see that this position was of course unduly skeptical. But twenty-five years ago, the political and legal landscape was quite different. There was reason to think that mainstream acceptance of gay rights would be a long time coming.

During the 1980s the HIV/AIDS pandemic devastated the gay community. In the 1986 *Bowers v. Hardwick* case, the Supreme Court declared that it was constitutional for states to pass laws that criminalized private, consensual sex between same-sex adults. President Ronald Reagan did not publicly address AIDS until 1987, six years into the crisis, after nearly twenty-three thousand Americans had already died from the disease. After campaigning in 1992 on a promise to lift the ban on gays and lesbians in the military, President Bill Clinton caved to resistant military and congressional leaders, signing a law popularly known as "Don't Ask, Don't Tell." This new policy excluded from service people who "demonstrate a propensity or intent to engage in homosexual acts," compelling lesbian, gay, bisexual, and transgender members serving in the military to remain in the closet. In 1996 Congress resoundingly passed, and Clinton signed, the Defense of Marriage Act (DOMA), which defined marriage as occurring only between a man and a woman.

The academy was no better. While I was finishing graduate school at the University of Notre Dame in the late 1980s, gay and lesbian students were allowed to meet only at the campus health center, presumably because the administration assumed that homosexuals were thought to be mentally and/or medically ill. In my first job at the University of Wisconsin–Milwaukee, several colleagues were openly hostile to gay rights. As late as the mid-1990s the flagship journal of the American Political Science Association regularly rejected manuscripts submitted on LGBT politics without even bothering to send them out for review, a practice known as a "desk rejection."

Looking back on this grim history, one can understand why so many of us did not anticipate that LGBT people would soon be free to have consensual sex privately without fear of state punishment, to serve openly in the military, and to marry with legal recognition. For quite a while, scholars focused on why such change was not likely to occur, relying on institutional and structural features such as judicial restraint and federalism to explain mainstream resistance to change.[3] Yet as early as 2012, a popular book on the LGBT movement declared "victory" in its title, referencing the "triumphant gay rights revolution" in its subtitle, and describing its contents as follows: "How a despised minority pushed back, beat death, found love, and changed America for everyone."[4] By 2017, political scientist Gary Mucciaroni predicted that the completion of the LGBTQ civil rights agenda was "virtually inevitable."[5] How did such enormous skepticism about recognition of LGBT rights turn into inevitable acceptance?

In part, talk of inevitability came from the propensity of mainstream social scientists and pundits to focus on public opinion polls, which have shown a remarkable increase in public acceptance of LGBT rights and liberties in recent years. Between 1986 and 2021, public support for consenting adult sex between gays and lesbians grew from 32 to 79 percent. Public support for inclusion of gays and lesbians in the military grew from 51 to 83 percent between 1977 and 2019, and 71 percent of the public supported the inclusion of transgender people in the armed forces. Between 1996 and 2021, support for same-sex marriage grew from 27 to 71 percent.[6] While these polls clearly show a dramatic increase in public support for LGBT rights and liberties, scholars have not been able to fully explain why this occurred, particularly at such a rapid rate compared to other large-scale shifts in public opinion. In addition, focusing on public polls risks reinforcing status quo power relationships, in part because social scientists typically assume that the preferences of elite political actors drive public opinion from the top down.[7] As Robert Lieberman has noted, "Prevailing institutional approaches in political science are limited in their capacity to account for change."[8]

To address this problem, Jeremiah Garretson has suggested that grassroots social movements play an important part in shifting public opinion.[9] He argues that the AIDS crisis led activists in radical grassroots groups like ACT-UP to target mainstream news media in outlets in their hometowns during the late 1980s and early 1990s. These representations of local gay people suffering from AIDS on television prompted more people to come out, leading more straight people to recognize their personal connection to gay people, which in turn produced greater tolerance in mainstream American society and, eventually, LGBT legal and political victories.[10] Garretson's creative melding of findings from the fields of public opinion, popular culture, and social movement studies offers important insights about political and legal transformation, but his work relies on the idea that gay representation is the driving force of change. Representations of LGBT people in popular culture surely has made a difference, as for example in *Ellen, Will and Grace, Orange Is the New Black*, and *Pose*. But Garretson's analysis begs a prior question: Why were mainstream outlets receptive to including representations of LGBT people in the first place?

Interlude: *Julie and Julia*

In 2009, in the midst of this transformation, I saw a mainstream Hollywood film called *Julie and Julia*. I was finishing up a book called *The*

New York Times on Gay and Lesbian Issues, a history of the paper of record's coverage of LGBT issues since 1851. I often go to see films while completing major writing projects, in part to get away from my own ideas and give my head some rest. I often fail to obtain this mental rest, and that certainly turned out to be the case in this instance. Puzzling through *Julie and Julia* turned out to be the basis for the book you are currently reading.

On the face of it, *Julie and Julia* has very little to do with gay issues. Rather, it focuses on the dynamics of two white heterosexual couples in specific political times, one in postwar France, one in post-9/11 America. Julie Powell (Amy Adams) is a young, low-level bureaucrat who is working in New York City for the Lower Manhattan Development Corporation fielding phone requests from distraught family members of 9/11 victims, while living in a run-down flat in Queens with her new-ish husband. Bored with the constraints of both her work and domestic life, she undertakes a yearlong project that involves cooking every one of the 524 recipes in Julia Child's classic work, *Mastering the Art of French Cooking*. Powell's project begins modestly, as a simple replication of Child's work, and then blossoms into a popular autobiographical blog, a full-length book, and eventually this major motion picture that creatively explores the resonances between her and Julia Child's commitment to their burgeoning careers and marriages.

The film moves back and forth in time between Julie Powell's life in post-9/11 New York City and Julia Child's life in post–World War II Europe, prompting the viewer to reflect on the changes in politics and culture of these time periods. Their reflections reimagine the past, providing a critical basis from which to judge historical events and practices, at times in a somewhat distorted manner. Temporal reflection is a standard feature of many forms of popular culture. Political scientist Michael Shapiro notes that modern cinema offers "a way of reading events that is more critical than mere perception" due to a kind of representation that prompts the viewer to "think about the time and value of the present."[11] This kind of reflection on time can help us to better understand (and complicate) major political transformations by rendering the past from the point of view of the present. The interpretation of the film *Julie and Julia* that follows briefly exemplifies how this can work, offering an interesting revisionist twist on 1950s purges of homosexuals from public service during the McCarthy period, rendered from the standpoint of burgeoning LGBT inclusivity of 2009.

My interest was piqued by a series of minor scenes toward the end of the movie, when Julia Child (Meryl Streep) and her husband, Paul (Stanley Tucci), an exhibits officer for the United States Information Service, begin to worry that he may lose his cherished posting in Paris due to rising McCarthyism in the United States.[12] When Julia asks why, Paul says, "Senator McCarthy doesn't like people like us." As she wonders aloud about what they have done, Paul responds, "We haven't done anything; that's not the point. The point is we were in [communist] China and that's practically sufficient." Shortly thereafter, Paul is sent to two comparatively uninspired postings: Marseilles, in the south of France, and a suburb of Bonn, Germany.

Suddenly, Paul is called back to Washington. In a letter to her best friend, Avis, Julia describes what she calls their "own version of Kafka," as we see three agents of the federal government interrogating Paul in a small, poorly lit room. As Julia describes it, he is being "grilled in a windowless room with a foot-high stack of papers ominously sitting on the table," while being asked about "friends, books, our years in China, our patriotism. They even asked him if he was a homosexual." Meryl Streep's Julia Child enunciates the word "ho-mo-sexual," emphasizing long *o* vowels, underscoring the apparent foreignness of the word at that time. We then see a flashback in which a federal agent asks Paul, "Are you a homosexual, Mr. Child?" Paul smirks while answering, "No, I'm not." As one of the agents responds, "*This* is not a joke, Mr. Child," Paul replies, "I'm well aware of that."

In the following scene, we see the Childs back together again in their bedroom in Europe. As Julia describes it, "Paul came home exonerated, but thoroughly bruised."[13] He calls the ordeal "a nightmare" that causes him to question whether his entire career, and perhaps his whole life, has been a waste. Interestingly, Paul Child and Julie Powell are both faceless bureaucrats who worry that their hard work does not amount to much in the end. Subsequently Paul is sent to Oslo for his last (out)posting before retirement.

What was the meaning of these seemingly insignificant scenes, and why were they included in this film? I came to see *Julie and Julia*, told from the standpoint of the frictional political time of 2009 for LGBT rights, as a revisionist account of the standard McCarthy era narrative that focused on the purge of State Department workers based on accusations of being communist. The government purged at least 2,611 "security risks," while an additional 4,315 resigned under pressure of investigation.[14] As David K. Johnson has noted, "Historians of the McCarthy era have given stunningly little attention to the Lavender Scare," the purge of gays and lesbians from public service, concentrating almost exclusively on allegations of communist affiliation.[15] Johnson comments that the purge was focused on men, in large part because women "have traditionally had less access to public space than men and therefore were less vulnerable to arrest and prosecution for their homosexuality."[16] This would have also been the case for Black people at that time, men and women alike. *Julie and Julia* includes the standard communist suspicion, but also indicates that sexuality was another cause for investigation during that period. Despite being set shortly after World War II, the film adopts a 2009 political and cultural sensibility that foreshadows the lifting of the ban on gays and lesbians in the military that is to come in 2011.

Julie and Julia not only highlights accusations of homosexuality as a basis for the purges, but also suggests that government agents doing the purging are in the wrong. Paul's private admission of distress certainly indicates victimization, while his smirking public resistance indicates a kind of heroic defiance in the face of real danger. Contrary to the political tone of the 1950s, this film represents the government as the villain, and the purported communist/homosexual as an innocent but damaged hero. The revisionist reversal of heroes and villains suggests that by 2009 an important but complicated transformation in public understanding of homosexuality had occurred since the 1950s.

As portrayed by Stanley Tucci, Paul Child is certainly not a specimen of robust male masculinity. He is much shorter than his wife, as well as somewhat effeminate in his cultural interests and personal affect. Although their relationship is represented as demonstrably heterosexual, it is unusual for the time in that it is portrayed as a partnership of equals. For example, they are both delighted when Julia's cookbook becomes popular in the period following the investigation, and her career eclipses Paul's. In a way, Paul embodies the coming together of mainstream straight culture with queerness in his own political time, but reimagined from the vantage point of 2009, a point of significant friction between traditional ideas of LGBT exclusion and new ideas of inclusion.

The temporal reversals and the reflections prompted by *Julie and Julia* suggested to me that pop culture can help us to more fully understand how such profound shifts in public acceptance of LGBT rights came about. Released in the midst of an enormous transformation in the American public's acceptance of gay and lesbian rights, *Julie and Julia* portrays that shift through the sympathetic character of Paul Child, foreshadowing even more profound changes to come. I include the example here because it was the source of inspiration for this book and because it shows how politics and culture can come together in certain time periods to produce new ideas and policy directions, a theme that will recur throughout this book.

Political Time and the Role of Ideas in American Political Development

As I will show in this book, ideas matter in politics. So does timing. American political development (APD) scholars such as myself explore political questions against the backdrop of both. We focus on the introduction of new ideas in "political time."[17] Ideas and timing produce political transformation when "opportune political circumstances favor it."[18]

In the early days of the field, in the 1980s, APD scholars focused on shifts in balance of power between the two major political parties, arguing that long periods of political order and stability are regularly followed by party realignments. There have been six, perhaps seven, such realignments in the history of US politics, and they have typically occurred during large-scale shifts in the ideas driving the governing party, often during major crises such as the Great Depression or the Civil War. Recognized realignments include the election of Thomas Jefferson in 1800, Andrew Jackson in 1828, Abraham Lincoln in 1860, William McKinley in 1896, Franklin Roosevelt in 1932, and Ronald Reagan in 1980. A relatively short period of political tumult during the shift is typically followed by a much longer period of status quo politics.

Realigning periods are quite politically unstable for a time. Mainstream political horizons are typically broadened during such periods, in a manner that makes radical political movements on both the left and the right much more visible than they normally are in US politics.[19] Realignments reset the parameters of mainstream political discourse, centering a new political vision that includes new political ideas, subjects, governing coalitions, legal doctrines, and policies. Political scientist Rogers Smith has called this process of change and stability the "spiral of politics." Ideas matter because they form the basis of newly emerging political coalitions and their policy directions. Smith argues that "ideas include notions of human identities; conceptions of interests, including but not limited to economic interests; ideologies and philosophies of how the world works and should work; and hopes and fears."[20] New ideas prompt once stable political coalitions to compete on different terms, reshaping themselves to more effectively capture governing institutions and create new policy through resulting deals and compromises. This process eventually produces a stable new political context, which endures until other fresh ideas and interests are introduced, and a new political spiral emerges. Successful ideas typically appeal to both elites and the public at large.

With respect to parties, realigning political times recur every forty years or so in US politics, and we are due. It is quite possible that we are in the midst of such a realignment right now, particularly since the one-term Trump presidency was largely a legislative wash apart from tax policy and judicial appointments, due to an inability to hold together the long-standing but rapidly fragmenting Republican governing coalition. APD scholars have called this kind of political failure a "disjunctive presidency," to indicate that the coalition supporting the long-dominant party is fragmenting, a phenomenon that typically occurs right before a long-standing balance of party power realigns. For example, Democrat Jimmy Carter was a failed, one-term president who could not hold together the fragmenting New Deal governing coalition, right before the Reagan landslide in 1980 ushered in years of Republican dominance based on small government and devolution of power from the national government to the states. Similarly, Republican Herbert Hoover was a failed, one-term president before Franklin Roosevelt and the New Deal Democrats came to dominate politics for many years thereafter.

Despite these recurring patterns across US history, many people find it impossible to imagine a different political order other than the one they are in at the moment. They presume that currently dominant political norms will always govern them—just as many scholars and activists, including me, had earlier assumed that mainstream acceptance of LGBT rights and liberties would not occur in our lifetimes.[21] Ironically, once a shift in political orders happens and change is institutionalized, many of these same folks insist that such change was inevitable, and some of them even claim that they saw it coming.[22]

In this book, I adapt the APD concepts of political time and ideas to track shifts in the mainstream acceptance of LGBT rights and liberties. In doing so, I move beyond older scholarship that emphasized structural and institutional obstructions to LGBT rights, as well as newer studies that fail to explain why mainstream acceptance finally occurred. The framework I use suggests that "human agency can defy the constraints of political and social structures and create new possibilities."[23] Competition between different sets of ideas creates a kind of friction in the political system, which produces change in mainstream politics, much in the way that dissonance in otherwise relatively consonant music produces movement.

A Classic Civil Rights Account of LGBT Rights and Liberties

Focusing on ideas and political time, the chapters of this book begin with narratives that explain how LGBT rights and liberties came to be accepted in mainstream politics. I call this explanation a classic civil rights narrative because it follows the pattern of the paradigmatic social movement in the US experience, the Black civil rights movement. Classic civil rights narratives emphasize the liberal state's slow but steady political inclusion of a group that had been overtly excluded in the past. This kind of story notes that America has sometimes fallen short of its aspiration to provide equal rights and privileges to all, while still anticipating a time when excluded groups will receive equal protection under the law.[24] I break this classic narrative into three major stages of development, each characterized by the dominance of different ideas regarding political inclusion: (1) traditional norms that reinforce exclusion, (2) transitional conflict between traditional norms and new, more inclusive ideas, and (3) concluding victory, during which time the more inclusive ideas become the new norm. Each stage marks a specific phase in the formation of rights and liberties as the interests of the state and the oppressed group diverge and then converge over time.

In the first or traditional stage, the state denies the excluded group the full rights and privileges guaranteed to other citizens based on the group's purported moral inadequacy and the threat that the very existence of the group poses to the state and its supporting institutions. Traditional ideas that support exclusion dominate in mainstream politics. Even private expression of homosexuality is disdained in mainstream law and politics. To the extent that LGBT inclusion in the military and marriage are even considered, they are thought to be wholly subversive of those institutions, of government more generally, and even of Western civilization more generally. The interests of the state and the excluded group are largely seen as divergent, and they regard each other warily at best, as security threats and existential threats. Little, if any, political friction is openly expressed in mainstream politics. The fledgling civil rights movement is only beginning to organize to gain state recognition of basic freedoms regularly accorded to other citizens outside the group.

In the second or transitional period, state exclusions continue. However, as the movement expands, it introduces ideas of inclusion. These ideas challenge the traditional norms upon which persistent unequal treatment is based, fostering the friction necessary for political and legal transformation in the future. Slowly, the excluded group begins to be cast not simply as a threat to the power of the state, but also as a victim of it. A long period of struggle ensues, with moments of movement triumphs and losses, as the drive for equal rights and liberties becomes noticeably visible in mainstream law and politics, alongside traditional norms favoring continued exclusion. State officials and the public sometimes concede, if somewhat reluctantly, that the excluded group is not simply a threat to the state, but also a victim of prejudice and rejection. This yields early signs of increasing public acceptance as well as some political and legal victories that are important, if partial. The movement advances ideas of inclusion at a national level, creating political friction by openly challenging traditional norms. While traditional norms remain largely dominant in mainstream politics, the political friction created by the movement's competing ideas about political inclusion results in a series of "compromises" that reflect and balance these competing ideas, pleasing neither side completely.

In the third or concluding stage of the conventional civil rights narrative, members of the excluded group are now seen as (more or less) full, rights-bearing citizens who can heroically defend the state and its institutions. Once excluded and vilified, the group is now assimilated into mainstream legal and political life, as the state and the public accept that the group's rights and liberties are worthy of protection. Traditional norms and assumptions are resoundingly rejected as the hearts and minds of a majority of the American people embrace a more inclusive national narrative. New laws and policies formally signal toleration and inclusion, offering a seemingly happy ending to a story with very troubled beginnings. This is a fine story that offers redemption for both the state and its citizens by highlighting the triumph of American ideals of toleration and inclusion over historical prejudice and exclusion. During this stage, ideas about LGBT inclusion become dominant in mainstream politics, eventually to the point that they become taken for granted. The old traditional norms remain visible, but they are reformulated to fit their new challenger status and typically fail to create significant political friction.

The classic civil rights narrative offers a fuller story, moving beyond mainstream political science methods by providing a staged account of the "spiral of politics," including an account of the origins, frictions, and shifts in political ideas that are necessary for political transformation. By integrating important factors such as social movement development, doctrinal shift, and policy adoption, classic civil rights narratives significantly improve on flatter polling analyses. But neither explains why these changes occurred. To do so, I believe it is necessary to add to this exploration concepts that are central to critical race theory and queer theory, such as the role of popular culture in political transformation, critical analysis of the costs of mainstream inclusion, and alternative conceptions of political time and subjectivity.

Critical Race Theory and Popular Culture

Critical race theorist Derrick Bell and political scientist Richard Iton have suggested that the standard civil rights narrative is not so much wrong as incomplete. Using pop culture, they offer a more complicated story of political change that addresses overlooked costs of inclusion and persistent racism. Pop culture allows them to get at these more complicated political dynamics to challenge the redemptive happy ending offered by the classic civil rights narrative. Excluded groups often must reshape their interests so they can converge more readily with mainstream interests. Victories are often quite fragile as interests can diverge as easily as they converge, turning into "backlash." Perhaps most importantly, victories are often not as complete as they may initially seem. These factors led Bell and Iton to conclude that modern Western democracies and their institutions are premised on racial, gender, and sexual power dynamics that persist in different forms over time. Greater inclusion in mainstream institutions requires once excluded groups to accept the terms of mainstream discourse, including these power dynamics. Despite apparent gains by excluded groups, power typically adapts well when it is effectively challenged, often generating clever new ways to oppress traditionally excluded groups.

A civil rights veteran and law professor, Bell used popular culture to try to understand what is missing from the standard civil rights story, becoming a key founder of critical race theory. His epic three-book series on Black civil rights blends historical data and pop culture into a fantastical science fiction narrative that reveals persistent racism in US politics, beginning at the founding of the country and running through the contemporary period, despite the passage of civil rights laws and other policies that seem to advance the cause of racial justice.[25] Designed to be accessible beyond the academy, his work made it on to the *New York Times* best seller list.

Iton suggested that mainstream political scientists mistakenly have characterized popular culture as "peripolitical, prepolitical, or nonpolitical."[26] Political scientists typically favor "real" politics, by which they mean electoral, institutional, and policy-making processes. They often dismiss popular culture as trivial or simply reflective of elite interests. Iton's work demonstrates how Black popular culture has played an important role in constituting the Black community, a counterpublic distinct from the mainstream, which broadened the meaning of politics, challenging mainstream assumptions and creating conditions for more critical ideas and radical politics to emerge.

Drawing on the work of Bell and Iron, this book is premised on the complex idea that pop culture frequently represents the interests of both the masses and elites, and can better capture the shifting divergence and convergence of the two.[27] That is, pop culture can both challenge and reflect dominant interests, and it often does so at the same time. Noted cultural studies scholar John Fiske also made this point some time ago: "Popular culture is the culture of the subordinated and disempowered and thus always bears within it signs of power relations, traces of the forces of domination and subordination that are central to our social system and therefore to our social experiences. Equally it shows signs of evading these forces: popular culture contradicts itself."[28] This apparent contradiction offers a more complex view of how power works, as well as how it might be transformed. Paul Passavant has noted that this kind of critical theory is "empirically grounded and normatively oriented." It aims to make political science (and related disciplines) more critically engaged "by broadening its perspective, sharpening or redirecting its attention, and by encouraging articulation of the normative implications of its evidence."[29]

Rather than thinking that culture "causes" political and legal change, this book offers a more dynamic or "mutually constitutive" relationship between popular culture and elite politics. This method suggests that major political transformation is often "nested within a broader context of cultural change" that intersects with and sometimes drives elite decision making, altering "who we are, what we want, and how we might satisfy our desires."[30] It can help us to better understand how the relationship between mainstream and radical culture, between publics and counterpublics, can produce significant political transformation.

Work on pop culture in LGBT politics has typically focused on representational breakthroughs such as the first television series that centralize queer characters such as *Ellen*, *Will and Grace*, and *Transparent*. While these milestones are surely important, I offer a more complex reading of how shifts in mainstream ideas produced broad public acceptance of LGBT rights and liberties. Following this model, I argue that pop culture broadened public understanding of privacy, gender and sex norms, and family forms, fostering public acceptance of a new LGBT political subject with equal rights and liberties. I close each chapter with a queer critical analysis that assesses the costs and contradictions of political inclusion in these areas of mainstream politics. A queer critical analysis of these dynamics is crucial for understanding the future of LGBT politics, given that the movement was founded on a radical rejection of state power during the uprisings at Stonewall in New York City, Compton's Cafeteria in San Francisco, and other sites of resistance in the late 1960s and early 1970s.

Queer Theory and Trans Centrality

Mainstream acceptance of LGBT rights and liberties has transformed both mainstream and queer understandings of the basic terms of the social contract. Queer or straight, past or future, our origin stories are all deeply embedded in mainstream ideas and institutions. At the same time, queer theory also aims to challenge received norms about "the true, the good, and the right," in part by questioning their apparent givenness.[31] As such, the complicated and often contradictory power dynamics that underlie Fiske, Iton, and Bell's understandings of pop culture also inform queer critical analysis. Norms about privacy, the military, and the family are regularly expressed through mainstream pop culture, constituting us and shaping the parameters of political discourse. While these norms are undeniably primary to the formation of the self and identity, as well as mainstream and radical politics, they do not completely determine their shape. As formative queer theorist Judith Butler has noted, it is "in relation to [the mainstream] framework that recognition takes place or the norms that govern recognition are challenged and transformed."[32] Jack Halberstam, also a noted queer theorist, adds that even if it were possible, adopting a scorched earth strategy to destroy mainstream ideas by "making a new orthodoxy out of negativity" would amount to an "epistemological self-destruction."[33]

Queering political time requires a "perverse turn away from the narrative coherence of adolescence—early adulthood—marriage—

reproduction—child rearing—retirement—death." It offers "a way of being in the world and a critique of the careful social scripts that usher even the most queer among us through major markers of individual development and into normativity."[34] It allows us to critically analyze the political world we find ourselves in through a queer lens, to imagine new, more expansive ways to reformulate the often violent foundations of political community, sexual freedom, and the family. Because queers have had to find ourselves in past political times, queer historians have sometimes reformulated time in a nonlinear way. Historian Carolyn Dinshaw speaks of a queer desire to "form communities across time," to open up "other modes of consciousness," a critical component of radical political change. She describes finding a "dreamed of collectivity realized long after the fact" in historical archives, "a history of mutually isolated individuals, dreaming similar dreams, arrayed before me in the aftermath of collective struggles and new identities."[35] However, there is no reason that these alternative, more radical modes of consciousness and connection must be found solely in the past. I conclude the book by looking to two imagined political communities represented in recent pop culture for new ideas about the transformation of political subjectivity, one grounded in the past and the other in the future.

To that end, the conclusion of the book offers a queer critical analysis of the stories of origin offered in *Hamilton* and *Sense8*. *Hamilton* centralizes Black political subjects in the story of origin of the American Revolution, focusing on the importance of racial inclusion. I argue that *Hamilton*'s representational politics, while important, cannot by itself produce transformational political change, in part because its narrative is disconnected from the radical past of Black Power as well as the radical revisioning of race in the contemporary Black Lives Matter movement in the present. To better understand how mainstream and radical ideas work interactively to produce political transformation, I explore an alternative story of origin found in *Sense8*, a Netflix television series that became a cult classic, created by the Wachowskis, two trans siblings who earlier created the *Matrix* films. Much less well-known than *Hamil-*

ton, Sense8 was critically acclaimed and had a substantial cult following. *Sense8* self-consciously connects the radical queer past to mainstream politics in a future-facing story that rethinks the meaning of sex, family, and the state, centralizing intersectional representations of race, gender, and sexuality, as well as foregrounding trans and other queer political subjects.

Overview

As noted earlier, I begin each chapter with a three-stage narrative of civil rights and liberties development, using pop culture to account for shifts in public acceptance of gay and lesbian inclusion in the right to privacy, military service, and marriage equality. These chapters analyze films and television series that are not obviously or directly related to LGBT issues. I argue that shifting understandings of moral norms about privacy, sex and gender norms, and the nuclear family foster greater popular acceptance of the three main pillars of contemporary LGBT rights and liberties. I offer fresh interpretations of popular films and television series to explore these shifts, focusing on the convergence and divergence of state and LGBT interests, and the way those dynamics shape both mainstream and LGBTQ politics going forward.

Chapter 1 explores the shift from community to individual moral standards through mainstream films about military service: *Casablanca* (1942), *An Officer and a Gentleman* (1982), and *Brothers* (2009). These films offer a fundamental reordering of expectations regarding public and private morality, a key component to decriminalizing sodomy and recognizing LGBT rights to private sexual expression. While this development is often celebrated as a move toward greater recognition of gay and lesbian rights and liberties, it comes at a clear cost. Increasingly cut loose from their earlier embeddedness in mainstream and LGBT communal life, both straight and queer people are now subject to significant moral confusion. Although the old standards have been displaced, to many it remains unclear what comes next. Some scholars and commentators have suggested that the right to privacy provides a thin or nonexistent standard upon which to base this new public standard of privacy. While the new standard may not have been as well articulated and circulated as it might have been, exacerbating concerns about social disorder and balkanization, I use the radical reformations offered in queer theory to move beyond confusion to an ethic of sexual mores that challenges the traditional state tendency to promote reproductive sex.

Chapter 2 outlines distinct shifts in male masculinity through the character of James Bond as he develops across twenty-six films over fifty years. At first, Bond represents traditional white masculinity in a largely unquestioned fashion, leaving no room for homosexuality other than as an eradicable danger or a marginal joke. In the second period, traditional masculinity is occasionally challenged and practiced in a somewhat more conflicted setting, opening the door for greater acceptance of those who regularly challenge mainstream sex and gender norms, including gays and lesbians. Contemporary Bond movies offer a new framing of masculinity that suggests that heterosexuality may pose as many pitfalls as homosexuality when it comes to serving the interests of the national security state. The unruliness of sexuality appears to undermine the disciplined allegiance that the modern state requires. *No Time to Die*, the most recent Bond movie, suggests that toxic masculinity's compulsive violence leads not only to the death of many enemies of the British state, but also to the death of Bond himself.

Chapter 3 focuses on the transformation of the nuclear family in pop culture, beginning with the early 1960s comedy *Leave It to Beaver*. Focusing on the foibles of young Beaver, who lives with his businessman father, stay-at-home mother, and older brother, the series offers humorous but ultimately serious moral object lessons to socialize Beaver into mainstream communal life, producing an eminently governable nuclear family. The nuclear family remains desirable in the late 1980s drama *thirtysomething*, but it is much more fraught due to the increasing difficulty of balancing work and family life for men and women alike. Released in 2013, *The Americans* focuses on a KGB-created family composed of two Soviet spies, total strangers who have two children to further their cover as a mainstream American family running a DuPont Circle travel agency and living in a Virginia suburb. Rather than idealizing the nuclear family or portraying it as a sought-after goal, *The Americans* reveals the nuclear family to be wholly constructed rather than natural. Sex and love and even children are instrumentally manipulated on a regular basis to further political goals, transforming basic assumptions about how marriage and family life really work beyond the façade of suburban America. *The Americans'* representation of alternative sexualities and its destruction of the nuclear family open space for greater acceptance of same-sex marriage equality.

But what lies beyond the nuclear family now that pop culture has helped the public better understand its dysfunctionality and exclusions? Now that LGBT people have made the compromises necessary to become rights-bearing citizens, can the movement continue to forward a politically transformative agenda? The book's conclusion addresses these questions by exploring two recent pop culture examples of the politics of movement and regime foundings: the enormously popular play *Hamilton* and the queer Netflix television series *Sense8*. Each rethinks the basic social compact, with new political subjects, practices, and institutions, often through real and fantastical violence, as is common in founding periods. Each offers a different measure of mainstream and radical politics. Each offers a distinct political vision to address the problems of our troubled times. *Hamilton* reformulates the past from the vantage point of contemporary political time through the lens of race. *Sense8* offers a complex understanding of how power works in political time, a vision of the future through an intersectional political consciousness that connects present political time to the future through queer characters, including a trans woman.

It is obvious that the future of liberal democracy is currently imperiled. At the very least, it needs significant transformation. It remains unclear where US politics is headed post-Trump. It is currently fraught with the perpetuation of fear-based, real violence. The book closes with

a discussion of *Sense8*'s use of fantastical violence to combat the politically enervating effects of this fear, connecting its story to present-day
politics, through a resilient political vision that has produced significant
political transformation in the past and is likely to do so again in the
future.

A Note on How to Read This Book

The interpretations I offer here do not amount to a comprehensive sur-
vey of pop culture, or even of the specific films and television series that
I discuss. That would be neither possible nor desirable. As Ta-Nehisi
Coates reminds us in his influential book *Between the World and Me*,
looking at pop culture in its entirety would likely yield an extremely
narrow political vision. He notes that when he was growing up, "black
beauty was never celebrated in movies, in television, or in the textbooks
I'd seen as a child. Everyone of any import, from Jesus to George Washington, was white."[36] Until very recently, this has also been the case for
LGBT people. The history of pop culture has been largely dominated
by straight white people. I do not wish to recapitulate that tired history.
As a result, the book does not offer a history of pop culture. Rather, it
uses pop culture to better understand political transformation. I offer
an interdisciplinary method, an approach to reading culture that better
captures the complicated dynamics of political change. I concentrate on
popular films and television series, in part because their mass appeal
suggests that they should "have a greater ideological impact on American culture."[37] My focus on mainstream pop culture is grounded in a
recognition of the power of mainstream politics à la critical race and
queer theory. I argue that the relationship between mainstream and
radical politics, mainstream public and LGBT counterpublics, produced
such change. To introduce my method on a smaller scale, I begin the
discussion in chapter 1 focusing on three films, *Casablanca*, *An Officer
and a Gentleman*, and *Brothers*. The analysis increases in complexity in
subsequent chapters. In chapter 2, I compare all twenty-six films of the

James Bond franchise and in chapter 3, 394 episodes of three television series, *Leave It to Beaver*, *thirtysomething*, and *The Americans*.

I selected these examples of pop culture because they encapsulate crucial moments in the shift of ideas that I discuss. As Carlo Rovelli has noted in his accessible synthesis of different ways that time has been conceptualized in the discipline of physics, social transformation typically occurs at many different sites. He notes, for example, that "slow, technical, cultural, and artistic advances made by innumerable workshops of painters and artisans were necessary before the Sistine Chapel was possible. But in the end, it was Michelangelo who painted it."[38] There is no question that other pop culture examples certainly could be used to illuminate how the basic terms of the social compact changed over time in a way that included LGBT people. My fondest hope is that the method and examples that I offer here will prompt readers to develop their own narratives about the way that pop culture can reflect and produce new political formations going forward. We need them now, more than ever.

1

From Criminal Perverts to Rights-Bearing Citizens

War Movies and the Right to Privacy

How did the public shift its view of gays and lesbians from criminal perverts to rights-bearing citizens? Many scholars failed to predict that privacy would be the first of the three pillars of LGBT rights to be recognized in mainstream law and politics, claiming that public disgust about sodomy would preclude its decriminalization.[1] Pop culture can help us to better understand how and why the public came to gradually accept this change. This shift was grounded in a new understanding of privacy based in a non-reproductive ethic of sexual mores.

The erosion of traditional standards of sexual morality was central to the decriminalization of sodomy and the inclusion of gay and lesbian sexual autonomy under the right to privacy in *Lawrence v. Texas*, the first pillar of equal rights for LGBT people. This enormous milestone for the LGBT movement changed the mainstream heterosexual community as well as the LGBT counterculture, in ways that neither have been able to fully anticipate or control. It opened the door for further development of LGBT rights and freedoms, even as it created an ongoing need in the LGBT community for continued recognition from heterosexuals and the state. By gaining state recognition through the right of privacy, the queer community became somewhat dependent on mainstream public approval.

This chapter begins with a brief historical summary of the three stages of political and legal change that culminated in *Lawrence*. I then turn to three mainstream films to explore the cultural roots of the shift from traditional, community-based moral law to individual autonomy as a basis for decision making, based on detailed readings of *Casablanca*

(1942), *An Officer and a Gentleman* (1982), and *Brothers* (2009). War films often present men in both their public and private roles, in service to their country as well as their families, frequently focusing on tensions between community and individual desires. The three films discussed here reveal a dramatic shift in public understanding of how the American state and society produce desire, and how these new ideas made it possible for the public to accept the private sexual autonomy of gays and lesbians more readily.

The inclusion of dissident sexuality fundamentally altered the traditional basis of public ethical understanding. When the Supreme Court recognized homosexuals as moral, rights-bearing people in *Lawrence*, it formally brought heterosexual and homosexual culture into something of a joint venture on uncertain terms to an unknown end. Once presumed to be criminals and perverts, homosexuals were now declared to be upstanding citizens with rights. Fallout and confusion were to be expected after a battle of that magnitude.

A Classic Civil Rights Account of the Right to Privacy

Sodomy was a criminal offense in the United States until its criminalization was declared unconstitutional in the 2003 *Lawrence v. Texas* case. Below I offer a summary of the classic narrative as it pertains to the repeal of anti-sodomy laws.[2] The classic civil rights narrative that is offered to describe these changes can be broken into three basic stages: the traditional, transitional, and concluding stages.

Traditional Period

Traditional norms held that homosexuality was an immoral perversion and a psychological disorder. Religious and secular community standards condemned it as a moral abomination. In the post–World War II period, all fifty states had sodomy laws, with all but two of them making it a felony. Homosexuals were barely tolerated in public. Many states and localities, including places as cosmopolitan as New York City, made it illegal for homosexuals to meet or work in state-licensed venues such as bars and restaurants. Police regularly raided gay bays and arrested gay patrons merely for socializing in public. Some arrests resulted in longer-term imprisonment. Those who were arrested were often named in newspaper accounts, and the arrests and resulting publicity often led to the loss of jobs, family support, and religious communities, and in some cases institutionalization, electroshock therapy, or suicide.

Although Stonewall patrons famously fought back against this treatment, laws criminalizing sodomy remained on the books for years to come in many localities.[3] While the Stonewall Rebellion is widely commemorated now as the beginning of the modern LGBTQ movement, it barely made a dent in public consciousness of homosexuality in its own time. It was reported on in the back pages of the city section of the *New York Times* in June 1969, as a local event with little national import. While a few brave souls such as Barbara Gittings and Frank Kameny demonstrated publicly for homosexual inclusion in mainstream institutions such as the Defense Department and the armed forces (see chapter 2), the LGBT movement was not yet organized nationally.

In 1965 the Supreme Court decided the case of *Griswold v. Connecticut*, striking down a law that prohibited married couples from using contraceptives in the privacy of their own homes.[4] This decision was consistent with an earlier report from the American Law Institute that recommend decriminalizing all "sexual relations, normal or abnormal, between consenting adults in private." However, *Griswold* made no mention of homosexuality. The individual right to privacy recognized there was linked to marital relations. Later Supreme Court cases extended the right to single people in 1972 and to the right to choose to have an abortion in the iconic case of *Roe v. Wade* (1973).[5] By 1977, even minors' right to use contraception was protected by the right to privacy.[6] But the Court refused to even hear a case challenging the constitutionality of laws criminalizing homosexual sodomy under the right to privacy. While the challengers argued that personal privacy trumped the state's right to regulate morality, the Supreme Court affirmed without comment the judgment of a lower federal court that found Virginia's criminalization of homosexuality, "even when committed in the home," to be a constitutional use of the state's power and "appropriate in the promotion of morality and decency."[7]

Transitional Period

When the Supreme Court finally did give a case challenging a state anti-sodomy law a full hearing in *Bowers v. Hardwick* in 1986, it upheld the law, emphasizing the "ancient roots" of criminal prohibitions on such behavior.[8] This case and the response to it exemplify the kind of political conflict that characterizes transitional periods in civil rights struggles. Traditional norms are both challenged and defended as the movement for inclusion expands and gains national visibility, prompting the public to consider the possibility of full rights and liberties for the out-group. Nonetheless, traditional norms typically continue to hold significant sway in the long and periodically quite pointed struggle that defines transitional periods.

Bowers was notable in that police officers had entered Michael Hardwick's home and found him having sex with another man. Although the prosecution dropped the charges without going to trial, Hardwick challenged the constitutionality of the law, claiming that it put him at constant risk of arrest as a practicing homosexual. Under Georgia law, sodomy was a felony that was punishable with a prison sentence of up to twenty years.

Lawrence Tribe, a professor of law at Harvard University, made the case for Hardwick, arguing that the government should not be allowed to play the role of "Big Brother" by monitoring private sexual activity between consenting adults. Michael Hobbs, the assistant attorney general of Georgia, claimed that the law was designed to promote community standards about what constitutes "a decent and moral society." Tribe argued that the government should have a better reason to justify the law

than simple "majority morality" because the case involved two important constitutional freedoms, the right to engage in private sexual relations and the right to be free from government intrusion in one's home.

The law had been found unconstitutional in lower federal courts. The
US Court of Appeals argued that homosexual relationships were "an intimate association protected against state interference," akin to marital
intimacy. Nonetheless, the Supreme Court refused to extend the right to
privacy to homosexuality, finding that the Constitution does not protect
private, consensual sodomy. Emphasizing the "ancient roots" of traditional criminal prohibitions on sodomy "deeply rooted in this Nation's
history and tradition," the Court said that it was "at best facetious" to
imagine that the Constitution protects "a fundamental right to engage in
sodomy." States were left to decide for themselves whether to criminalize
sodomy based on community moral values.

The Court split 5–4 over the ruling, rendering a decision that reflected
growing divisions in mainstream society about private same-sex sexual
behavior. Justice Byron White wrote the majority opinion. After he retired from the Court, White conceded in a public forum that he had
made an error: "When I had the opportunity to reread the opinions a
few months later, I thought the dissent had the better of the arguments."[9]
Michael Bowers, the attorney general of Georgia after whom the case
is named, was later found to have had an adulterous affair for over ten
years, in violation of the Georgia law against adultery, which was also
grounded in traditional morality.

Supporters and opponents of the ruling agreed that the case signaled
a very serious setback for the movement for gay and lesbian rights.
The Reverend Jerry Falwell, head of the Moral Majority, applauded the
traditional roots of the Court's decision that "recognized the right of a
state to determine its own moral guidelines" because it "issued a clear
statement that perverted moral behavior is not accepted practice in this
country." Atlanta lawyer Gil Robison, a member of the Atlanta Campaign for Human Rights, said that it was "ironic that the conservatives
who are interested in getting government off people's backs would ap-

plaud this." Other gay and lesbian leaders predicted increased police harassment and difficulty obtaining professional licenses dependent on "a good moral character." Child custody rulings involving gays and lesbians were also expected to be negatively impacted.

Although the *Bowers* ruling undoubtedly had very negative consequences for gay and lesbian rights, it did serve as a rallying point for the gay and lesbian movement, as evidenced by protests of the ruling that followed in various cities across the country. Several thousand gays and lesbians gathered in Washington, DC, at the Supreme Court building in a highly visible nonviolent protest several months later. The 1987 March on Washington for Gay and Lesbian Rights drew an estimated 200,000–500,000 people, marking the largest gathering at the Court since a 1971 protest of the Vietnam War. The Lambda Legal Defense and Education Fund, perhaps the most prominent defender of gay and lesbian rights at that time, doubled its budget in the year following the ruling, as contributions to movement organizations increased dramatically. However, twenty-five states still had laws that criminalized homosexual sodomy. Although they were often unevenly enforced, these laws nevertheless had important consequences. As many had predicted, laws criminalizing sodomy were often used to justify differential treatment between gay and straight people, particularly in the areas of employment, child custody, and adoption.

In 1994 the Court itself issued an important ruling in *Romer v. Evans*, striking down an amendment to the Colorado constitution that would have permanently prohibited localities within the state from including gays and lesbians in civil rights protections already on the books. As the first major Supreme Court ruling in favor of gay rights, the ruling provided new hope that the Court might overturn *Bowers* in the not-too-distant future. By 1998, even the Georgia Supreme Court had decided to overturn the sodomy law that had been upheld in the *Bowers* case, stating that the state's constitution offered greater protection for the right of privacy than the US Constitution. Several other states had decriminalized sodomy. However, nineteen states still had sodomy laws on the books at the time, continuing to criminalize private, consensual sodomy between adults. The transitional period set the stage for the Court's dramatic ruling overturning these laws that was to come in the now iconic case of *Lawrence v. Texas*.

Concluding Period

In the third and concluding stage of the classic civil rights narrative, members of the excluded group come to be seen not simply as threats to the state or victims of it, but as (more or less) full citizens who can heroically defend the state and participate (more or less fully) in public life. By 2003, only thirteen state sodomy laws remained on the books, largely in the southern region of the country. In *Lawrence v. Texas* (2003) the US Supreme Court concluded that the right to privacy included homosexual sodomy, overturning the *Bowers* ruling. It is hard to overstate the importance of this case for the LGBT movement, which transformed gays and lesbians from criminals into rights-bearing citizens.

By a 6–3 vote, the Court found sodomy laws unconstitutional, arguing that they demean homosexuals and threaten their individual rights to live as free and dignified people. As noted earlier, gay and lesbian attorneys in the audience wept visibly, as Justice Anthony Kennedy read portions of the majority's opinion from the bench, his voice breaking at times, as he too appeared to be moved by the historic importance of the landmark ruling that established the first pillar of rights for gays and lesbians. I also wept in my office as I heard the news. Gays and lesbians were now being recognized as rights-bearing citizens in mainstream law and politics. The ruling would have an impact on the shape of the LGBTQ community and movement going forward. For years, the LGBTQ community had been constituted into a "counterpublic," a community distinct from the mainstream with its own cultural contexts and ethical standards. Gay and lesbian inclusion in the mainstream would affect both communities in profound and often unanticipated ways.

Kennedy said that the *Bowers* case had been decided incorrectly, arguing that the right to privacy covers homosexual as well as heterosexual intimacy, as part of the core freedoms available to all Americans. In doing so, Kennedy made it clear that the right to privacy was not simply about reproductive sex, but rather about the right of individuals to live freely and to make autonomous decisions about the most important aspects of their lives. In a concurring opinion that emphasized the equal protection clause of the Fourteenth Amendment, Justice Sandra Day O'Connor argued that the moral disapproval of a group is an inadequate basis for state law that "runs contrary to the values of the Constitution."

Justice Antonin Scalia dissented from the majority's ruling in *Lawrence*, arguing that the Court had no basis for making such a sweeping decision overturning the Texas law and *Bowers*, and accusing the Court of signing on to the "homosexual agenda." But even he understood that the ruling signaled the end of the dominance of traditional values and community morality as the basis for continued LGBT exclusion. He correctly predicted that the *Lawrence* decision would lead to the legalization of same-sex marriage.

In the wake of the decision, gays and lesbians celebrated in the streets of various cities across the country. Legal experts called the decision historic and transformative. Activists likened *Lawrence* to *Brown v. Board of Education*, saying that it would mobilize the LGBT movement, just as *Brown* had done for the civil rights movement. While opposition to decriminalizing sodomy certainly remained, that position had been rendered a challenger view at best. How did the public come to accept these changes over time? What new ideas were needed to gain mainstream acceptance? An analysis of three mainstream films—*Casablanca*, *An Officer and a Gentleman*, and *Brothers*—can help to answer these questions.

Pop Culture on the Shift from Moral Law to Individual Rights

In *Casablanca*, a traditional form of public morality prevailed during the World War II period, calling for the sacrifice of individual desires in the name of higher communal values and clearly delineated lines between good and evil. All three major characters repress their personal desires in order to fight the clear moral evil represented by the Nazis. In a general context of self-sacrifice where heterosexuals are regularly expected to repress sexual desire for the greater good, it seems only reasonable to expect homosexuals to do the same and conceal their sexuality.

This traditional ethic of self-sacrifice, along with the heroic nature of servicemen, begins to be questioned in the post–Vietnam War era film *An Officer and a Gentleman*. In this transitional period, we learn that some servicemen have used the traditional ethic of self-sacrifice to dodge their public and private responsibilities, as the past is reread through the lens of the central character, Zack Mayo, who was severely neglected by his serviceman father. The film revolves around the son's apparently successful struggle to live up to traditional ethical standards by becoming both an officer and a gentleman, despite his father's failure to fulfill the model of honorable service in the field and at home. Rather than demanding the sacrifice of personal desire in the name of higher public values as in *Casablanca*, this film suggests that Mayo's ability to follow through on his private commitments allows him to strengthen his dedication to his public responsibilities as an officer. This represents an important shift from the absolute opposition of private desire and public good in *Casablanca*'s traditional model. *Officer* also suggests that traditional standards have hypocritically been used by straight men to shield their dishonorable behavior from view. *Officer*'s challenge to several assumptions that drove the traditional model reflect growing public acceptance of personal desire and individual privacy. However, consistent with the nature of transition, some traditional elements remain strong in this narrative. Rather than pitting personal against community desire, the transitional narrative seems to suggest their alignment, fostering greater acceptance of individual privacy and sexual autonomy, at least among straight people.

Officer does not directly discuss homosexuality (except when used as a slur to question an officer candidate's masculinity), and for the most part neither did the public at this time. To the extent that homosexuals were thought of at all, the public largely assumed that gay men were incapable of living up to the standards to which Mayo successfully aspires, believing that homosexual personal desire would necessarily render them incapable of becoming either gentlemen or officers. As a consequence, homosexuals still remained largely trapped within the traditional frame in the public sphere, not worthy of greater privacy.

Brothers completes the transition from public morality to privacy as the traditional moral compass of an apparently heroic Marine and devoted family man is destroyed by his service in Afghanistan. In this film, the serviceman's brother, a "common criminal," comes to be seen as the more heroic of the two, and privacy is used to stave off public disciplining of this serviceman when he comes home shattered and violent. The serviceman's emotional volatility and rage-fueled violence are a legacy of his father, a troubled Vietnam War veteran who is "coping" with the traumatic effects of his service largely by means of alcohol. In this film, ethical standards to which officers and gentlemen once aspired seem illusory at best in the fog of war, undermining traditional morality as a clear basis for solving difficult ethical problems that arise during armed conflict. However, as portrayed in *Brothers*, the erosion of public morality comes at a clear cost, and privacy turns out not to be all that it was cracked up to be, as the film suggests that disorder, trauma, and moral confusion appear to ensue when a common moral standard for ethical behavior is lacking.

Traditional Moral Law: *Casablanca*

Made in 1942, *Casablanca* is one of the most beloved films of all time. It won three Academy Awards, including Best Picture and Best Actor, and is widely recognized as iconic, appearing at or near the top of many "best of" lists, with some critics hailing it as the best film ever.[10] While *Casablanca* certainly acknowledges the draw of desire, the power of the moral law is the real force of the film. The higher causes of freedom and resistance to Nazi evil compel the lead characters to sublimate their individual romantic desires. While Rick Blaine (Humphrey Bogart) and Ilsa Lund (Ingrid Bergman) are not virtuous in the sense of being chaste, they are ultimately able to deny their individual desires in service to higher public values, weighing the public over the private much more heavily in their moral calculations.

The story, set shortly before the Japanese attack on Pearl Harbor in December 1941, unfolds in Rick's Café Americain, a successful night-club and casino located in Casablanca, which is patronized by a diverse group with widely ranging political values. Rick apparently is willing to serve anyone in order to make money, including corrupt local officials, Germans loyal to Nazism, Vichy French, expatriate Americans, and des-perate refugees trying to leave the area by obtaining the two letters of transit that would facilitate easy departure from the region.

Not a traditional Hollywood hero, Rick represents himself as a cyni-cal individualist, a lawbreaker who is willing to work the system to get ahead. He claims to resist the moral law's model of self-sacrifice, insist-ing, "I stick my neck out for nobody." But his actions repeatedly belie this assertion, suggesting that he has done so on a variety of occasions. Even though he appears to be emotionally unattached to his current girlfriend, he makes special arrangements for her to be taken home safely when trouble emerges at the café. He ran guns to Ethiopia follow-ing the Italian invasion there and fought with the Republicans against the Fascists in the Spanish Civil War. While he insists that his motives were purely self-interested and monetary, the audience is left wondering whether those were his only motivations.

Rick's actions lead Louis Renault, an opportunist police captain, to comment, "If I were a woman, and I were not around, I would fall in love with Rick." His offhand admission is consistent with Vito Russo's argument in *The Celluloid Closet* that many Hollywood movies of this era regularly identify morally compromised characters with the sugges-tion of homosexual desire.[11] Renault's moral failings when it comes to sex are later confirmed when it becomes clear that he regularly exploits the vulnerability of women with visa problems by compelling them to have sex with him in exchange for help leaving the country. His corruption casts further doubt on Rick's earlier assertion that he operates solely on the basis of financial self-interest. When Rick learns that Renault has blackmailed a Bulgarian woman and then refused to facilitate her passage, Rick arranges for her fiancé to win at his roulette table, affording the couple the ability to book safe passage back to their homeland, an action that is directly contrary to his monetary self-interest.

As the story continues to unfold, an old flame from Rick's past enters the café. Ilsa Lund, a Norwegian with whom Rick earlier had a torrid affair, had left him just as they were about to flee France together in advance of the Nazi occupation. Ilsa compels Sam, the café's pianist, to play "As Time Goes By," Rick and Ilsa's song. Eliciting both tears and anger from Rick, the famous lyrics of this song foreshadow both the power of desire and its apparent triviality in the face of higher values:

> You must remember this
> A kiss is just a kiss,
> A sigh is just a sigh
> The fundamental things apply
> As time goes by.

Ilsa needs the letters of permission now in Rick's possession so that she and her husband, Victor Laszlo (Paul Henreid), a concentration camp escapee and fighter in the Czech resistance, can continue his important anti-fascist work in America. Emphasizing his leadership in fighting the forces of evil, Laszlo leads the crowd in Rick's bar in a rousing rendition of "La Marseillaise," drowning out a group of Nazis who are singing a patriotic German song rooted in conflicts with the French.

It soon becomes clear that Ilsa has given up her true love, Rick, to support the higher cause of her husband. She still desires Rick, even though he is at first somewhat suspicious about her true feelings, knowing that she and Laszlo are desperate for the letters of transit.

Reasserting self-interest as his sole motivation, Rick insists, "I am the only cause I'm interested in." As a desperate Ilsa pulls a gun on Rick and demands the letters lest her honorable husband be killed, she finally breaks down and explains that she initially mistook her admiration of her husband and his work for love. As she and Rick fall into a passionate embrace, Ilsa explains that she had to leave him in France, because she had discovered that Laszlo had not in fact perished in the concentration camps as she had earlier believed. Moral law and communitarian values, expressed in the form of the battle against Nazism, compelled her to sacrifice her true love. But her resolve to continue to stay with Victor is weakening given the enormity of her desire for Rick. While she initially believes that she will stay with Rick and that he will facilitate Victor's departure for America, Ilsa continues to underscore the moral dilemma, asserting, "I don't know what's right any longer," and insisting that Rick "must think for both of us, for all of us." As he responds, "All right, I will," Ilsa again highlights the conflict between public morality and individual desire, stating, "I wish I didn't love you so much."

As Rick reveals his intention to use the letters to take Ilsa with him, Captain Renault reminds him that he was never all that interested in women. Revealing the depth of his love for Ilsa, Rick responds, "She's not just any woman." After Rick gains Ilsa's assurance that she will trust him no matter what happens, Renault arrives at the airport to arrest Victor for murder, commenting, "Love, it seems, has triumphed over virtue." However, this is not yet the end of the story. Rick intervenes, forcing Renault at gunpoint to allow Victor onto the getaway plane, along with Ilsa. When she objects, Rick reminds her that she asked him to "do the thinking for all of us," and urges her to deny her individual desire for the greater good, just as he has done. There is apparently no escape from this higher moral standard. Rick reminds Ilsa that doing otherwise would cause her regret "maybe not today, maybe not tomorrow, but soon and for the rest of her life." She belongs to Victor, and Victor belongs to the world.

In the end, all three of the main characters deny their personal desires for a greater good, a higher purpose. Rick notes this collective self-sacrifice, stating, "I'm no good at being noble, but it doesn't take a genius to see the problems of three little people don't mean a hill of beans in this crazy world." In the end, everyone must give up love for virtue and the greater good of combating evil, as represented by the Nazis. This is underscored when Captain Renault allows Rick to remain free, even after he shoots Major Strasser, a Nazi who has been hunting Laszlo down throughout the film.

Casablanca is a story of enormous sacrifice and disciplining of powerful heterosexual desires. The pursuit of love and desire, even the great love and desire of Rick and Ilsa, pales in comparison with the need to combat the tremendous evil of the Nazis. Traditional public morality requires enormous self-sacrifice. Those who are not able to do so are morally suspect. Expecting homosexuals to sublimate their desires is only consistent with the sacrifices being made by mainstream heterosexuals to maintain traditional norms and institutions in the face of fascism.

Pop Culture on Transitional Morality: *An Officer and a Gentleman*

One of the highest-grossing films of the year, *An Officer and a Gentleman* sold over thirty-eight million tickets in 1982 and received critical acclaim for developing complex characters grappling with serious moral dilemmas.[12] It also earned six Oscar nominations, making history when Louis Gossett Jr. became the first African American man to win a Supporting Actor award. Its signature song, "Love Lift Us Up Where We Belong," also won an Oscar and was in heavy rotation on mainstream radio stations, expanding the audience for the film's main themes.

Officer partially challenges and partially reinforces the dominance of traditional morality and the sacrifice of individual desire that was evident in *Casablanca*. Whereas in *Casablanca* devotion to country and higher values regularly trump personal needs and love interests, the hero in *Officer* has to attain love to become both an officer and a gentleman. This journey is complex, as the film reveals the earlier generation's claim of honor and sacrifice for higher values to be troubled at best. But rather than forgoing the quest for honor in light of this failure, the hero slowly comes to expand his narrow understanding of self-interest and embrace true love, which in turn allows him to live up to his public obligation to the military, thus fulfilling the aspirations of the film's title, as the hero becomes both an officer and a gentleman.

As in *Casablanca*, the main character of this story is not the standard Hollywood hero. Zack Mayo (Richard Gere) is a naval aviation officer candidate who enters training willing to break the rules and work the system to further his self-interest. After Zack's mother committed suicide when he was still a child, he was sent to live with his long-absent father, a naval serviceman stationed in Southeast Asia. A callous, judgmental man who drank to excess and consorted with prostitutes in the presence of his son, he made it quite clear that he had neither interest in nor aptitude for being a father and a role model. Zack's behavior in officer candidate school suggests that the callousness of his father has led Zack to become a detached, self-interested loner. While the other officer candidates in his training class are supporting each other as they struggle through rigorous training exercises conducted by Sergeant Foley (Louis Gossett Jr.), Zack is busy taking advantage of his classmates' vulnerability by selling them pre-shined shoes and belt buckles (which he procures on the cheap from an enlisted man) so that they can meet Foley's stringent inspection requirements.

The film revolves around Zack's conflict with Sergeant Foley, who is training him publicly to become an officer, and his townie girlfriend, Paula (Debra Winger), who is training him privately to become a husband. As Zack sees it initially, both Foley and Paula threaten to stand in the way of his goal of being a naval aviation officer, as they both challenge his firm belief that he's alone in the world and only in it for himself.

For his part, Foley questions whether Zack is too self-interested and too much of a loner to make a good officer. When Foley discovers that

Zack has been exploiting other candidates' need for inspection-quality shoes and belt buckles in order to make a quick buck, he tries to get Zack to voluntarily drop out of the program. Zack refuses, but during a weekend of endless discipline and verbal abuse from Foley, Zack does break down under pressure and concede that he has nothing else in his life but the program, a crucial admission of need and vulnerability.

Zack's relationship with Paula is equally fraught. He originally picks her up at a Navy- sponsored dance he attends with his friend and fellow officer candidate Sid (David Keith), who picks up Lynette (Lisa Blount) at the same dance, aiming for fun and sex without commitment throughout the duration of the program. As Zack slowly opens up to Paula over the course of the weeks-long naval training session, she comes to understand the lingering loneliness and hurt he feels as a result of his mother's suicide. As he continues to foreground his independence, insisting that "you're all alone in the world," she perceives a more complex self underneath his tough façade, responding, "I bet most people buy that line when you feed it to them, huh?"

As his personal relationship with Paula deepens, Zack also begins to bond with the other officer candidates. In contrast with his earlier self-interested behavior, when he has a chance to break the camp's obstacle course record, he instead offers moral support to the lone woman candidate as she struggles to scale the climbing wall, helping her to avoid disqualification from the program. At the same time, Paula begins to fall in love with Zack, even as she continues to insist to him that she's in it solely for fun. Her mother warns her against trying to trap him into marriage by becoming pregnant, something she herself tried to do in her youth with another officer candidate, only to be abandoned by him in her time of need when she became pregnant with Paula, another example of how honor and self-sacrifice were never really a given even in the armed forces. Meanwhile Paula's best friend, Lynette, has been dropping hints that she is pregnant, hoping to entrap Sid into doing the honorable thing by marrying her.

These story lines all come to a head when Sid has a severe anxiety attack in an altitude simulator and nearly drowns. In the wake of this incident, he quits the officer training program, prioritizing self-preservation over self-sacrifice. Realizing that he has been pursuing service in the Navy out of obligation to his family and in the memory of his brother who died in the Vietnam War, he abandons the Navy. While the shadow of Vietnam looms large, it ultimately does not compel Sid to sacrifice his individual interests. However, his apparent freedom from the traditional heroic framing does not ultimately enable him to fulfill his personal desires. While Sid has kept a long-standing girlfriend at home despite his relationship with Lynette (again, putting the lie to the traditional fiction that officers are gentlemen), he nevertheless succumbs to Lynette's hints that she is pregnant and asks her to marry him and return with him to Oklahoma. She rejects him because he has left the program and is no longer a desirable candidate for officer or husband. Zack and Paula judge Lynette severely for her ruse, suggesting that a moral code has been breached. Zack calls her "a cunt," and Paula insists that she would never be able to do what Lynette has done. They subsequently find that Sid has hanged himself in the hotel room where he and Lynette used to have their weekend liaisons. Reliving his mother's suicide, Zack berates Sid for not saying goodbye to him, and retreats back into his lonely self, asking, "Why can't I ever learn?" (presumably, not to care for people, as it always seems to end in disaster).

Even though Paula tries to assure him that he's not responsible for either his mother's or Sid's death, Zack immediately detaches himself from her, everyone, and everything, saying, "I don't want anyone to love me. . . . I don't need you, anybody. I don't need the Navy." Returning to the base, Zack tries to drop out of the program and detach from the Navy, but Foley won't allow it. Zack angrily undertakes a public martial arts battle with Foley, who ultimately wins and tells Zack that he can quit if he wants to. In the end, Zack does not quit, recognizing Foley's positive influence on him, and Paula's as well. The movie ends with Zack carrying Paula out over the threshold of the factory where she works, with the strains of "Love Lift Us Up Where We Belong" rising in the background, underscoring the redeeming and transformative effect of good love. Zack has successfully become both an officer and a gentleman, overcoming his father's shortcomings through the soft love of a good woman and the tough love of an honorable sergeant.[13]

Officer offers a transitional representation of the relationship between public morality and privacy, between honor and personal desire. The film breaks with the traditional frame by allowing its romantic leads to fulfill their personal desires, but it suggests that doing so, in the end, facilitates honorable military service and traditional community values. Rather than being sublimated as in *Casablanca*, private desire promotes traditional heroism and the fulfillment of official duty. This film suggests that the public and private model of the officer and gentleman may still be fulfilled, just not through self-sacrifice. Although Zack does not sacrifice personal desire, he does discipline it into a traditionally monogamous heterosexual relationship, as private desire becomes the key to developing into an honorable and heroic serviceman. Perhaps this somewhat more flexible understanding of the relationship between public morality and personal desire is permissible in this context because *Officer* is not set in the context of war, let alone World War II, in which the lines between good and evil seemed so very clear.

An Officer and a Gentleman challenges the traditional assumption that sacrificing individual desire for the greater good is necessary when it comes to sex. The fulfillment of desire actually allows Zack to better serve his country. *Officer* also suggests that the traditional narrative about honorable men sacrificing for the greater good is at least somewhat fanciful. Zack's father is shown to be morally suspect even though he spent his entire life in the armed forces. But *Officer* is also a transitional narrative and as such it does not completely dismiss traditional norms. Sexual desire must still be disciplined, as Zack must learn to accept the strictures of heterosexual monogamy. In addition, the shift away from traditional values portrayed in the film was thought to apply only to heterosexual men in mainstream politics and society in the 1980s. Homosexual personal desire was largely thought to render gay men incapable of acting in a gentlemanly fashion. It would be impossible for homosexuals to become public heroes in this transitional narrative frame, as Sergeant Foley's repeated characterization of substandard trainees as faggots and pansies makes clear. While Foley's clear devotion to Zack suggests possible change on the distant horizon, at this time the public largely continued to assume that gay males would be unable to live up to the standards that Zack's heterosexual romance taught him to fulfil both privately and publicly. Neither gentlemen nor officers, homosexuals remained trapped within the frame of traditional norms, subject to exclusion in the form of persistent moral and legal condemnation.

Pop Culture on Concluding Morality: *Brothers*

Brothers, a 2009 Hollywood remake of a 2004 Danish film, focuses on the aftereffects of war on individual servicemen returning home. It received a good deal of attention when it was released, in part due to the top-line actors in the cast (Tobey Maguire, Jake Gyllenhaal, Natalie Portman, Sam Shepard, and Mare Winningham), with critics praising the depth of their performances, especially Maguire's. Despite receiving nominations for Golden Globes in the Best Actor (Maguire) and Best Original Song (U2, "Winter") categories, it drew a smaller audience than *Officer*, perhaps because of the difficulty of its themes. It starts off in the standard triumphalist form of a war movie, suggesting that those who have followed all the rules will be richly rewarded and regarded as heroes. However, it ends with a more complex message that suggests that moral clarity is uncertain at best after the war is over. While servicemen still aspire to heroism and honorable behavior in their public lives in *Officer and a Gentleman* (admittedly in a somewhat different form than in *Casablanca*), the very existence of these virtues comes to be questioned in *Brothers*.

Brothers begins by suggesting that the line between right and wrong, hero and villain is quite clear. In that sense it is initially reminiscent of a traditional narrative. Sam Cahill (Maguire) is a Marine captain preparing for his fourth tour of duty in Afghanistan and a devoted family man married to his high school sweetheart, Grace (Portman), with two daughters. He appears to be a squeaky-clean hero who has done everything right in both his private and public life. Contrary to both *Casablanca* and *Officer and a Gentleman*, this hero is not a rule breaker in any obvious way. His brother, Tommy (Gyllenhaal), on the other hand, appears to be nothing but a rule breaker. A volatile single guy with substance abuse issues, he has just been released from prison after serving time for armed robbery. Although Sam is supportive of Tommy, Grace doesn't like him, fearing that he will be a bad influence on her girls if he spends too much time in their seemingly picture-perfect home. Sam's father (Shepard), a Vietnam vet, is angry and a serious drinker. He has a history of abusing his kids and creating problems for their long-suffering mother (Winningham), once again challenging the notion that servicemen of previous eras are heroic and honorable on and off the battlefield.

Traditional heroism and honor are challenged yet again, as the behavior of rule followers comes to be questioned and the actions of rule breakers appear redemptive. When Sam is redeployed to Afghanistan, word soon follows that he has been killed in a helicopter crash. Seeking to help his sister-in-law and redeem himself in her eyes, Tommy arranges for his contractor friends to remodel her kitchen (suggesting that the picture-perfect house is not so perfect after all). Unbeknownst to them, Sam is not dead; rather, he and one of his men, Private Joe Willis (Patrick Flueger), are being tortured in the mountains of Afghanistan. Meanwhile, Tommy has become increasingly close with Grace and her girls, regularly participating in family activities. While drinking and smoking marijuana together late one night, he and Grace loosen up and share a kiss as she confesses that she is not the good girl that she has always appeared to be. They immediately pull away and become much more cautious in their subsequent interactions, but continue to spend time together as Tommy maintains his relationship with Grace's girls.

Back in Afghanistan, Sam's captors succeed in breaking him, forcing him to denounce his mission on video. Once broken, and under threat of not being able to see his family ever again, he is forced to choose between his own life and that of Private Willis. Unwilling to give up the hope of returning home to his family, Sam beats Willis to death with a lead pipe, creating a terrible secret that he shares with no one upon his subsequent rescue and return home. He becomes emotionally volatile because of this trauma, alternating between extreme withdrawal and explosive fits of rage. Convinced (wrongly) that Tommy and Grace have been sleeping together, Sam brings the tension to a head when he destroys the new kitchen with a fireplace poker that resembles the pipe that he used to kill Willis. Pulling the gun that he has been carrying around with him since his return home, he then threatens to kill Grace and Tommy.

This scene completely destroys the moral clarity that seemed to be a given before the war. Here, convicted criminal Tommy appears to be the good guy, as he protects Grace and the girls from Sam's rage and attempts to get him to drop the gun. Sam's behavior reveals the disappearance of traditional heroism. As the police arrive, the conflict moves outside the private confines of the house and into a much more public space, the front yard. When the police try to talk him down by recognizing Sam as a war hero, he replies by waving the gun around and shouting, "I'm not a hero! Do you know what I've done?" Tommy's response highlights the private nature of the conflict, as he tries to get the police to back off by saying, "This is a family matter," while also calling out to Sam, "You're my brother, you're my family." Sam affirms this as he drops the gun, crying out, "I'm drowning, Tommy." When next we see Sam, he is being treated for mental trauma at a VA hospital, held in a locked-up unit, recalling the way that Tommy was living behind prison bars at the beginning of the movie. This complete reversal challenges all that we had taken for granted about who the heroes and villains are in this narrative, what constitutes honorable behavior, and whether moral standards (traditional or otherwise) are as clear as they once seemed.

After Grace threatens to leave Sam if he doesn't tell her what happened when he was being held prisoner, he finally breaks down and confesses to killing Willis. But even this act of contrition does not right the moral universe and restore normal life. There is no clear right and wrong in the post-9/11 world of violence and torture. In the meantime, Tommy has apologized to the victim of his armed robbery. Those who were once clear heroes are now broken, left without a moral compass in a world of seemingly terrible choices. Those who were once morally suspect have now been redeemed and are even seen as honorable.

By the end of the film, it is unclear whether Sam, Grace, and their family will stay together, or whether Sam will make it at all, as he wonders in a voice-over, "I don't know who said only the dead see the end of war. I've seen the end of war. The question is, can I live again?" As the film concludes, we hear the Irish rock band U2 singing "Winter" in the background: "Now I'm twenty-five / I'm trying to stay alive / In a corner of the world / with no clear enemies to fight." This confusing new moral universe lacks a compass, leaving individuals to struggle with their families and selves in a confusing private world that seems devoid of clear moral standards.

Brothers casts considerable doubt on the romantic notion that traditional moralizing was ever all that it seemed to be. Military servicemen of the Vietnam era and post-9/11 world no longer seem to be the officers and gentlemen they were made out to be in days gone by. The erosion of belief in traditional morality that is displayed in *Brothers* is an important step in shifting public understanding toward privatizing morality, a key component in the drive to decriminalize sodomy. Such a shift undercuts the ethical foundation of the notion that homosexuals are by definition perverse and dangerous. In a moral universe where a convicted criminal like Tommy can come to be seen as heroic in both private and public life, LGBT people can too. The public moral standard that characterized gays as moral degenerates and led to a long pattern of condemnation has been eviscerated, much as it was in *Lawrence v. Texas*.

In *Brothers* these revelations appear to come at a considerable cost. This postwar shift appears to create private havoc and public uncertainty, apparently leaving individuals to negotiate complex moral problems on their own and undercutting the basis for collective moral action. What happens in the wake of this evisceration of traditional standards remains uncertain at best in *Brothers*, just as it was in *Lawrence*.

Conclusion

Casablanca, *Officer*, and *Brothers* portray a shift from traditional, community-based morality to private, individual-based morality. In *Casablanca*, private desire is repressed to further the greater community good. In *An Officer and a Gentleman*, individual desire both reinforces and challenges traditional values in the private and public sphere. In *Brothers*, traditional standards of public morality have completely eroded. These shifts reflect a slow but gradual reformulation of mainstream understanding of the relationship between sexuality, public morality, and the right to privacy.

The development of these new ideas in mainstream culture had important ramifications for the decriminalization of sodomy, the first pillar of the drive for LGBT rights. Privatizing desire significantly undercut the basis for continuing to criminalize allegedly deviant sexual behavior. As part of this process, mainstream, heterosexual culture slowly acknowledged and then included homosexuality in its drive to privatize sexual choice. As queer theorist and English professor Michael Warner has noted, "Any organized attempt to transform gender or sexuality is a public questioning of private life."[14] In this case, government became more limited in a manner consistent with a more libertarian stance toward governing, leading to greater acceptance of the humanity and rights claims of homosexuals. Building on the momentous events at Stonewall and the creation of a national LGBT movement in its wake, the shift to privacy served to further open the closet door for many sexual deviants, producing a decriminalized political and legal identity.

These developments fostered more vociferous demands for additional LGBT inclusion, but they also created a continuing need for mainstream recognition and acceptance, producing both opportunities and limitations for future movement development. The shift to decriminalization undercut the traditional moral narrative and the politics of disgust it fostered, replacing it with the right to privacy, contingent on consent and lack of harm. In the process, a new kind of encounter was forged between the gay and lesbian community and the mainstream that created interdependence between two formerly antagonistic entities.[15]

The monumental shift away from traditional morality toward an individual right to privacy was bound to create moral confusion, a kind of domestic version of the fog of war portrayed in *Brothers*. Sam is left without family and a stable self, as well as enormous fear about what will happen next. This is not because there is no moral standard beyond exclusionary traditional moralizing and conservative community values, as some politically and culturally conservative commentators have declared while proclaiming the end of Western civilization as we have known it. That of course is hyperbole at best. But it is fair to say that the new standard was not as specifically articulated as it might have been.

What would it mean to move toward a non-reproductive ethic of sexual mores that challenges the state's traditional inclination to promote reproductive sex? In *Lawrence*, Justice Kennedy offers a view of this grounded in mainstream values about liberty and individual autonomy. "Love is love" is a kind of boiled-down popularization of this jurisprudence. From this mainstream perspective, the basic idea is that gay and straight people really want the same thing deep down: to be loved, and to be able to express that love privately. But what would public, non-reproductive sexual ethics look like from the standpoint of the LGBT community, a counterpublic whose story of origin is grounded in the slogan "Smash the Church, Smash the State"?

From Enemies of the State to Heroes Fighting on Its Behalf

The James Bond Film Series and Military Inclusion

How were LGBT people transformed from existential threats to the state into potential heroes fighting on its behalf? In a historic policy shift that some likened to the end of racial segregation in the military, Congress voted in December 2010 to lift a long-standing ban on lesbians, gays, and bisexuals serving openly in the military. The ban was officially lifted in 2011 when President Barack Obama formally certified that the military was prepared to allow lesbian, gay, and bisexual members to serve openly. Prior to this shift, numerous studies identified a variety of legal and political variables that explained why inclusion had not yet occurred, and why it was not likely to for some time.[1] When some change did occur with the passage of the "Don't Ask, Don't Tell" policy, many scholars characterized it as compromised at best, reinforcing the idea that thoroughgoing policy shift was unlikely in the foreseeable future. As a result, the forces of institutional and ideological resistance to lifting the ban have been well documented. Why they were overcome is much less clear. This chapter explores the cultural roots of that development. Using the James Bond film series as a basis for tracking shifts in public understanding, I argue that changes in public understanding of sex and gender norms reflected and fostered support for lifting the ban first on gays and lesbians in the military, and later transgender people, integrating LGBT people into a major mainstream institution.

The chapter begins with a historical summary of the three stages of political and legal change that culminated in the lifting of the ban. I then explore the twenty-six films of the James Bond series, demonstrating three distinct shifts in sex and gender norms that foster greater acceptance of gays and lesbians in public service. The result is a new form of contemporary male masculinity that jettisons the idea that sexuality, whether homosexual or heterosexual, is an existential threat to the state. LGBT people are not only accepted, but sometimes even portrayed as heroic. In the end, it is male masculinity's toxic and seemingly genetically based addiction to violence that brings Bond and his failing empire down in the end.

A Classic Civil Rights Account of Military Inclusion

In this section, I break the classic civil rights narrative that describes gradual inclusion of LGBT people in the armed forces into three parts: the traditional, transitional, and concluding stages.[2]

Traditional Period

Scholars have suggested that thousands of LGBT people have served in the US armed forces over time, alternatively disciplined or accepted, often depending upon military need and commander discretion. For example, during the Revolutionary War, Lieutenant Gotthold Enslin was discharged for practicing same-sex sodomy. At the same time, Captain Friedrich von Steuben was revered as a brilliant leader even though he had relationships with at least three men during the war, two of whom he later adopted and made his heirs.[3] It is difficult to know exactly how many LGBT people have served throughout US history, in no small part because punishment for even identifying as LGBT could sometimes be quite severe. Documentable examples such as Enslin and von Steuben suggest that it is likely that there are many more unknown cases of such service.

In the first or traditional stage of the classic civil rights narrative, members of the excluded group are denied the full rights and privileges guaranteed to other citizens based on traditional assumptions about the group's moral inadequacy and the threat posed to national security. The

interests of the state and the interests of homosexuals were seen as dia-
metrically opposed. Each regarded the other as a threat to its basic security and, at times, its very existence. During World War I and World
War II, official policy excluded LGBT people by screening at entry into
the armed forces and dishonorably discharging those who were able to
elude screening. The first large-scale purge of suspected homosexuals
occurred at Newport Naval Training Station in 1919.

During World War II, the military began to view homosexuality as
a psychological dysfunction that could serve as grounds for exclusion
or discharge. Purges continued, destroying the careers and reputations
of many homosexual servicemembers. At the same time, other homosexuals continued to serve and were tolerated in many units, in part
due to the continuing need for troops. In a documentary entitled *Before
Stonewall*, lesbian servicewoman Sergeant Johnnie Phelps recalls General Dwight D. Eisenhower ordering her to conduct a purge of lesbians
serving in her WAC unit. Phelps agreed to do it but told Eisenhower that
the first name on the list of those to be discharged would have to be hers.
Overhearing the discussion, another WAC said that Phelps's name might
be the second name on the list, but that the first name would have to be
her own, leading Phelps to explain to Eisenhower that a purge would
decimate their unit. According to Phelps, Eisenhower immediately decided to abandon the purge.

The military also tolerated drag shows during World War II. Some
scholars argue that the modern gay and lesbian movement has its roots
in this culture, as many first became aware in the military that they constituted a significant percentage of the general population.[4] After the
war, many gay and lesbian veterans relocated to port cities, establishing
gay subcultures in cities such as New York and San Francisco, both of
which later became central to LGBT activism.

Despite these aberrations, traditional arguments dominated during
this period. Homosexuality was seen as morally wrong, medically aber-
rant, and threatening to the state. These beliefs resulted in an official
policy of exclusion, even if it was sometimes applied unevenly. After

World War II, "blue discharges" were often issued to prevent homosexual soldiers from receiving benefits even though they had served without a court-martial or a prison sentence. Blue discharges fell in between honorable and dishonorable discharges and are said to have been called blue because they were printed on blue paper.[5]

During the Cold War period, LGBT people continued to be characterized as threats to the very existence of the state. As discussed in the book's introduction, in response to fears of communist infiltration, Senator Joseph McCarthy and his allies prompted the State Department to discharge thousands from service on morals charges in the early 1950s. "Sexual perversion" was seen as a security risk that made homosexuals particularly vulnerable to blackmail from communist enemies, and therefore unfit to serve.[6] Given the stakes, gay and lesbian attempts to organize during this period were very brave if somewhat tentative. In the early 1960s, a handful of well-dressed, clean-cut gays and lesbians including Mattachine Society members such as Frank Kameny and Barbara Gittings protested exclusion from government service in cities such as Washington, DC, and Philadelphia. While these groups were often small and fleeting, their efforts paved the way for challenges to the ban that were much more visible in mainstream politics.

Transitional Period

In 1975 Sergeant Leonard Matlovich came out and challenged the ban on gays in the military. Although individual efforts like Matlovich's did not immediately result in policies of greater inclusion, they did make the issue of exclusion more visible than it had ever been in mainstream politics. As a result of his challenge, Matlovich became the most well-known homosexual in the country at that time, appearing on the cover of *Time* magazine.

A decorated career Air Force member, Matlovich had served three tours of duty in Vietnam and later as a trainer in race relations. After he declared his homosexuality to his commanding officer in order to challenge the ban, the Air Force recommended that Matlovich receive a general (i.e., less than honorable) discharge. Raised as a strict Catholic and once a committed conservative supporter of the Republican Party, Matlovich argued that it was his patriotic duty to fight for the inclusion of gays in the military, a battle he viewed as parallel to Black civil rights struggles. After an Air Force panel found him to be unfit for military service, a federal appeals court ruled his dismissal unlawful. The Court argued that current policy gave the military too much discretion, making it impossible for the court to determine whether improper factors played a role. Five years after initially declaring his homosexuality, Matlovich won a further victory when a court ordered the Air Force to reinstate him with back pay. He ultimately settled with the Air Force for $160,000 in exchange for an agreement that he would not try to enlist in any branch of the service. Despite Matlovich's triumph in court, the military continued to discharge gays and lesbians on a regular basis. The military ban did not mention transgender people, but at least one person was expelled for "homosexual tendencies" based on her marriage to a trans man who had been a WAC.

Transitional periods in civil rights struggles are characterized by such conflict. While traditional norms remain well represented, arguments challenging the assumptions behind these norms gradually become more ascendant. Opponents of lifting the ban often argued that allowing homosexuals in the military would undermine morale, order, and discipline. Some also said that homosexuality was immoral. Supporters of lifting the ban noted that these were the same kinds of arguments that were made earlier to maintain racial segregation in the armed forces, adding that the military needed anyone who was willing and able to serve, regardless of whatever prejudices people may hold about sexual orientation.

After Matlovich's important breakthrough, individual exclusions continued to be challenged in the federal courts, resulting in both victories and losses for gay and lesbian challengers.[7] The LGBT movement had gone national by this time, partially in response to continued opposition from the political right. Interest groups that addressed a wide variety of gay and lesbian issues had been established, including the National Gay and Lesbian Task Force and the Human Rights Campaign, as well as more specialized organizations focused on inclusion in the armed forces.

Although much of the media's coverage of this issue focused on gay men, women and especially women of color were discharged from service at a much higher rate, especially in the Navy, which at that time was beginning to send more women to sea. The ban resulted in the discharge of nearly ten times more women Marines than men, including an extensive purge of women who were alleged to be lesbians at the Marines' Parris Island Recruit Training Depot in 1988.

In the following year, a federal appeals court issued a stunning ruling that found the military ban unconstitutional, prohibiting the Army from excluding people from service because of their sexual orientation. Likening discrimination against homosexuals to that of other minority groups such as African Americans, Judge William Norris said that the military's arguments that homosexuals would harm morale and discipline did not meet a heightened constitutional standard. While the core ruling finding the ban unconstitutional was later overturned, openly gay and African American Sergeant Perry Watkins, the challenger in this case, was allowed to re-enlist because the Army had repeatedly allowed him to do so over his fourteen-year career with full knowledge that he was a homosexual.[8]

Despite the government's continued resistance to lifting the ban, a Pentagon research center issued a report, again contending that excluding homosexuals was discriminatory. Noting that anyone with a secret is subject to blackmail, the report argued that homosexuals were no more susceptible than heterosexuals to such pressures, thus undermining a central argument that the government had been using to justify the exclusion of gays from the military. Defense secretary Dick Cheney (who has a lesbian daughter) agreed, characterizing the argument as "an old chestnut." Nonetheless, Pentagon sources quickly disavowed the report as biased. Two years later, Congress's General Accounting Office found that enforcing the ban cost the government at least $27 million a year. Later that same summer, both the *Army Times* and the *Air Force Times* newspapers came out in favor of ending the ban.

In 1992 candidate Bill Clinton pledged to lift the ban on gays in the military. Once he was elected, he presented his plan to the public, arguing that the country needed everyone willing and able to serve. However, there were many signs that neither Congress nor the military would accept a change in the policy. Key congressional leaders such as Senator Sam Nunn and military leaders such as General Colin Powell, chair of the Joint Chiefs of Staff, argued that including homosexuals would undermine morale, order, and discipline. Several military leaders argued that lifting the ban could lead to mass resignations and recruiting difficulties. Some said that they resented such a major policy change coming from a president they thought of as a draft dodger. Although President Harry Truman issued an executive order to end racial segregation in the armed forces in 1948, Clinton instead opted to negotiate with Powell.

Navy officials had resisted when a federal judge ordered reinstatement of openly gay servicemember Petty Officer Keith Meinhold, who was discharged for stating on national television that he was a homosexual. In response to the Navy's inaction, Judge Terry Hatter reissued the order, stating, "This is not a military dictatorship. Here, the rule of law applies to the military." When the Navy complied with this second order, Meinhold commented that his presence in the Navy would effectively disprove the military's argument that gay servicemembers undermine good order, morale, and discipline in the ranks.

Testifying before the Senate Armed Services Committee on President Clinton's proposal to end the ban on gay men and lesbians serving openly in the military, Colonel Fred Peck made headline news when he announced, "My son Scott is a homosexual. I think he's a fine person. But he should not serve in the military." While denying that he was homophobic, Peck testified that openly gay soldiers would damage morale and could face physical danger or even murder at the hands of many in the ranks, a foreshadowing of the violence that was to come in this period.

The conflict between opponents and advocates of greater inclusion eventuated in "compromise" legislation in 1994, popularly known as the "Don't Ask, Don't Tell" policy. In an odd twist, this policy weaponized privacy against LGB individuals, allowing them to serve, but not openly. Instead, LGB servicemembers were compelled to remain in the closet to avoid the formal threat of dishonorable discharge as well as the informal threat of violence.

Despite the promise of this new policy to reset the terms of gay participation in the military, the rate of gay discharges increased dramatically, affecting over a thousand servicemembers a year, and more than thirteen thousand by the time the ban was later lifted. Reports of anti-gay harassment also rose, including the murder of Private Barry Winchell, who was beaten to death by a member of his own unit wielding a baseball bat as Winchell slept. Petty Officer Third Class Allen Schindler was stomped to death and mutilated by two of his fellow sailors at a US naval base in Japan, shortly after coming out as gay to his commander. Some sailors noted that these murders were part of a pattern of harassment against gays at the base. Prior to his death, Schindler described life on his ship as a "living hell" for gay sailors.

Cast as a compromise, the policy failed to satisfy both opponents and advocates of lifting the ban. It allowed LGB people to serve, disappointing those who sought an absolute ban. Because the policy forced servicemembers to remain closeted, it also disappointed those who were ready to hold Clinton to his campaign promise to lift the ban entirely. Nonetheless, in a classic civil rights account, a compromise like "Don't Ask, Don't Tell" represents significant, if incremental, progress toward the goal of full inclusion, indicating an important public reframing of LGBT servicepeople as victims rather than villains.

Concluding Period

In the third or concluding stage of the classic civil rights narrative, the hearts and minds of the American people have changed enough to fully displace traditional exclusionary assumptions. By the time Barack Obama was first elected president in 2008, 69 percent of the American public believed that gays should be able to serve openly in the military. This number included groups across the ideological board, including 58 percent of Republicans and 60 percent of those who described themselves as weekly churchgoers.

After brokering an agreement with Congress in 2010, Obama announced his intention to lift the ban. Congress signed the repeal into law and the president signed it, contingent on a sixty-day waiting period, during which time the armed forces certified that the shift would not harm military readiness. In the 2011 signing ceremony, Obama fully repudiated the traditional idea that gays are immoral and a threat to the state. He noted that gays and lesbians have long provided heroic service to the country, dispelling official antagonism between the state and the LGBT movement, at least as regards inclusion in the military and public service. The LGBT movement's interest in inclusion and the state's interest in fielding an armed force capable of continuing to undertake two wars appeared to come together. As of 2013, same-sex spouses of those who serve in the military have been entitled to the same rights and benefits as opposite-sex spouses.

In 2016 the Department of Defense repealed regulations that banned transgender people from serving in the military, providing a seemingly happy ending to a story with very fraught beginnings. The interests of LGBT people and the state appeared to converge in a redemptive narrative that highlights the ability of American political institutions and the public to embrace ideals of toleration and inclusion over time, eventually triumphing over historical prejudice and exclusion.

Contrary to what the classic civil rights narrative would have us believe, conflicts of this magnitude are typically not easily put to rest.

Shortly after his surprising victory, President Donald J. Trump tweeted in 2017 that transgender people would no longer be able to serve in the armed forces. However, Joint Chiefs of Staff chairman General Joseph Dunford indicated that transgender people would continue to serve until he received direction from General James Mattis, secretary of defense. Shortly thereafter, several transgender servicepeople challenged the proposed ban in court. Trump then directed the Department of Defense and the Department of Homeland Security to create a plan to implement a transgender ban on military service by February 2018. Meanwhile, a federal district court barred the Trump administration from excluding transgender people. The Department of Justice asked a federal appeals court to stay the ruling, claiming that including transgender people imposes extraordinary burdens on the military and may harm military effectiveness. After the court denied the administration's request, the Pentagon indicated that it would begin to accept transgender applicants as of January 2018, if they could show a stable gender for at least eighteen months prior. Between April 2019 and January 2021, transgender people who had medically transitioned were not allowed to serve. Those who had not transitioned were required to enlist under the gender they were assigned at birth.

Just a few days after he took office in January 2021, President Biden appeared to provide the redemptive ending called for in classic civil rights accounts, as the transgender ban was fully lifted with no remaining restrictions on LGBT people in the armed forces. This inclusion signaled a massive shift away from traditional ideas about LGBT people, transforming them from perverse threats to heroes in the public mind. Why did this shift happen? Below I argue that the answer lies in shifting understandings of sex and gender norms across the twenty-six movies in the James Bond film series.

The James Bond Film Series on Sex and Gender Norms

The longevity of the James Bond series makes it an excellent site to explore long-term cultural shifts in popular ideas about sex and gender norms, particularly as they are expressed in the context of the military and service to the state. Some scholars have cautioned that pop culture in general and the James Bond series more specifically have not typically been out in front in this area, in part because they have often reflected mainstream production and cultural values.[9] There is, of course, no doubt that traditional understandings that reinforce regressive gender and sex roles appear throughout the Bond series. However, consistent with my earlier argument that pop culture is often contradictory, the Bond franchise also provides ample challenges to status quo gender and sex norms over time.

The Bond series has had an enormous cultural impact over roughly sixty years. While they have usually not been critically acclaimed, the Bond movies are the fourth most successful film series in history in terms of box office draw.[10] James Chapman argues that "Bond films have been the most popular and enduring series in motion picture history."[11] According to the documentary *James Bond: The True Story*, more than half the people in the world have seen a 007 film. While Bond works for the British secret service, he is deeply embedded in American popular culture.[12] No less an American icon than President John F. Kennedy contributed to the success of the early films in the series by placing *From Russia with Love* on his list of top ten favorite books.[13] He also held a White House screening of *Dr. No*, which was released as the Cuban Missile Crisis was coming to a head. In the documentary *Everything or Nothing: The Untold Story of James Bond*, Kennedy is reported to have said, "I wish I had James Bond on my staff."

According to Metro Goldwyn Mayer (MGM) Studios, Bond's target audience is very broad, including men and women ages thirteen to fifty-nine. However, the National Research Group (a Hollywood-based research firm) has found that men over thirty-five are most likely to identify as Bond fans.[14] Advertisers believe that this demographic will be interested in drinking the kind of vodka that is used in Bond's "shaken, not stirred" martinis and wearing a Rolex watch like Bond's. Scholars suggest that this consumption is closely related to a desire to take on the flavor of Bond's masculinity, much in the way that vodka "takes on the characteristics of whatever it is mixed with."[15] This is consistent with several popular treatments of the Bond series written by men who, as adolescents in the late 1960s and early 1970s, experienced their first Bond movies as an opportunity to develop sexual fantasies that have shaped their consumption of the series ever since. These range from trade books such as Simon Winder's *The Man Who Saved Britain: A Personal Journey into the Disturbing World of James Bond* to Benjamin Svetkey's piece "50 Years of Bond," which appeared in *Entertainment Weekly* magazine to mark the release of *Skyfall*.[16] Relatedly, Claire Hines has argued that a special connection exists between Bond and *Playboy*. Created in 1953, the same year that Ian Fleming published the first Bond novel, *Playboy* was the first American magazine to publish one of Fleming's spy stories. It "embraced Sean Connery's cinematic Bond as uniquely expressive of its aspirational masculine ideal," at one point associating his trademark introductory line ("Bond. James Bond.") with its own charismatic publisher: "Hefner. Hugh Hefner. Oops. It's an easy mistake to make."[17] There is little doubt that shifting sex and gender norms in the Bond series would be influential for a broad swath of the public.

Sex, Gender, and Sexuality Norms

The Bond character represents male masculinity in a heroic form, in the context of service to the government as a secret agent throughout the Cold War period and beyond. Ideas about sex, gender, and sexuality are often central to the construction of film heroes, including ideas about who is most fit to serve their country.[18] While most scholarly treatments of the Bond series include at least some discussion of gender roles, there is much less discussion of homosexuality and, to my knowledge, none that link gender or sexuality directly to public opinion or to public policies that affect LGBT inclusion.[19]

Formative queer theorists such as Judith Butler and Eve Sedgwick have argued that gender roles are intimately related to homosexuality and gender identity.[20] When traditional sex and gender roles are followed, binary sex maps directly onto gender. Thus, biological maleness is directly related to aggressive masculinity and biological femaleness to passive femininity, a repetitive pattern that Butler has referred to as "the myth of sex and gender convergence." She calls it a myth because in her view there is nothing natural or given about biological sex, or of males necessarily being masculine and females feminine. She argues that these seemingly natural arrangements are in fact social and political constructions that serve to distribute power, rewarding those who stay within traditional sex and gender norms and disciplining those who challenge them. Heteronormativity helps to hold the myth in place by naturalizing and rewarding opposite-sex relationships, which are premised on a binary wedding of female femininity to male masculinity, further embedding the convergence of sex and gender, calling to mind the popular phrase "opposites attract." Demonizing homosexuality is part and parcel of this process. Traditional moralizing punishes deviants, pushing them away from challenging the mythic convergence and back into the closet.

Butler's theory suggests that public acceptance of traditional sex and gender norms would align with a public policy that excludes lesbian and gay people from public service, just as challenges to traditional sex and gender norms could open space for greater inclusion. Sedgwick's work suggests that refiguring the closet would be central to such a development, as continued demonization of homosexuality encourages gay people to remain hidden deep in the closet. As gender and sex roles change, sexual identity is likely to shift along with them, moving from largely private or closeted, to an open secret that is somewhat acknowledged yet not embraced, to proudly and publicly out.

In the sections that follow, I focus on shifting representations of heroes and villains by tracking changing ideas about sex, gender, and sexuality norms in the twenty-six films of the Bond series. I argue that a shift in mainstream understanding of these norms led to a reconfiguration of gay identity from villain to hero, and that this critical development reflects and fosters growing public acceptance of inclusion of LGBT people in the military.

Sex, Gender, and Sexuality Stages in the Bond Series

There have been three distinct shifts in Bond's representation of masculinity, each of which entails a specific construction of homosexuality in relation to state interests. These shifts in ideas about sex and gender in mainstream culture help to explain why LGBT inclusion in the military came to be accepted. In the first or traditional period, Bond represents a traditional form of aggressive male masculinity, which dominates a relatively passive form of female femininity. If homosexuality comes up at all, it is addressed obliquely, dismissed as laughable among strong masculine types, or killed off when such traits are hinted at in less masculine types who clearly threaten the state's interests. Lesbians who exhibit any traditionally feminine traits are easily converted back to heterosexuality by Bond's charms, while women who perform female masculinity are seen as a threat to the state and are killed off. In short, the Bond of this period suggests that homosexual interests always diverge from the interests of the state, and therefore must be eradicated.

In the second or transitional period, traditional masculinity begins to be challenged. Thus, traditional masculinity is practiced in a somewhat more conflicted setting, while a far less passive form of femininity emerges when Bond's superior, M, begins to be played by a woman (Judi Dench). The new M makes her displeasure with Bond's dalliances quite clear and he begins, ever so slightly, to offer a new and somewhat less sexually aggressive form of masculinity. The representation of homosexuality also shifts, as it begins to be more publicly acknowledged, if still somewhat obliquely. It is treated largely as an open secret, and a few comments directly reference the then-emerging "Don't Ask, Don't Tell" policy, always with accompanying snide references to Bond's ongoing heterosexual philandering. While homosexuality is acknowledged more directly during this period of the Bond series, the closet remains firmly in place, consistent with "Don't Ask, Don't Tell," which allowed LGB people to further their interest in serving in the military if they were willing to become complicit with the state's continuing desire to conceal homosexuality.

The Bond of the third or concluding period offers a new framing of gender and sexuality that highlights male masculinity's growing vulnerability. Feminine characters are often in a position of equal or superior power to Bond institutionally as well as interpersonally, making sex frequently as dangerous as work. Homosexuality is embraced in the concluding period by no less a heroic specimen of male masculinity than James Bond, who unabashedly suggests that it is possible that he himself may have had same-sex sexual encounters. Spoiler alert: despite these shifts, toxic masculinity proves to be Bond's undoing in the end.

Bond on Masculinity and Sexuality in the Traditional Period

James Bond is played by Sean Connery, George Lazenby, and Roger Moore in the traditional period, which accounts for roughly two-thirds of the movies in the series. Bond is an archetype of traditional masculinity in these early films, reinforcing traditional gender and sexuality norms and policing those who challenge them. He is handsome, tough, sexually aggressive, intelligent, professionally successful, egotistical, and cold-blooded in his pursuit of enemies of the state. There is much commentary about Bond's sexual prowess, including various double entendres about his penis. He is blatantly sexist and sleeps with women whenever he chooses and always on his own terms. He regularly stalks, harasses, and assaults women to get them to do his bidding.

Part of Bond's appeal is his swagger, which, according to John Cork and Bruce Scivally, "comes not just from his good looks" but also "from a particular confidence, a certainty within himself."[21] I will argue that

Bond's "certainty" is one of the important elements that shift over time, giving way to greater vulnerability in the concluding period. Interestingly, Sean Connery's certainty about what he called his "violent side" also shifted over time. In 1965 (during the traditional period) Connery stated, "I don't think there is anything particularly wrong about hitting a woman." Given the opportunity to retract that statement in a 1987 interview with Barbara Walters during the transitional period, Connery noted, "I haven't changed my opinion." Later, during the concluding period, he conceded that he had been wrong.[22]

When bad girls use their feminine wiles to try to lead him to his death, he sleeps with them to get vital information and coldly kills them afterwards, disposing of them with remarkable ease. Although the female lead characters, collectively known as the "Bond girls," often have featured roles, they typically represent traditional female femininity and are regularly dominated by Bond's traditional male masculinity. In *Bond Girls Are Forever*, a 2002 documentary about the women who have played these roles, Halle Berry comments that Bond girls are "the epitome of femininity." Beautiful, sexy, and exotic, they sport names such as Pussy Galore, Honey Ryder, Holly Goodhead, Mary Goodnight, and Xenia Onatopp. Unlike the bad girls, who receive their just deserts for trying to outfox Bond with sex, the Bond girls survive, perhaps due to their compliance with his demands. Feisty though they may sometimes be, they submit. The relationship between Bond's outsized masculinity and his freewheeling heterosexuality is highlighted early and often in this period. Presumptive gays and lesbians who transgress traditional gender and sexuality norms by failing to pair maleness with masculinity and femaleness with femininity are severely punished, typically with death.

In the first movie in the series, *Dr. No*, Sean Connery's Bond is compelled to accept a bigger gun from M, the head of the UK's Secret Intelligence Service (MI6), as he becomes a 00 agent with a license to kill. M describes Bond's previous weapon as light enough and small enough "to fit in a lady's purse." After this exchange, Bond is shown having sex with a beautiful woman whom he had earlier bested at the card table. In a subsequent scene he has sex with his next conquest twice, checking his watch to make sure there is enough time for a second go-round before the car he has called for them is scheduled to arrive. When the car does appear, Bond puts the girl in and she is taken away by the military; we come to understand that he has known all along that she has been trying to set him up to be killed. But he has outfoxed her. This begins a long pattern of having sex with women before either killing them or turning them in to others who will do the job for him, calling attention to Bond's extreme cold-bloodedness when it comes to women and sex.

His third conquest in *Dr. No* is Ursula Andress, who plays Honey Ryder. When she asks Bond whether he has a woman of his own, there is a long pause, and then an interruption that allows him to avoid answering, a pattern that is repeated throughout this period. As *Dr. No* reaches its conclusion, Bond overcomes a nuclear reactor threatening the Western world. As an enormous explosion results, he and Honey float offshore, apparently having sex in a small wooden boat. The regular practice of closing each film with Bond sleeping with the female lead continues until the concluding period of the series, except for *On Her Majesty's Secret Service* (1969) (discussed below), in which Bond is briefly domesticated.

Bond's relationship with Miss Moneypenny, the secretary of Bond's boss, M (the head of Britain's MI6), is also gendered, producing a traditional masculine and feminine relationship between hero and subordinate in a teasing and unrequited manner. In the second film of the Bond series, *From Russia with Love* (1963), Bond calls the office while sleeping with a woman, telling Moneypenny that he will be in shortly but that he is currently "reviewing an old case." When Moneypenny hears the woman slap Bond's hand, she responds, "Your old case sounds interesting." When Bond finally arrives at the office, M asks why Bond has been delayed. Rolling her eyes, Moneypenny retorts knowingly, "It'll be a miracle if he can explain where he's been all day." Despite her knowledge of Bond's wandering ways, she still pines after him, as presumably all women do. When he receives an assignment to Istanbul, Moneypenny says, "Maybe I should get you to take me there one day." Bond responds, "Darling Moneypenny, you know I never look at another woman."

Thunderball (1965) further reinforces Bond's traditional masculinity, while also making it clear that the hero will severely punish other men who deviate from traditional gender norms. In the opening action sequence, Bond watches a funeral from a distance while arranging to meet a female companion "later." Directly after the funeral, he calls on the grief-stricken widow, who is wearing a black dress and veil. Upon entering her home, Bond promptly punches her in the face and a fight ensues that reveals Bond's rival to be a man in drag. Bond kills the man in drag by choking him with a fireplace rod, and, despite being chased by two other foes in hot pursuit, he adds insult to injury by taking the time to throw several roses on the dead body with a smirk, suggesting that males who dare to cross the sex and gender line will in no way be tolerated.

You Only Live Twice (1967) extends this disdain for alternative masculinity, rejecting the possibility that traditional heroes such as James Bond could even consider homosexuality. As Bond continues his unrequited yet flirtatious relationship with Moneypenny, she unsuccessfully tries to compel him to repeat to her the new password, "I love you," before leaving on a trip to Japan. Later he must repeat the password to identify himself to the male head of the Japanese secret service, who must in turn respond in kind before any other business can transpire. This exchange is quickly laughed off by both men, each of whom represents a robust specimen of traditional masculinity. When his Japanese counterpart informs Bond shortly thereafter that men always come first in Japan, Bond reaffirms his adherence to dominant masculinity by responding, "I just might retire here," as he is subsequently offered several unnamed girls to keep him company during the night ahead. Colonialist and Orientalist themes abound in the Bond series. For example, when Bond asks a lover in Hong Kong why "Chinese girls taste different," she responds in a painfully caricatured accent, "Why, you think we better?" Bond patronizingly responds with a metaphor that highlights his pleasure in consuming varying cultural objects: "No, just different, like Peking duck is different from Russian caviar. But I love them both."

These representations of traditional masculinity and femininity, of conquest and passivity, continue throughout this period, running through the representation of Bond by Roger Moore. In Moore's first and most popular Bond film, *Live and Let Die* (1973), in the opening scene Bond wakes up in bed with a woman who looks up at him and asks, "One more time, again?" When his boss, M, arrives unexpectedly to give Bond a new assignment, his unnamed bedmate discreetly picks up her clothing, which has been strewn about the living room, and tries to sneak out the door undetected. In the meantime, Miss Moneypenny has come into the apartment and hidden the woman in a closet, removing her from the view of M and making Moneypenny's form of female femininity knowingly complicit in Bond's male masculinity. After Moneypenny and M leave, Bond picks up where he left off, using his special magnetic watch to pull down the zipper in the back of her dress, offering the tongue-in-cheek comment "sheer magnetism" as they begin the requested second sexual encounter of the evening.

Humor aside, Moore's Bond is every bit as cold-blooded as Connery's when it comes to women and sex. When the CIA sends an African American agent named Rosie to protect him in Haiti, he immediately comes on to her. While she initially rejects him, they do have sex on the beach the next day, after which he kills her, knowing all along that she was double-crossing him. When Rosie pleads with him before being shot, "You wouldn't kill me, after what we've just done," Bond reveals his contempt for female femininity, responding, "I certainly wouldn't do it before," and shoots her. Bond subsequently seduces a virginal Tarot card reader named Solitaire (Jane Seymour) by literally stacking the deck with the Tarot card marked "The Lovers" to persuade her that having sex with him is her fate. Afterwards, we learn that losing her virginity has destroyed her ability to see the future. Nonetheless, she too asks him for a second encounter, and he complies right before he leaves for his next adventure, saying, "No sense in going off half-cocked." After he has vanquished the enemy, the film concludes with Bond asking Solitaire where she would like to go. "Anywhere where we can find one of these," she responds, pointing to a bed. When they arrange to take a train to their next destination, they're asked, "What can you do on the train for sixteen hours" as they are then shown riding off down the tracks in their sleeper car, Bond and his girl together again.

It is worth noting that even during the traditional period, there is something of a break in Bond's otherwise rampant traditional masculinity, although it is rather brief and quickly reversed. *On Her Majesty's Secret Service* (1969) begins with George Lazenby's Bond saving a woman who is attempting suicide by drowning herself at the beach. As Bond fights off enemy agents, she speeds away in her car. After discovering that she is the Contessa Teresa "Tracy" di Vincenzo (Diana Rigg), Bond meets up with her again at a nearby hotel casino. Before too long they have sex, shortly after a scene in which he unapologetically slaps her in the face for offering his enemies information about his whereabouts. She herself suggests that she had been prostituted by Bond because he paid off an earlier bet that she was unable to cover in the casino.

As it turns out, Tracy is the daughter of a powerful mob boss, who comments that "what she needs is a man to dominate her, who will make love to her enough to make her love him." Bond refuses the one million pounds that her father offers in exchange for marrying her, instead accepting information about Bond's archenemy, Blofeld. While Tracy almost immediately falls in love with Bond, he continues to have sex with an array of other women, in one instance arranging to sleep with three women over the course of three hours in a single evening, perhaps overcompensating for the domesticity to come: eventually, Bond does ask Tracy to marry him and she, of course, accepts. Because "an agent shouldn't be concerned with anything but himself," he understands that he will "have to find something else to do" other than spying. When Tracy asks him whether he's sure about leaving the service, he responds that he loves her and "will never find another girl" like her. This is

James's first real hint of any sort of emotional attachment to any of his many conquests.

Here the Bond series appears to be engaging with the popularity of Diana Rigg, who also played Emma Peel on *The Avengers*, a spy show that made a big cultural splash in the United States, where it ran from 1965 to 1967. Peel was designed to be a character that would have "man appeal"; her name was drawn from a shorthand reference to this idea: "M. Appeal." The independence that she had gained due to the loss of her husband, however, allowed her also to be seen as much smarter and more aggressive than most female characters on television at that time. Including Tracy in this film allowed Bond to engage with this new cultural phenomenon—at least momentarily. While Rigg's Tracy is undoubtedly stronger than the typical Bond girl (she was, after all, able to domesticate James Bond), he is not married long enough to even get her out of her wedding dress before she is killed by Bond's archenemy, Blofeld, suggesting that all such attempts to curb traditional masculinity are doomed to failure.

Domestication is rolled back even further by the return of Sean Connery as Bond in *Diamonds Are Forever* (1971). In one sense, the franchise and its representation of traditional masculinity carry on as if George Lazenby and his brief foray into domesticity had never even existed. Connery returns to the fore, as undomesticated and sexually aggressive as ever—perhaps even more so to compensate for his short-lived marriage. To reestablish the traditional sexuality of the Bond of yore, the film also introduces two exceedingly odd (or one could say queer) characters who substantially deviate from traditional masculinity, Mr. Kidd and Mr. Wint. At Blofeld's direction they undertake several unsuccessful plots to eliminate Bond. While there is no direct mention of their sexuality, many scholars have understood them to be homosexual lovers.[23] Early on in the movie they are shown heading off into the sunset, virtually hand in hand, after having murdered two men who stood between them and a cache of South African diamonds. Characterized as "unsympathetic" as well as "deadly, effete, and ugly," these presumptively homosexual characters fail to kill Bond, and in fact are killed off by him.[24] This development is consistent with Vito Russo's argument that a wide variety of Hollywood films of this period, including spy movies, eliminated characters who were coded gay as punishment for their deviance and perversion.[25] With the return of Connery, the rampant womanizing associated with Bond's robust masculinity means that heterosexuality no longer poses a threat to the secret agent's success in the way that it did during the Lazenby/marriage moment. Nonetheless, even the mere suggestion of homosexuality seems to be a problem in need of elimination. As queer theorists have argued, demonizing homosexuality in this manner valorizes heterosexuality, a central theme in the Bond franchise if there ever was one.

As *Diamonds Are Forever* did with the characters Wint and Kidd, *From Russia with Love* (1963) offers a sexually deviant character without directly acknowledging her as such, this time one who represents as female masculinity and lesbian. Thoroughly butch, and the Number 3 agent below Blofeld, this ruthlessly violent and aggressively unfashionable colonel in the Russian military features hair severely pulled back, thick dark glasses, and chunky black shoes fitted with a retractable venomous knife. She is the very antithesis of the typical hyperfeminine Bond girl. As the BBC documentary short *Ian Fleming* notes, such lesbian-themed material offered "risqué undertones for the time." Be that as it may, the film was entirely in keeping with traditional sex, gender, and sexuality norms that dominate in the traditional period, as Number 3 is killed off in due course. In addition, the rampant heterosexuality that grounds Bond's male masculinity is portrayed as so strong that more feminine lesbians can't resist his charms and are regularly converted back to heterosexuality.

In *Goldfinger* (1964), one of the most popular and (somewhat) critically acclaimed films of the Bond franchise, the provocatively named Pussy Galore (Honor Blackman) is introduced as a foe just as Bond awakens after being knocked out, in the nick of time to save himself from a laser beam inching perilously close to his genitals.[26] As he awakens he looks at Pussy and says, "I must be dreaming," and flirts with her in typical Bond fashion throughout the next several scenes. Despite an appearance of female femininity, Pussy does exhibit some masculine traits, as suggested by her piloting a plane to deliver Bond to his rival, her boss, Mr. Goldfinger. Here Pussy hints at lesbianism, telling him with great annoyance, "You can turn off the charm. I'm immune." Further, when Goldfinger asks her to woo Bond as a means of getting information out of him, she makes it clear that she's not interested. Not in the habit of taking no for an answer from any woman, gay or straight, Bond continues to hit on her, even after (especially after?) learning that Pussy heads up her own presumptively lesbian girl gang of pilots, called "Pussy Galore's Flying Circus." Eventually, Pussy succumbs to a literal and figurative roll in the hay with Bond. A scuffle between the two in a barn leads to a forced kiss from Bond, followed by sexual activity that is presented as more consensual. And indeed, the movie ends in a typical manner, with Bond in a clinch with Pussy, lesbian or not.

In short, the pairing of Bond's aggressive version of male masculinity and voracious heterosexuality dominates the ultimately submissive female femininity of all his conquests. Homosexuality plays hardly any role in this period. When it does appear, it is represented as deviant and in need of elimination (in the case of effeminate men like Kidd and Wint or butch women such as Number 3), or conversion (in the case of more effeminate lesbians who are more able to conform to traditional sex and gender norms, such as Pussy Galore). While homosexuality poses no direct threat to Bond himself due to his unquestioned masculinity, it is a trait possessed by several of Bond's enemies, a marker of evil. As such it represents a grave danger to the state that must be eliminated or converted, depending upon the extent of the challenge it poses to traditional gender norms.

Bond on Masculinity and Sexuality in the Transitional Period

In the transitional period, Bond offers a somewhat more restrained form of traditional masculinity, as a variety of female characters begin to challenge various aspects of Bond's heretofore unquestioned behavior. This begins slowly, as Timothy Dalton's Bond is gently questioned about his behavior, and gains steam when Pierce Brosnan's Bond is aggressively challenged by the new head of the British secret service, M, played for the first time by a woman, Judi Dench. As women in public life become more assertive in the workplace during this period and obtain positions of leadership, stereotypically masculine behavior begins to be represented as unattractive and vaguely distasteful, contrary to the Bond brand, which represents him as au courant. Women begin to be seen as equal or even superior to men. At the same time, plenty of traditional masculine and feminine behavior persists during this period, despite M laying down the (newly emerging) law with Bond. Homosexuality is refigured as something of an open secret that continues to be judged, but now, sometimes, with a wink and a nod.

Timothy Dalton's Bond appears in two films during the late 1980s. In *The Living Daylights*, Bond refrains from killing Kara Milovy, even though she aims to assassinate a defecting KGB officer. Suspecting that she is not a professional killer, he exercises uncharacteristic restraint and shoots the rifle out of her hands instead. Back at headquarters, as he and Miss Moneypenny review her profile, they observe the photo of this stunningly beautiful concert cellist on an oversized screen. Moneypenny wryly comments, "That girl must be very talented." Rather than responding in the traditionally aggressive manner of his predecessors, Dalton's Bond offers a politically correct response that offers no hint of being tongue-in-cheek: "I assure you, my interest in her is purely professional." Although Bond does sleep with Milovy later, this does not occur until well into the film, and she is the sole object of his attention from that point forward. Although he is patronizing toward her (as well as brutal with the mistress of his enemy), he nonetheless exhibits a surprising attachment to Milovy, even as the movie concludes in the traditional manner, with the Bond girl in his arms once the enemy has been vanquished.

License to Kill (1989) also exhibits traditional masculine dominance, but in a new tack, much of the most blatant behavior of this sort is dismissively attributed to the machismo of Bond's South American enemy, Franz Sanchez. When the Bond girl asserts that she should be called Ms. rather than Miss and asks why she rather than he should pretend to be a secretary, Bond laughs her off, saying, "We're south of the border and it's a man's world." Consistent with the transitional form of masculinity in this period, traditional masculinity is both challenged and reinforced. While the film offers a measure of critique of the purportedly more sexist norms of Latin America, Bond is nonetheless able to continue to practice masculine domination undaunted, presumably due to the location of the action in the global south, where, on his telling, it is impossible to do otherwise. However, his relationship with the Bond girl in this film is also tinged with assertions of gender equality, as they repeatedly kid each other about who should initiate sexual contact. That said, the film closes in the traditional manner, with the two in a clinch. Bond has once again initiated, while laughing at her earlier attempts to do so.

This transition between the traditional and the concluding forms of masculinity becomes even more visible when Pierce Brosnan takes over as Bond. In his first film, *GoldenEye*, both M and Moneypenny directly challenge the sexist behavior that was standard issue in previous Bond films. This 1995 movie was the first to be released since the dissolution of the Soviet Union, a signifier of the end of the Cold War and a momentous transition in its own right. In each of the previous films, Bond flirted with Ms. Moneypenny, fostering her unrequited love for him. However, when Brosnan's Bond attempts to continue this practice in *GoldenEye*, Moneypenny responds with a concern about the dangers of interpersonal relations at work: "This sort of behavior could qualify as sexual harassment." The term "sexual harassment" was not even in mainstream circulation during the traditional period. By 1995, its meaning had become well known to many in the United States, thanks in part to now-Justice Clarence Thomas's 1991 Senate confirmation hearings, during which his former employee Anita Hill accused him of exactly that behavior. Judging from the enormous popular interest and response to this development, Hill described a practice that many women apparently had regularly experienced in the workplace for some time, notwithstanding the lack of name for it.

Yet the transition to more contemporary forms of masculinity and femininity did not conclude decidedly during this period. This is exemplified by Moneypenny's response when Bond asks what the penalty would be for sexual harassment. Here, she quickly slips back into their traditional flirtatious patter, reinforcing his typically aggressive form of male masculinity, saying, "Someday you'll have to make good on your innuendos." Yet, immediately after this scene, Bond is dressed down by the new M, in what has become a well-known, perhaps even iconic, scene in the series. As noted earlier, this was the first Bond film in which M was played by a woman. Art imitated life as the new director of the British secret service in real life was a woman at that time as well. In this scene Dench asks (but really tells) Bond, "You don't like me, Mr. Bond? Good, because I think you're a sexist, misogynist dinosaur, a relic of the Cold War, whose charms are wasted." Dench's M represents a new kind of woman for the Bond series, one who is not only every bit his equal, but is institutionally superior to him. Accordingly, there is no need for her to accept his authority or the traditional gender norms that support it. Destabilizing the traditional alignment of female sex and passive femininity, she concludes, "If you think I don't have the balls to send a man to die, you're wrong."[27]

Tomorrow Never Dies (1997) continues to displace the presumptive superiority of traditional masculinity. When Bond's mission is transmitted via phone from Moneypenny, her position seems to have expanded beyond mere receptionist. Upon hearing the Danish woman whom Bond is in bed with, Moneypenny comments with a smirk, "You always were a cunning linguist, James," a not very indirect reference to oral sex, as M enters Moneypenny's office eyebrows archly raised. "Don't ask," says Moneypenny to M. "Don't tell," responds M to Moneypenny, directly referencing the "open secret" policy regarding gays in the military in place in the United States at that time.

When a British submarine appears to have been sunk by Chinese missiles, M counsels restraint to avoid provoking World War III. Meanwhile, Admiral Roebuck of the British Navy argues for full retaliation as a show of military might in the wake of the attack, a difference of judgment that he characterizes as being based on gender and differences in physical anatomy. "Sometimes I think you don't have the balls for this job," he shouts at M. "Perhaps," she calmly replies, "but I don't have to think with them all the time either." In the end, the prime minister accepts the admiral's judgment and decides to send in the fleet to retaliate, signifying the ongoing power of the traditional framing. However, in deference to M's authority, he grants a forty-eight-hour reprieve from all action to allow her to investigate further, a decided nod in the direction of greater equality that also characterizes the transitional period.

Gender themes continue to be explored as the story unfolds further, with traditional norms being both reinforced and challenged. We quickly learn that M was correct to suspect that multimedia magnate Elliot Carver had privately orchestrated the attack, in order to instigate a spectacular conflict that would surely sell more newspapers and gain attention for his new global networks. Because Bond has had a clandestine affair with Carver's wife in the past, M instructs him to "pump her for information." Moneypenny saucily comments, "You'll have to decide just how much pumping is needed," while Bond replies, "If only that were true of you and I, Moneypenny."

Upon reintroducing himself to Ms. Carver, Bond is slapped squarely across the face, as she upbraids him for abruptly leaving her without explanation after they were last together. When she later comes to visit Bond at his hotel, he tells her to leave, stating that she has made her loyalty to her husband clear: "You made your bed." Would the Bond of the traditional period have cared one way or the other? In any case, she replies, "Yes, but I'm here now," and even though he has told her in no uncertain terms to leave, she stays, challenging his ability to control the situation. In no time he admits that he left because he felt vulnerable and that she had become too close. The Bond of the traditional period would never make such admissions. With that they reunite, falling into bed as she sighs, "I've missed you."

In this film, Bond's secret service agent counterpart is a woman from China, Wai Lin. She and Bond have more or less equal and complementary skills. She is nothing if not tough, an excellent fighter with training in the martial arts and extensive knowledge of Eastern weaponry. As such, Wai uses her skills to rescue Bond from seemingly certain death on more than one occasion. Their ability to survive depends on their ability to cooperate, as evidenced by a sustained chase scene in which they are handcuffed together while being shot at and riding at top speeds on a motorcycle, highlighting their mutual need. In this sense, Wai helps to transition Bond (and the audience) to the women who will soon regularly equal Bond on his own terms. In the end, however, Wai succumbs to his advances, occupying the more traditional position of the Bond girl by falling into his arms at the end of the movie, after Bond has saved her from mortal peril. With a British submarine lingering in the background, she murmurs after a long kiss, "They're looking for us, James." In traditional Bond fashion, he responds, "Let's stay undercover," apparently his solution to any predicament, including the challenge that this new kind of woman has posed to him throughout much of the film.

This pattern of moving back and forth between challenging and reinforcing traditional gender norms continues in the two remaining films in the transitional period, *The World Is Not Enough* (1999) and *Die Another Day* (2002). Both are chock-full of traditional masculine and feminine behavior, including ribald sexist cracks, the typical Moneypenny and Bond double entendres, and 007 winding up in bed with the Bond girl, after having slept with other women throughout the films. At the same time, new challenges to traditional gender norms abound. Judi

Dench's M asserts her power over Bond by removing him from duty after he sustains job-related injuries that render him uncharacteristically vulnerable. In addition, Bond must also contend with women who are professional equals, such as Halle Berry's Jinx Johnson, an NSA agent in *Die Another Day*. Yet the viewer's introduction to Johnson is through Bond's binoculars as he watches her come out of the water in slow motion à la *Baywatch*, highlighting the viewpoint of the traditional male gaze as she sports a bathing suit that is a colorful orange version of the now-iconic white bikini that Ursula Andress wore in the very first movie in the Bond franchise, *Dr. No*. However, while Andress's Honey Ryder was out collecting shells in her bathing suit, Berry's Johnson, like Bond, is chasing a North Korean terrorist who has threatened to provoke nuclear war. Johnson and 007 are professional equals, but they also quickly wind up in bed in the traditional manner of all the Bond girls. However, Johnson is no passive recipient of Bond's charms. She is on top of things, literally and figuratively, representing the challenge to traditional masculinity that accompanies sleeping with workmates during this period.

Meanwhile, M adds another female agent to the case, Miranda Frost, who has never once mixed business with pleasure during her three years of service in MI6. When M cautions her about Bond, Frost replies, "I think it would be foolish to get involved with someone in the community, especially James Bond." Yet it is Frost who winds up using her feminine wiles to woo Bond into bed, in order to have an opportunity to empty his gun so she can later double-cross him without worry of being killed. Here it appears that the women in the workplace who are most worthy of suspicion are those who (falsely) suggest that they are willing and able to maintain a bright line between public and private relationships. Underscoring this point, back home in London, the most consistently loyal woman to Bond in the series, Miss Moneypenny, is using a virtual reality machine created by Q, the spy equipment quartermaster, to fantasize in living color about Bond returning home to ravish her on her desk, suggesting her inability to maintain the line between work and play (if only in fantasy).

In sum, the Bond of the transitional period occasionally offers a different, less traditional version of masculinity, while also regularly contending with more aggressive and increasingly more equal females, both at work and at play. While subordinate Moneypenny seems content to fold back into traditional femininity after occasionally commenting on some of the more outrageous features of Bond's traditional masculinity, his sexism is criticized openly by his superior, M, who is clearly unwilling to suffer any of his shenanigans during this period. She regularly takes him to task and removes him from duty when necessary, even against his protestations. However, she does not ask about his sexual escapades and has made it clear that she is uninterested in anyone telling. Don't ask, don't tell indeed.

While Bond's escapades continue regardless of M's open disdain, the Bond girls are increasingly gaining in power, sometimes occupying positions of professional equality with Bond. He is clearly more physically vulnerable at times, and his personal vulnerability also seems to deepen somewhat in this period. His attachment to women is often more emotional than the detached debauchery of Connery and Moore in the traditional period. Not only does transitional Bond rescue the girls out of duty and valor as in the old days, he also seems personally gratified upon doing so rather than simply professionally fulfilled. And sometimes, these new Bond girls reciprocate and rescue him. While homosexuality seems to be largely invisible in any sort of embodied form in the Bond films of the transitional period, it is present in the form of several references to "Don't Ask, Don't Tell," a policy that institutionalized it as an open secret in the US armed forces, a clear connection between shifting gender and sexuality norms in film and in the public sphere. Moneypenny and M both wish that Bond's womanizing would be less out in the open and more of an open secret, reflecting a shift in understanding of sexuality that also indicates the beginning of a change in the previous distinctly binary relationship between heterosexuality and homosexuality.

Bond on Masculinity and Sexuality in the Concluding Stage

The most recent Bond films have been referred to as a "rebooting" of the franchise, as Daniel Craig plays a less experienced and more vulnerable Bond in his first film, *Casino Royale* (2006), setting the stage for a more vulnerable and darker 007 to emerge in *Quantum of Solace* (2008), *Skyfall* (2012), *Spectre* (2015), and the last of Craig as Bond, *No Time to Die* (2021).[28] A reboot is often used to reinvigorate a series that has grown stolid. The Craig films offer an intriguing reconfiguration of Bond's masculinity that reflects a more contemporary understanding of gender, aligning with a decidedly more inclusive attitude toward homosexuality. As was the case in the traditional and transitional periods, Bond is still portrayed as a stylish, globe-trotting secret agent whom women desire and men envy. However, aggressive masculinity and moralizing about homosexuality no longer fit that bill. In this period, male masculinity and female femininity are represented as roughly equal. Only villains continue to embrace the more traditional, now thoroughly caddish version of masculinity. Gay sexuality no longer needs to be eliminated or laughed off as in the traditional period, or marginally tolerated while largely kept under wraps as in the transitional period. Indeed, to do so would challenge Bond's long-standing representation as au courant. In the concluding period, Bond embraces homosexuality, and suggests that he, James Bond, perhaps the most dominant action-adventure hero of all time, has himself had same-sex encounters. In the end, Craig's Bond is done in by a virulent form of toxic masculinity, suggesting that male masculinity, not sexuality, was the most dangerous practice all along.

In *Casino Royale*, Bond has passionate sex only with women he loves. This deep attachment makes him incapable of performing his duties as an agent. While Connery and Moore's traditionally masculine Bond had a brand of sexual potency and detachment that rendered him uniquely fit for a highly successful career as a secret agent, Craig's form of masculinity is capable of emotional intimacy, endangering his ability to put the interests of the secret service first. As *Casino Royale* moves toward its conclusion, Bond becomes attracted to a woman named Vesper Lynd, consummating the relationship with sex so passionate that it knocks items off an adjoining table. A later scene is reminiscent of the famous Burt Lancaster/Deborah Kerr beach encounter in *From Here to Eternity*, during which Bond tells Vesper that he loves her. After returning to the hotel, he resigns his position as a secret agent, has sex with her again, and tells her that he is going to marry her. Shortly thereafter, Bond learns that Vesper apparently has double-crossed him, highlighting the riskiness of sexuality, particularly in the workplace. Despite vowing to kill her, when faced with an opportunity to do so, Bond instead attempts (unsuccessfully) to save her as she drowns trapped in a cage immersed underwater, underscoring both the depth of his love and the threat that it poses to the state.

Bond also openly embraces homoeroticism for the first time in the series, suggesting a growing connection between contemporary masculinity and increasingly visible homosexuality. Whereas the Bond of the traditional period would have either laughed off homosexuality as inconsequential or killed it off as a threat to the state, in *Casino Royale* Bond rejects both options, and appears to embrace it—at least somewhat. When Bond does go home with a woman he feels no attachment to in Nassau, he abruptly leaves her right before sleeping with her in order to chase after her husband in Miami Beach. When he finally catches up with the husband, the two men engage in a very homoerotic knife scene in which they rhythmically thrust back and forth with rather phallic-looking knives in a sexually suggestive manner.

In a subsequent scene that is more overt, Bond's masculinity is threatened by Le Chiffre, a private banker to global terrorists. After having had Bond stripped and taken to a poorly lit interrogation room, Le Chiffre threatens him with emasculation, in a low and intense voice threatening to torture him until there's "nothing left to tell you're a man." As Bond is placed on the frame of a chair with the seat cut out so his naked rear end is fully exposed from the bottom, Le Chiffre looks him over admiringly, commenting, "You take good care of your body, Mr. Bond," while strok-ing his face gently. As he repeatedly wields a bludgeon through the hole in the bottom of the chair, Bond responds with a smirk, while scream-ing in apparent pain. A literal bottom in this scene, Bond presents as a masochist, taking some control of the situation by asking for more and expressing enjoyment in the pain of being dominated, a direct challenge to older forms of masculinity and sexuality. Bond disarms Le Chiffre by requesting more of the same, saying he has an itch that needs scratching "down there," and commenting, "Now the whole world will know that you've itched my balls." As Le Chiffre threatens to cut off his genitals, saying, "I'll feed you what you seem not to value," another man bursts into the dungeon-like scene to save Bond, just in the nick of time.

After the release of *Casino Royale*, Daniel Craig publicly invited a gay scene in the next Bond movie, offering full frontal nudity. "Why not?" he asked. "In this day and age fans would have accepted it."[29] Although such a scene ultimately was not included in the following movie, *Skyfall* did address same-sex sexuality even more directly than *Casino Royale*, leading one writer to entitle his review "The Bi Who Loved Me," an obvi-ous play on an earlier Bond film drawn from the traditional period, *The Spy Who Loved Me* (1977).[30] The contemporary Bond of the concluding period does not care about being perceived as gay or bi. He may be un-containable by modern sexual taxonomies, or not care about them at all.

During yet another scene of captivity and bondage, Bond's new arch-enemy, Raoul Silva, has tied him to a chair for interrogation, recalling the torture scene in *Casino Royale*. Silva berates Bond for his loyalty to M. As he suggests that M betrayed Bond by sending him out into the field knowing full well that he had been unable to pass his physical, psy-chological, and technical tests, Silva unbuttons Bond's shirt and strokes his chest, neck, cheek, and inner thighs, saying, "There's a first time for everything." Rather than eliminating, laughing off, or ignoring the sug-gestion of same-sex sexuality, as would have been his typical response during the traditional and transitional periods, Bond embraces the pos-sibility head-on, quickly retorting, "What makes you think this is my first time?" His refusal to be intimidated by the possibility of same-sex sex while coming out as a potentially willing participant affords him a modicum of power, destabilizes Silva at least momentarily, and allows Bond to regain a measure of control of the situation.

In addition, the Bond of the concluding period initially does not flirt with Miss Moneypenny in the manner of all the other Bonds, in part because her character does not even appear in either *Casino Royale* or *Quantum of Solace*. When Moneypenny does reemerge in *Skyfall*, she appears as a field agent rather than a receptionist, although viewers do not learn her true identity until much later in the film. Prior to that, no one would suspect that it was her, given the much greater and more active role that she plays compared to the Moneypenny of the earlier films. This new Moneypenny wields an equal if not superior power to Bond's, as she nearly kills him while following M's order to shoot an enemy in her sights, even though she is fully aware that she may wind up taking out Bond due to the lack of a clear shot. Although she hesitates for a moment, her professional detachment leads her to shoot, hitting him and leaving him presumed to be dead. Moneypenny has become a professional equal, a steely field agent who is willing to shoot to kill even at the risk of losing a valued colleague. She is no longer a subservient receptionist simply there to do his bidding or for comic relief.

A different representation of power is also reflected in their personal relationship, as for example when Moneypenny later appears at Bond's room unannounced late at night when he is shaving. As Moneypenny completes the job by shaving his throat with a straight-edge razor, this charged erotic scene reveals a new, more fully vulnerable side, suggesting that his life is once again in her hands. As the scene cuts away, they seem to have transformed a once chaste if flirtatious relationship into a close, apparently passionate sexual intimacy initiated by Moneypenny, who now appears to be both an interpersonal and a professional equal.

Nonetheless, Bond is still quite capable of having sex without emotional attachment, as he sleeps with a nameless foreign woman while licking his wounds on a remote island off the coast of Turkey, after having been shot by Moneypenny. He returns to duty after hearing of a terrorist attack in London, demonstrating his deep attachment to his country and possibly to M. There he has a brief, perhaps somewhat more emotionally intimate relationship with Severine, a woman with ties to his enemy Silva, a former agent who has since become hell-bent on terrorizing MI6 and M in particular. Identifying a tattoo on her wrist as signifying that she grew up as a prostitute in Macau, Bond offers to help her escape her bondage to Silva, her master. It is never entirely clear whether he is attached to her or using her to get information about Silva. Viewers are left questioning whether his feelings for her or his declining marksmanship skills lead him to be unable to shoot a glass full of scotch off the top of her head to save her life. However, he is not ruthless toward her in the way of Silva, who, despite having known her since her youth, thinks nothing of casually killing her with one quick shot after a clearly shaken Bond has aimed well wide of her and the glass of scotch. That said, Bond exits the scene with only the callous comment, "A waste of good scotch."

His apparent indifference makes more sense as it becomes increasingly clear that the real Bond girl in *Skyfall* is not Severine, but M, whom *Entertainment Weekly* dubbed "the ultimate Bond girl."[31] The relationship between Bond and M is certainly not sexual; if anything, she is a maternal figure for him. However, their relationship is far more emotionally intense than his standard hookups with the Bond girls in the traditional and transitional periods. It is born of a deep emotional attachment, even love, that has developed over the years, despite their rocky beginnings during the transitional period.

In the brave new world of the concluding period, Bond's masculinity has become less dominant and more sensitive, while femininity has emerged as tougher and more powerful than ever before. This shift creates substantial risk for both M and Bond, who are both increasingly vulnerable interpersonally and professionally. The aging and traumatized Bond can no longer pass the psychological, physical, and technical tests necessary to return to the field. At one point he is unable to shoot without trembling visibly. For her part, M is increasingly at risk of los-ing her position as head of MI6. She is told early on by Gareth Mallory (Ralph Fiennes), the chair of the Intelligence and Security Committee, that she should begin to plan for "voluntary" retirement, largely due to her inability to prevent national security breaches from high-powered hackers such as Silva. Though professionally vulnerable, she still retains enormous institutional power, as evidenced by the fact that she over-rides Mallory's order to dismiss Bond after he fails his tests. When Mal-lory asserts that she is "sentimental about him," she responds, "As long as I'm head of this department, I'll choose my own operatives," and he backs off. While M may well be at risk of losing her job, she clearly re-tains ultimate authority when it comes to MI6.

As the plot builds, it becomes clear that Silva wants to kill her to take his revenge on her for selling him out in exchange for Chinese prisoners when he was still an agent under her command. Bond brings M to his childhood home in Scotland, the Skyfall estate, where he seeks to protect her from harm. Protecting her requires that Bond explode his traditional family home, eliciting his observation, "I never liked this place." Despite his desire to protect her, in the end M succumbs to a gunshot wound. Though Bond is unable to save her in the way that he used to protect the other Bond girls, he does catch her before she falls to the ground. In a moment of obvious tenderness before her death, he responds, "I'm game if you are" when she supposes that "it's too late to make a run for it." Her last words are, "I did manage to get one thing right," leaving no doubt as to the depth of their relationship and whether Bond has done her proud. Revealing an entirely new level of vulnerability, Bond cries openly, shuts her eyes, and kisses her gently on the forehead. As the film ends, view-ers learn that the old M will be replaced by a new M (Ralph Fiennes), as male masculinity reclaims institutional power at MI6. However, there is no doubt that male masculinity will remain ambiguous and unsettled throughout the concluding period.

No Time to Die brings Daniel Craig's run as Bond to a close. As A. O. Scott notes, this final film is "uncommonly preoccupied with memory and leave-taking," indicating a significant reflection on time.[32] The film opens with a little girl named Madeleine Swann (Léa Seydoux) shooting and then running away from the central villain, Lyutsifer Safin (Rami Malek) after he has killed her drunk and largely incapacitated mother. By this time even young girls are capable of (nearly) lethal violence, even though older women such as her mother still appear to have no choice except to succumb. The opening credits roll shortly thereafter, complete with various Bond totems. However, this new opening also includes symbols of the British Empire falling through the sands of time in an oversized hourglass, an ominous sign indicating a significant shift in global politics.

Bond's sole love interest in *No Time to Die* is Madeleine, the now fully grown woman who was once the young girl presented in the opening scenes. But rather than falling back into his old womanizing ways, Bond appears to be on the road to monogamous and domestic bliss. There are no Bond girls in the movie. He sleeps with no one except Madeleine, not even a saucy and skilled young CIA agent named Paloma who later will help him out of a jam in Haiti. However, Bond is haunted by the past, most significantly by Vesper Lynd's betrayal of him back in 2006's *Casino Royale*. While he and Madeleine are vacationing in Italy, Bond visits Vesper's gravesite, presumably trying to make peace with that betrayal. When he is unexpectedly ambushed, he immediately suspects that Madeleine has betrayed him, just as Vesper did, and he leaves her.

Five years later, the new male masculine M (Ralph Fiennes) has made a serious error. He has commissioned a secret project called Heracles, which is designed to launch nanobots into the DNA of Britain's enemies. But the plan has gone awry. Lyutsifer has gotten ahold of the toxic weapon and plans global-scale mass destruction. Even though Bond has retired to Haiti, his old friend from the CIA Felix Leiter (Jeffrey Wright) recruits him to foil Lyutsifer. Upon his return to London, Bond discovers that his 007 agent number has been reassigned to Nomi (Lashana Lynch), a Black woman much younger than Bond. When she asserts that "things have changed since you retired," he resists: "In my experience, things don't change that much." And indeed, he does supplant her, reclaiming his 007 status, eventually with her approval, another apparently successful restoration of male masculinity.

Madeleine does have a secret she was keeping from Bond. Not only did she shoot Lyutsifer when she was young, she is also the daughter of a now-deceased member of SPECTRE, the sinister organization that Bond has been battling since the beginning of the series. These facts have long been tidily swept behind the façade of her professional life as a psychologist and her private life as a single mother of a child. When they reunite five years after their earlier breakup, Bond eventually learns that the child is his, and he tends to her lovingly. As Anthony Lane puts it in his review in the *New Yorker*, "Everyone agrees that the age of the lady-killer is dead, unmourned, but are we ready for Bond the babysitter?"[33]

Ready or not, we do not have to suffer him for long. Bond cannot be a family man, even if he wants to. In the end, his own violence prevents him from domesticating. As Bond violently attacks Lyutsifer to save humanity from the toxic DNA hack that M foolishly had produced, the vial of it that Lyutsifer is holding in his hand breaks open. As Bond is infected, Lyutsifer exclaims, "You made me do this!," underscoring Bond's role in spreading the uncontrolled toxic masculinity that takes him down in the end. Although Bond has saved the world yet again, toxic masculinity has rendered him unsuitable for family life, lest he infect those closest to him. Alas, toxic masculinity spoils the party, once and for all. Bond is no more capable of family life than Lyutsifer, who sees himself and Bond as "mirror images of each other, . . . two heroes in a tragedy of our own making." Toxic masculinity has made Bond's domestication impossible. Try as he might to do otherwise, he can really only be a globally gallivanting secret agent. The problem is, the world that produced him as an agent is quickly passing. He and his form of male masculinity are, as Judi Dench's M once said, a relic of the Cold War period. He cannot adapt to the diverse new world that is emerging, complete with Black women 007 agents. Try as he might, Bond cannot shake the rampant violence long associated with male masculinity. It is not sexuality, whether homosexual or heterosexual, that is the true source of the problem. Rather, it is the uncontrolled violence of toxic male masculinity that ultimately threatens not only Bond's family, but also the world at large. Bond now carries it with him in his very bloodstream—it has literally been discovered to be in the very DNA of white straight men like him. M passed it to Lyutsifer, who passed it to Bond. They are both killed by the missiles that Bond has told M to launch "before there's nothing left to save." The story ends with Bond isolated on an island, dying to save the world from toxic masculinity: Lyutsifer's as well as his own.

In the concluding period, sex and gender norms shift in a manner that opens space for greater recognition and integration of gays and lesbians. While women are by no means treated the same as men at home or in the workplace, either in the Bond series or in public life, they have developed a significant measure of agency, power, and authority, both professionally and personally. In earlier periods women were largely vehicles for a titillating subplot or two in the Bond series. But here they appear in increasingly complicated forms, as central characters who must be directly contended with and sometimes even obeyed. At the same time, a rebooted Bond becomes increasingly vulnerable, both personally and professionally. As feminine and masculine roles are destabilized, allowing women to become more powerful and men more vulnerable, the Bond series opens the door to a previously unthinkable possibility for a central hero: a male who is unquestionably masculine as well as open to same-sex encounters and being thought of as gay or bisexual. If even James Bond can be liberated from the stereotyped prison of gender and sexuality, why can't the military? In the end, it turns out that gay sexuality and gender aberration were not the threat they were once thought to be. Toxic masculinity lies at the root of the problem all along, threatening both the state and family.

Conclusion

Popular culture in the form of the James Bond series provides a rich context for analyzing shifts in popular understanding regarding the inclusion of LGBT people in the military. Consistent with several of the teachings of foundational work in queer theory, the series provides strong evidence of a connection between shifts in gender, sex, and sexuality. As male masculinity shifts from dominating female femininity in the traditional period, to being challenged by female femininity in the transitional period, to sharing a more or less equal playing field with female femininity in the concluding period, related shifts occur with regard to sexuality. As gender norms shift, so too do norms about sexuality. Homosexuality is ridiculed, converted, and killed in the traditional period, allowed to exist as an open secret in the transitional period, and openly embraced during the concluding period. Pop culture allows us to gauge these gradual changes in public understanding over time, as well as their import for public policy governing LGBT people in the military. Official policy shifts from exclusionary purges, to the partial inclusion of "Don't Ask, Don't Tell," to the full inclusion associated with lifting the ban. In this sense, the Bond series aligns with the three-period form of a classic civil rights narrative, as once despised gays and lesbians become fully assimilated citizens who offer heroic service to the state.

Yet inequalities and discrimination have also persisted against LGBT people even as the movement's interest in greater inclusion in public service seems to have gradually converged with the state's interest in recruiting more men and women to join the military. Shortly after the federal government lifted the ban and cleared the way for gays and lesbians to serve in the armed forces openly, several states refused to process benefits for married gay and lesbian soldiers with families based in their jurisdictions, denied discounted housing to gay and lesbian married couples, and excluded same-sex spouses from retreats run by chaplains designed to ease the stress of multiple deployments and relocations. In addition, incidents such as the Tailhook scandal, Abu Ghraib, and the increasingly visible rape culture in the armed forces suggest that heterosexuality in the workplace may create at least as many risks as homosexuality when it comes to fostering the interests of the national security state.[34] These developments suggest that the unruliness of sexuality, not just homosexuality, undermines unit cohesion and militarized nationalism, and that sexual violence is elemental to the military.

The apparent unruliness of sexuality—hetero as well as homo—may make it especially well suited to challenge the orderly power of the national security state. LGBT movement leaders such as Barbara Smith have long argued that striving for full inclusion in the military decentered a more radical, more liberatory form of sexuality that was once central to the LGBT movement, weakening its connections to racial and gender justice movements that were succinctly suggested earlier on by the Stonewall era rallying cry, "Smash the Church, Smash the State."[35] These scholars worry that LGBT inclusion in the military will come at the cost of disciplining and channeling radical sexuality into the patriarchal, colonial, hierarchical structures of the military. They are committed to "smashing the state" in order to clear the way for more radical and grassroots-generated decision-making arrangements.[36] Others have argued that while a critique of the state is necessary to promote political transformation, a blanket rejection of the state is problematic as it is grounded in an improbable if not impossible fantasy about escape from power.[37] In either case, attention to persistent inequality and oppression is likely to open up and sustain more critical civil rights narratives and ongoing criticism of the state.

Increasing women's representation, equalizing the gender playing field, and coming out loudly and proudly did not neatly resolve the problem of power and oppression for women and gays in real life or in the Bond series. Despite her obvious power in the male-dominant world of national security, the authority of Judy Dench's M is questioned throughout *Skyfall*. As has often been said of other female trailblazers, Dench's M is damned as a bitch if she wields power effectively and damned as a weak girl if she does not. Even Bond himself is disdainful of her ruthless, balls-out decision making, particularly when it is directed at him. It is worth remembering that Bond instantly replies "bitch" when M's name is mentioned in a word association test that Bond must take to regain his status in the field after she has removed him due to an injury that was the result of Moneypenny's shooting. In addition, M's job as the head of MI6 is at risk when she is being blamed for not effectively neutralizing Silva. In the end, M dies and the threat of a gender backlash emerges in the form of Ralph Fiennes's character, Gareth Mallory, who takes over the helm of MI6, thus menacing the shifts in gender, sex, and sexuality that have been represented in the series thus far.

And what of Bond himself, newly out as an apparent member of the extended LGBT family? The ability of Daniel Craig's Bond to perform even the most basic tasks associated with his job is persistently questioned by the end of his run. In the end, it is toxic male masculinity that takes him out, not uncontrollable sexuality, be it hetero or homo. This hardly aligns with the happy ending of inclusion and redemption demanded by the classic civil rights form. Unruly sexuality, both hetero and homo, is likely to continue to threaten the purported stability of the modern security state and its supporting institutions. But the surprising conclusion of *No Time to Die* suggests that the death blow for the long-failing British Empire, and perhaps of Western democracy itself, comes from toxic male masculinity, which needs to be exterminated for the world to survive let alone produce new practices of sex, gender, and sexuality in a differently imagined global context.

The greater assimilation of LGB people that emerges toward the end of the Bond series may provide a brighter political backdrop highlighting the dark existential threat that toxic masculinity poses to us all. Contemporary Bond, thoroughly rebooted along gender and sexuality lines, returns to his roots—his family estate, Skyfall—only to observe it being blown to bits by the conclusion of the film. Change as he might, Bond and his altered, though still toxic form of violent male masculinity do not survive yet another fatal explosion at the conclusion of *No Time to Die*. Pop culture provides a platform on which to analyze these shifts and to imagine an LGBT movement with similarly explosive potential. The challenges to the nuclear family discussed in the next chapter continue this exploration.

3

From Dangerous Pedophiles to Respectable Parents

Television Families and Marriage Equality

Political scientists have often overlooked the central role the family plays in constituting political power, instead defining politics largely as elections, institutions, and policy making. Yet the first place most people learn about politics is in their families of origin, where basic values and beliefs about power, freedom, and authority are transferred from one generation to the next. From the very start, family and state work together to produce (and undermine) power and freedom. As Julie Novkov and Carol Nackenoff's aptly titled collection of essays *Stating the Family* suggests, the relationship between family and state should be taken seriously by anyone who wants to understand how political life is being ordered and transformed in political time.[1] For them, the key question is not whether the family is political, but rather what are the politics of the specific family form that the state is promoting in a given time and place.

Marriage is, of course, a key element of the traditional nuclear family form that dominated in the post–World War II era. It is also a major adult rite of passage in mainstream American society. In 1971 two gay men, Jack Baker and James McConnell, challenged the constitutionality of a Minnesota law that made it illegal for the state to grant them a marriage license. Although they had been married by a Methodist minister in 1970, the state's highest court turned down Baker and McConnell's request for a license. That ruling was upheld by the US Supreme Court when it refused to review the case "for want of a substantial Federal question." Fifty years later, in 2021, secretary of transportation Pete Buttigieg and his husband, Chasten, were for the most part warmly received when they announced the birth of their two adopted children, Penelope and Joseph. Pete Buttigieg is the first out gay member of the cabinet as well as the first openly gay man to run for president. Press coverage included a photo of the Buttigiegs in a hospital bed holding their new babies, much the way one might see a new mom with her baby right after having given birth. The contrast between 1971 and 2021 could not be more distinct. Gays and lesbians, once seen as dangerous pedophiles who threatened the family, had become respectable parents. How did this happen?

In this chapter I argue that television families' shift away from the traditional nuclear family form is crucial to understanding the relatively rapid acceptance of same-sex marriage in mainstream politics, as well as more radical efforts to subvert or queer the nuclear family. I start with a classic civil rights account of this shift and then focus on three iconic television series, *Leave It to Beaver*, *thirtysomething*, and *The Americans*. In *Beaver*, the nuclear family is assumed to be given and natural, the path to personal happiness and social stability. In *thirtysomething*, the nuclear family is in transition, remaining desirable but becoming far less attainable. And in *The Americans*, the nuclear family is shown to be completely constructed and, in the end, doomed to failure. This failure opens up space for consideration and acceptance of alternative family forms.

A Classic Civil Rights Account of Marriage Equality

Traditional Period

Gay and lesbian marriages like Baker and McConnell's were not recognized by the state in the traditional period. To the extent that gay and lesbian couples were thought of at all, they were assumed to be outside of or a threat to traditional marriage and family. Same-sex marriage equality became more visible during the highly charged debate over the ratification of a proposed amendment to the US Constitution that was designed to protect equal rights regardless of sex. Popularly known as the Equal Rights Amendment (ERA), it aimed to grant women equal rights to men. Despite the focus on women's equality, opponents regularly suggested that the ratification of the ERA would compel states to recognize same-sex marriages. When the ERA failed, its supporters bitterly asserted that such arguments had "intentionally distorted" the meaning of the amendment, directly contributing to its defeat. The ERA was not the only seemingly unrelated issue that raised the specter of same-sex marriage in the 1970s.

When Dade County (Miami), Florida, was considering whether to repeal a law that protected the civil rights of homosexuals in 1977, a former beauty pageant queen by the name of Anita Bryant launched a campaign opposing it. Called "Save Our Children," Bryant's campaign focused on the sinful nature of homosexuality, maintaining that gay pedophiles were threatening children and their families. Bryant's campaign was successful. Not only were civil rights protections for homosexuals in Dade County repealed, but the Florida state legislature also approved bills that outlawed same-sex marriage and prohibited homosexuals from adopting children.

The handful of same-sex couples who unsuccessfully applied for marriage licenses in the 1970s did so for a variety of reasons, including hospital visitation, co-adoption privileges, joint property ownership and inheritance rights, workers' compensation benefits, family leave, immunity from being compelled to testify against one's partner, as well as various other legal, insurance, and tax advantages. In the traditional period, these challenges were typically dismissed as laughable or dangerous deviations from the traditional nuclear family.

Transitional Period

The transitional period was characterized by various legal and political battles between defenders of the traditional nuclear family and those who challenged it in the name of gay rights. These struggles became more visible in mainstream politics in the 1980s in part because of health issues that arose during the AIDS crisis, as well as in response to the high-profile struggle of Karen Thompson to gain the right to see her long-term lesbian partner, Sharon Kowalski, who had been severely disabled in a 1983 automobile accident. After the accident, Kowalski's father won legal guardianship over Sharon, denying Thompson any visitation or access to her. While a married partner would have immediately been recognized as the rightful guardian of a disabled spouse, Thompson was initially not allowed to care for Kowalski, even though both women consistently said that they wished to remain together as a family.

The Kowalski case highlighted the precarious status of same-sex relationships and became a centerpiece of the drive for legal recognition of gay and lesbian partnerships. In 1989 marches and vigils were organized in twenty-one cities on August 7 to mark "National Free Sharon Kowalski Day." Around that time, the city of San Francisco, long recognized as a center of gay culture, with gay residents there comprising an estimated 15 percent of the city's population, became the first major city in the country to allow "domestic partners" of city employees to be included on their health coverage. Designed to parallel marriage licenses given to heterosexual couples, the measure provided a basis for requesting hospital visitation rights equal to those regularly given to married couples. Across the country, in New York, another city with a very visible gay community, Mayor Ed Koch extended the city's bereavement policy to include unmarried employees, giving them the same right to paid leave after the death of a partner. This action followed an important court decision that allowed a gay man to inherit his deceased partner's rent-controlled apartment. In 1991 a judge finally concluded that Thompson was Kowalski's rightful legal guardian. William Rubenstein, director of the Gay Rights Project at the ACLU, commented that the Kowalski ordeal "exemplifies the difficulties lesbians and gay men have in safeguarding our relationships," adding that it "underscored why we need legal protection, and created a terrific incentive to fight for these kinds of marital rights and recognition of domestic partnership."

As gay and lesbian partnerships were slowly coming to be recognized in instances such as the Kowalski case, some began to speculate that Hawaii might become the first state to legalize same-sex marriage. In 1993 that state's Supreme Court announced that the current ban on gay and lesbian marriage could be interpreted as a violation of the state constitution's prohibition against sex discrimination. The Court relied on a 1967 US Supreme Court decision, *Loving v. Virginia*, which held that it was unconstitutional to prohibit mixed-race marriages, even though all Blacks and all whites were prohibited from marrying across race, much the way that all women and all men were prevented at that time from marrying within their own sex.

Noting that marriage is a basic civil right, the Hawaii Supreme Court asked the state to defend its decision to exclude same-sex couples from marriage in a subsequent trial. By long-standing custom, US states have recognized marriages performed in other parts of the country, even when the requirements for such marriages—such as those related to the age of consent—differed from the recognizing state. However, in 1995 Utah became the first state to pass a law explicitly denying recognition to out-of-state marriages not conforming to Utah law. Similar bills followed in South Dakota and Alaska.

Responding to this controversy, Congress passed the Defense of Marriage Act (DOMA) by overwhelming margins of 85–14 in the Senate and 342–67 in the House. President Bill Clinton, a Democrat, signed the bill into law in 1996. DOMA defined marriage as a union between one man and one woman and permitted states to deny recognition to same-sex marriages performed in other states. Ralph Reed, the executive director of the Christian Coalition and an important defender of the traditional nuclear family, described this law's passage as "a huge victory for the pro-family movement."

Back in Hawaii, the state was unable to provide adequate evidence to defend its claim that only heterosexual marriages were in the best interest of children. Voters subsequently approved a referendum to make same-sex marriage unconstitutional by a 2-to-1 margin. The Hawaii Supreme Court allowed the ban to stand, effectively ending the drive for recognition of gay and lesbian marriages in the state. By that time, thirty states and Congress had passed laws banning gay marriage.

Despite this resistance, Vermont began to offer civil unions to gay and lesbian couples in 2000. Nina Beck and Stacy Jolles, one of three gay couples fighting for legal recognition, said that they were doing so because Jolles had been prohibited from seeing Beck during a medical emergency related to labor complications that resulted in Beck being sent to the hospital. Rather than admitting her, as they would have done for any heterosexual spouse, staff asked Jolles, "Who are you? Do you have legal papers to be there?" Noting that state courts overturned laws prohibiting mixed-race marriages long before the US Supreme Court did so in 1967, Beck and Jolles's lawyer argued that it was time for Vermont to lead the way in a similar fashion with regard to same-sex marriage. The Vermont Supreme Court ruled unanimously that the state had to provide the same benefits and protections to gay and lesbian couples that it does for heterosexual married couples, including health insurance, tax breaks, inheritance rights, and hospital visitation. Grounding the ruling in "recognition of our common humanity," the Court said that the legislature should pass a law allowing for either same-sex marriage or a form of domestic partnership that would entitle gay and lesbian couples to state recognition and benefits. Defenders of the traditional nuclear family called the decision "judicial tyranny" that contradicted the Bible and thousands of years of tradition, while supporters of same-sex marriage responded that the Bible and tradition had also condoned slavery and other deplorable practices.

The Vermont legislature opted for a compromise, a common strategy during transitional periods, recognizing "civil unions" that would give gays and lesbians virtually all the benefits of marriage at the state level. Some gay rights advocates were disappointed that the final decision fell short of actual marriage. Many likened civil unions to the "separate but equal" racial segregation of the Jim Crow era. Defenders of traditional marriage were also critical, including the Roman Catholic bishop of Burlington, who called it "a very sad day for the majority of Vermonters." A group opposed to civil unions called Who Would Have Thought was invoking a long-standing myth connecting same-sex relationships with child molestation by implying that Governor Howard Dean supported pedophilia. Vermont eventually approved same-sex marriage nine years later.

As was the case with Hawaii, the recognition of civil unions in Vermont engendered strong reactions in other states. Nebraskans voted to amend their constitution to ban not only gay marriage but also civil unions and domestic partnerships. Some said that the language of the Nebraska amendment was so broad that it could invalidate binding contracts in place between same-sex couples such as powers of attorney, wills, and medical directives. Supporters of the ban argued that it was not about bigotry, but simply a matter of drawing the line before "a man and a dog can get married." By 2003, the number of states that had adopted laws prohibiting the recognition of same-sex marriages had risen to thirty-seven. However, states such as Connecticut and Rhode Island had begun to permit same-sex marriage.

In one of the biggest developments of the transitional period, the Supreme Court of Massachusetts declared in 2003 that same-sex couples have the right to marry on the grounds that the state constitution "forbids the creation of second-class citizens." The ruling, deemed a "political earthquake" by some experts, made Massachusetts the first state in the nation to grant legal recognition to same-sex marriages. Governor Mitt Romney pledged to pursue an amendment to the state constitution that would overturn the ruling. On May 17, 2004, same-sex marriages began to be performed in Massachusetts and efforts to amend the constitution subsequently failed. Defenders of the traditional nuclear family pledged to seek an amendment to the US Constitution. By this time roughly forty-two million residents, or about 15 percent of the country, lived in states offering some form of legal recognition to gay and lesbian couples at that time. Nearly one in five same-sex couples lived in these states. Yet these changes had prompted a new swath of resistance to marriage equality in states and localities across the country, making the ultimate outcome of the conflict anything but certain.

President George W. Bush indicated his opposition to same-sex marriage in his 2004 State of the Union address. This led Mayor Gavin Newsom, who had attended the speech, to the unusual step of allowing same-sex marriages to be performed in the city of San Francisco, in apparent contradiction of a California state law that prohibited it. He argued that the state law was unconstitutional, and that the constitution required him to provide equal treatment to all his constituents. While opponents said that the marriages were worthless and that the mayor was acting above the law, supporters argued that Newsom was acting responsibly by taking a courageous stand against unjust legislation. Newsom explained his position as follows: "He is the president of the United States, and I am just a guy who does stop signs and tries to revitalize parks. But I also know that I've got an obligation that I took seriously to defend the Constitution. There is simply no provision that allows me to discriminate."

In the twenty-eight days that followed, over four thousand same-sex couples were married, while opponents argued that the new policy amounted to "municipal anarchy." Many couples said that they viewed their participation as an act of civil disobedience. Not knowing how long the opportunity would remain, thousands of gay and lesbian couples from locations across the country came to San Francisco to be married. Two weeks after San Francisco began to recognize same-sex marriages, Bush announced that he supported an amendment to the US Constitution that would ban gay marriage. Arguing that marriage is "the most fundamental institution of civilization," Bush called for a constitutional prohibition on same-sex marriage, while conceding that states should be free to recognize gay unions short of marriage. Democrats characterized the proposal for an amendment as an attempt to "drive a political wedge" into the presidential race.

Meanwhile, events in San Francisco apparently inspired other localities to recognize same-sex marriage, however briefly. In New Mexico, a county near Albuquerque briefly issued licenses to same-sex couples, as did the town of New Paltz, New York, where Mayor Jason West said that he was "willing to go to jail to uphold these marriages. This is a stand any decent American should take." West was eventually fined and charged with a misdemeanor for issuing nineteen illegal licenses. Marriage licenses were also issued for a time in Multnomah County, Oregon, which includes the city of Portland, and Asbury Park, New Jersey. In a move that underscored the pointedness of the ongoing conflict, Willamette County, Oregon, took the unusual step of refusing to issue any marriage licenses—to either gay or straight couples—in order to assure equal treatment under the law.

The Supreme Court of California halted same-sex marriages in San Francisco the following month. In 2005 voters in Kansas adopted a constitutional amendment banning same-sex marriage, making it the eighteenth state with a constitutional prohibition, while thirteen other states considered similar amendments that year. Connecticut joined Vermont in offering civil unions, along with New Jersey the following year.

In a blockbuster ruling, the Supreme Court of California legalized same-sex marriage in 2008, saying that "in view of the substance and significance of the fundamental constitutional right to form a family, the California Constitution must be properly interpreted to guarantee this right to all Californians, whether gay or heterosexual, and to same-sex couples, as well as opposite-sex couples." The decision was made by a split court, with a 4–3 vote on the ruling. While supporters of gay rights welcomed the decision, arguing that same-sex marriage harmed no one, opponents pledged to fight the ruling, saying that "the court brushed aside the entire history and meaning of marriage in our tradition."

Over seventeen thousand same-sex couples had been married in the state by the time a referendum on the issue appeared on the California ballot during the 2008 presidential election. The referendum, known as Proposition 8, passed with 52 percent of the vote, halting same-sex marriage in California for the second time. Although he pledged during the campaign to be a champion for gay rights, Barack Obama opposed same-sex marriage during his first presidential campaign, on the basis of his religious beliefs. Financial backing of over $5 million from the Mormon Church in the final days of the campaign for Proposition 8 was also said to be a significant factor in its success, leading thousands to protest outside the headquarters of the Mormon Church in Salt Lake City, Utah, where gay rights supporters carried signs with slogans such as "Mormons: Once persecuted, now persecutors."

Proposition 8 also led to a new wave of activism in the gay community, dubbed by some Stonewall 2.0. Activists successfully encouraged gay rights supporters to join in a series of large-scale protests after Proposition 8 passed. When thousands turned out at demonstrations in cities across the country, many called it a watershed moment on a par with Stonewall and protests held during the height of the AIDS crisis in the 1980s, calling it "the greatest civil rights battle of our generation." Despite these developments, activists on both sides of the debate acknowledged that the momentum had at least temporarily swung in favor of those who oppose same-sex marriage.

Some believed that the debate was effectively over in 2009, when the Supreme Court of Iowa overturned a law that limited marriage to a man and a woman, becoming the first state outside the Northeast or the West Coast to recognize same-sex partnerships. The state had earlier refused to protect slave ownership well before the Civil War, was the first to allow women to practice law, and desegregated its schools nearly a century before the US Supreme Court ruled in 1954 that the country must do so. As David Twombley, a sixty-seven-year-old gay man and member of one of the six couples that had challenged the law, said, "There's been a perception that it couldn't happen here. But yes, it happened, right here in Iowa. There's something about that, about it happening in the heartland that has got to accelerate this process for the whole country."

The Iowa decision appeared to turn the momentum back toward those favoring same-sex marriage, as activists in New England initiated a campaign called "Six by Twelve," identifying the goal of having all six states in New England (Vermont, Massachusetts, Connecticut, Maine, New Hampshire, and Rhode Island) recognize same-sex marriage by 2012. After Maine and New Hampshire legalized same-sex marriage in 2009, this goal seemed inevitable to many, with only Rhode Island remaining. However, in the November 2009 election, the people of Maine rejected same-sex marriage in a statewide vote, reversing the momentum in the debate once again and becoming the thirty-first state to block gay marriage through a public referendum.

Concluding Period

Two important US Supreme Court cases concluded the debate about the legality of same-sex marriage, *United States v. Windsor* (2013), which found a key section of the Defense of Marriage Act (DOMA) unconstitutional, and *Obergefell v. Hodges* (2015), a landmark case that guaranteed to same-sex couples across the nation a constitutional right to marry. Two residents of the state of New York, Edie Windsor and Thea Spyer, were married in Toronto in 2007. Their marriage was subsequently recognized in New York state in 2008, but not by the US federal government, due to the Defense of Marriage Act (DOMA), which was still in place at that time. After Spyer died, Windsor was subject to over $360,000 in estate taxes, even though heterosexual surviving spouses were not subject to such taxes. Windsor sued the federal government in 2010, seeking a refund. The Supreme Court found in favor of Windsor, stating that DOMA's exclusionary definition of spouses and marriage had no purpose but "to disparage and injure." Many knowledgeable observers anticipated that a nationwide right for same-sex couples to marry would soon follow.

Following the *Windsor* case, various federal appeals courts began to find state-level bans unconstitutional, leading thirty-six states to issue marriage licenses to same-sex couples. However, the Sixth District continued to assert that states had a right to exclude same-sex couples from marriage. James Obergefell (along with several other couples) challenged the constitutionality of this ruling. Obergefell had travelled from Ohio (where marriage was not yet legal) to Maryland (where marriage was legal) to marry John Arthur, his gravely ill spouse, shortly before Arthur passed away. Obergefell sued to have his name included as the surviving spouse on Arthur's death certificate. In *Obergefell v. Hodges* the Supreme Court found that the fundamental right to marry extends to same-sex couples, definitively concluding that all fifty states must issue marriage licenses regardless of whether one seeks to marry a same-sex or opposite-sex person. Many declared *Obergefell* to be the most important case in the struggle for equal rights for LGBTQ people, the crowning achievement of the movement's activism in the post–World War II era.

The civil rights account of same-sex marriage detailed above helps to explain how same-sex marriage came to be accepted in mainstream law and politics. But why did this happen? Below, I will argue that new ideas about alternative family forms in popular television shows challenged the dominance of the traditional nuclear family, fostering greater mainstream acceptance of same-sex marriage.[2] While the pop culture analysis in previous chapters focused largely on one element of other shifts, this chapter explores shifting representations of a variety of values that are typically transmitted through families, including norms about gender, economics, time, difference, and discipline.

Leave It to Beaver and the Traditional Nuclear Family

As television became more popular after World War II, the traditional nuclear family became the dominant family represented there. Well-known programs like *The Adventures of Ozzie and Harriet* (1952–1966) and *Father Knows Best* (1954–1960) set the norms for family life in this era. The family was typically represented as white, heterosexual, child-centered, suburban, and economically comfortable. As historian

Stephanie Coontz has noted, "Our most powerful visions of traditional families derive from images that are still delivered to our homes in countless reruns of 1950s television shows."[3]

In this section, I focus on *Leave It to Beaver*, a black-and-white television series that ran in 234 thirty-minute episodes over six seasons between 1957 and 1963. *Beaver* continues to be associated with the traditional nuclear family in the popular imagination more strongly than any other series of the postwar era. It has been televised in reruns almost continually since its original run and is currently streaming on Hulu as of this writing.[4] A feature-length *Leave It to Beaver* film was released in 1997 and was given a three-star rating by renowned film critic Roger Ebert.[5] *Beaver* is also popular in social media. For example, June Cleaver's fashion choices are discussed on Pinterest, blogs, and Etsy.[6]

Beaver is also a popular reference point for public intellectuals of various ideological stripes. In an online journal called the *Imaginative Conservative*, Michael De Sapio has championed the moral superiority of *Beaver*, arguing that it draws from "the wellspring of the moral imagination, creating characters and situations which have become archetypes."[7] On the other side of the ideological spectrum, a humorous collection of essays edited by Deborah Werksman entitled *I Killed June Cleaver: Modern Moms Shatter the Myth of Perfect Parenting* parodies the traditional family presented in *Beaver*.[8] Love it or hate it, *Beaver* continues to hold an important place in the popular imagination.

Plot and Characters

The series revolves around Theodore "Beaver" Cleaver, his older brother, Wally, stay-at-home mother, June, and businessman father, Ward. The Cleaver family lives together in a white, suburban development called Mayfield, in a split-level single-family home with three bedrooms and two baths, bounded by a classic white picket fence, suggesting a middle-to upper-middle-class level of affluence.[9] Beaver is eight years old when the show begins. He has many friends but does not like school or girls (until the final year of the show) and is not much of an athlete. He seems to genuinely care about others, even though misunderstandings, mistaken judgments, and self-interested motives all regularly lead him off the path of good behavior. By contrast, his big brother, Wally, is a very good student and star athlete who dates regularly. Given their four-year age difference, Wally is much more knowledgeable than Beaver about the rules that govern private and public life, although he too has much to learn.

Beaver is a light comedy offering object lessons that teach the boys how to become happy adults. The humor largely stems from young Beaver's misunderstandings about how to address everyday issues at home and at school.[10] Mild amusement results when Beaver tries to resolve (to him complex, but to the viewer simple) situations without getting into (too much) trouble, often creating (ultimately harmless) havoc in his wake.

Each episode reveals a new difficulty for Beaver and/or Wally. Their foiled solutions often involve at least some deception, suggesting that discipline for their misbehavior looms large in the background. At some point Ward typically steps in to clarify the morally correct way to address matters, and then metes out well-deserved punishment as Beaver and Wally are socialized into mainstream family and social life. The result is an eminently governable nuclear family, which the boys will presumably reproduce in due course as adults, given its centrality to personal and societal happiness. Nothing terribly complex happens. Viewers are treated to a few laughs and every problem is neatly resolved within a half-hour period. At a deeper level, *Beaver* reveals how the nuclear family transmits political norms and values about gender, economy, discipline, and difference to the next generation.

The Politics of Gender

Traditional gender norms were typical in the post–World War II nuclear family, and they are front and center in *Leave It to Beaver*. Women keep house and provide childcare; men bring home the bacon and dispense discipline. Even though June is a college graduate who worked briefly as a bookkeeper, now that she is a respectable middle-class married woman she no longer works outside the home, as that would reflect poorly on her husband. She is a full-time homemaker whose main function is to raise her boys and keep house, all while wearing a dress and pearls.[11]

As the man of the house, Ward supports the family financially. A World War II veteran, he is now a successful white-collar professional who works for a large company. The proverbial king of the castle, he rules the family in a firm but just manner, while June occasionally wields softer power that smooths over Ward's harder edges. Marriage domesticates Ward's presumptively aggressive nature. Within the boundaries of these gender norms, the Cleavers' marriage appears companionable, loving, and respectful.

Gender themes arise throughout the series as Beaver and Wally learn traditional lessons about what it takes to become a man, including appropriate personal appearance and successful dating practices. Few things are more humiliating to Beaver and Wally than being forced to cross the gender line or being bested by a girl. In just the third episode of the series, Beaver comes home with a black eye after having run away from a fight, much to Ward's great dismay, as he explains to Beaver that a man must always defend himself. After receiving boxing lessons from Ward, Beaver diligently heads over to the perpetrator's house to settle the score. In the meantime, Wally discovers that Beaver was punched by a girl, Violet Rutherford. Horrified that Beaver might abridge gender norms by publicly hitting a girl, Ward and Mr. Rutherford race to find their children, only to learn that they went out for an ice cream soda after Violet (naturally) declined further aggression.[12]

Later in the season Beaver suffers humiliation at school after being forced to wear a suit with short pants bought for him by his never-married Aunt Martha, who is visiting the Cleavers. Having learned how to demonstrate his manliness earlier in the season, Beaver immediately punches a boy who calls him a "sissy." As Beaver sadly heads out to school the next day wearing the short pants, Ward calls him into the garage and gives him more appropriate clothes to wear, further reinforcing the importance of maintaining a strict gender line.[13] In a later episode, Beaver talks his parents into allowing him to buy an expensive "Eskimo" sweater that he has been eyeing in a store window. He is mortified when several girls at school are wearing the very same sweater. Beaver ditches it at the local movie house and then lies to his parents, saying that some bullies took the sweater from him. The jig is up when the movie theater calls the Cleavers to let them know that they've found Beaver's sweater.[14]

Wally also faces gender trouble when he is cast in a satirical school play as a dress-wearing dancehall girl. To evade humiliation, Wally tricks his friend Eddie Haskell into switching parts with him. He then regrets it when Eddie gains a lot of attention for playing it broadly, introducing a new wrinkle into the gender norms that Wally is learning: it is okay to cross the gender line as long as you make it known that you understand that doing so is laughable.[15] More humiliation arises when it appears that Wally's new girlfriend is several inches taller than him. The crisis is averted when she accommodates Wally's fragile ego by appearing for the dance in low-heeled shoes, with a flat hairdo that removes any trace of her physical dominance.[16] Still more gender trouble ensues when Wally invites another girl to a formal dinner dance at the country club and she picks him up in her father's car, a clear abridgement of gender norms. Wally's friends tauntingly suggest that perhaps he rather than his girlfriend should be wearing the corsage.[17]

Season 2 is especially brutal for Wally, who becomes confused when he receives little attention after scoring a touchdown, typically a surefire way to reinforce his masculine bona fides. He quickly discovers that no one cares about football anymore because all his male friends are now bragging about shaving. Desperate to join in, Wally visibly nicks himself and Ward scolds him in front of Eddie Haskell for shaving before he has a full beard, leading his friends to disparagingly nickname Wally "baby-face." Wally doubles down and goes to a barber, not knowing that Ward has told the barber to give Wally a shave to make up for embarrassing him in front of his friend. Despite all these travails, Wally learns a valuable lesson from Ward: shaving is part of "being a man."[18] When Wally adopts a new hairdo called the jellyroll in a subsequent episode, Ward and June become concerned that it makes him look like a gangster, freak, and tango dancer, all "outsiders" well beyond what is acceptable in their little town. When Wally's friend Lumpy Rutherford also adopts it, his father complains to Ward that his "strapping boy came home looking like a rather ugly girl." Beaver adopting the hairdo is the last straw for June. She uses her soft power to ask Wally to understand that the haircut is as embarrassing as the time when Beaver wore one of her old hats to Sunday school, leading Wally to wash the new style out of his hair.[19]

In terms of dating, Ward and June worry that Wally will wind up with the "wrong" girl, meaning one who will dominate him, want to marry right away, and/or is more experienced.[20] Their concerns often seem to be triggered by seemingly harmless incidents, such as when they worry that Wally's new girlfriend has his letterman's sweater. After they see the girl with his sweater and hear her publicly bragging to other girls that she has Wally wrapped around her finger, Ward and June question him about the whereabouts of his sweater. When he responds that it is in his locker at school, Ward calls him out for lying and counsels that "women never want a sweater just because they're cold." By the end of high school (and the series), Wally has learned valuable lessons that will prepare him to find the right girl when he enters college the following fall.[21]

Unlike Wally, Beaver is quite resistant to learning the ins and outs of dating for most of the series. For example, Beaver is incensed when Violet is directed to sit on his lap in a crowded car as the Rutherfords and the Cleavers head to a picnic together. Once there, Mr. Rutherford coaxes Violet to give Beaver a kiss while he takes a photo, which is later printed in his workplace newspaper under the caption "A Future Merger?" After much teasing at school, Violet and Beaver claim mutual dislike.[22] This kind of trouble reemerges as late as the fourth season, when Beaver is forced to kiss a girl in a school play. Again, the problem is resolved when both parties claim no interest in each other.[23]

In the fifth season Beaver actively begins to seek out girls. His social-ization to dating and mating rituals occurs in fits and starts. After asking a girl at his dancing class out on his first date, he decides that girls are not worth the effort when his date dances with another boy.[24] In the final season, Beaver finds himself in a bind when he accepts one girl's invitation to the graduation dance, as well as a subsequent invitation from a prettier girl whom he likes better. Following Eddie Haskell's ad-vice, Beaver tries to get the first girl angry so she will uninvite him, and then feels bad when he realizes that she knows that he finds the other girl more attractive. By the time he calls it off with the second girl, the first girl already has found another date for the dance, leaving Beaver to spend the night alone in his room.[25]

As the series ends, Beaver is still learning about gender. When he suddenly gets interested in a fast-talking pretty girl, he begins to ques-tion the wisdom of leaving town on a six-week summer bus tour across America, lest his friend Gilbert move in on the girl while Beaver is away. Beaver persuades Gilbert to go with him, only to find out that another friend, Whitey, is now under the girl's spell, being charmed by the very same lines she had used on both Beaver and Gilbert earlier![26] Beaver has clearly graduated to the stage of dating where June and Ward will now anxiously worry about him coming under the sway of a bad girl, and presumably will be successfully socialized during his high school years, just as Wally was.

Political Economy

Episodes regularly include lessons about key elements of the postwar political economy such as money, work, markets, and capitalism. Ward and June instill traditional values in the boys about how to carefully steward money by working hard, saving carefully, investing cautiously, and repressing impulsive purchases. For example, after Wally and his friends have cornered the neighborhood chore market to raise money for their baseball team's uniforms, Beaver learns that the water main will be turned off for several hours and sets up a black-market, cold water delivery scheme with what we would now call surge pricing. Ward lectures him about taking advantage of Wally's friends, who become angry at him when they realize that most of their money has gone to buy Beaver's inflated water. Beaver gives them back their money as everyone learns that the electricity will be turned off that evening. Having learned alternative ways to manipulate markets from Beaver, Wally and his friends buy candles and resell them at a profit in the neighborhood to pay for their new uniforms, including one for Beaver, who becomes their water boy.[27] Working somewhat outside regulations apparently pays off, even if the cost is Ward's scolding. This is but one of many money-making schemes that teach the boys various lessons about the vagaries of market capitalism. In a later episode, the boys try to sell terrible-smelling perfume door to door in their neighborhood to earn a new projector from the distributor, only to find that no one wants to buy the foul-smelling product. Ward intervenes in the market, promising to reimburse various neighbors if they will buy a bottle from the boys. When the projector arrives at the house, Ward realizes that it is a cheap piece of junk. He secretly replaces it with a snappy new model, using benign deception to reinforce the value of hard work. The boys realize what Ward has done but decide not to say anything, as capitalism appears to require multiple levels of deception and manipulation.[28]

Yet Beaver does have his limits. When Ward agrees to pay for half of a canoe if Beaver will earn the rest of the cost, Beaver starts catching frogs and selling them for twenty-five cents apiece—at least until he learns that the frogs are being experimented upon. He abandons the frog money-making scheme, and Ward again intervenes in the market, agreeing to let Beaver clean his car for the remaining balance on the canoe.[29]

After Ward has a sober talk with Beaver about the monthly household bills, Beaver buys a book entitled *I Became a Millionaire in Twelve Months* and gives it to Ward, thinking that it will liberate him from his worries. When Beaver finds that the book has been stashed in a kitchen junk drawer rather than in Ward's personal library, Beaver climbs into a tree and hides. He finally comes down when Ward explains that you cannot become a millionaire by reading a book and that he had told Beaver he had put it in the library to avoid hurting his feelings. Beaver comes down, having learned a valuable lesson about how hard it is to become rich.[30]

In the aptly titled episode "Stocks and Bonds," Ward teaches the boys basic principles about the stock market, getting them to use twenty-five dollars of their own savings to buy a stock of their choice. Ward tries, but fails, to steer them away from a speculative stock called Jet-Electro, which Eddie Haskell has recommended on the basis of its "swinging" name. After a quick rise, Jet-Electro crashes due to the loss of a lucrative government contract. The boys are crushed until they learn that Ward had already sold off their Jet-Electro holdings before it dipped below its original market value, substituting the much more stable Mayfield Power and Electric.[31]

Beaver remains subject to the harsh realities of traditional market capitalism through the last season of the series. When Ward puts Beaver in charge of his own finances, Beaver is enticed into joining a record club that obligates him to buy more expensive "bonus" records unless he sends back a form that explicitly rejects them. When Beaver racks up a huge debt, Ward puts Beaver on a payment plan. Having learned his lesson, Beaver immediately alerts Ward the next time a "bonus" record offer arrives in the mail, shouting, "Dad, they're after me again."[32]

Authority and Power, Discipline and Violence

Families during the post–World War II era were thought to be well behaved and orderly largely due to the direction of husbands, who were expected to govern their wives and children, schooling them when they inevitably became confused about appropriate social and household norms. Beaver and Wally would be lost without Ward's firm but just guidance, along with June's merciful sensibilities. This combination of hard and soft power conveys important traditional lessons about power and authority that produce deception due to a fear of discipline and violence.

A pattern of deception emerges in the very first episode of the series, revealing Beaver's take on power and authority. When Beaver's teacher gives him a note to take home to his parents, his friends convince him that he is about to be expelled. Beaver's first move is to try to destroy the note, which he crumples into a ball and hides under his desk. When his teacher asks him for the signed note the next day, Beaver lies and says that he could not deliver it because the family's stove exploded. After his teacher insists that he deliver it, Beaver "loses" the note on the way home from school and Wally creates a fake response from June that assures his teacher that Beaver has been whipped for his (unspecified) bad behavior. When the horrified teacher calls June into school for an explanation and explains that all she wanted was permission for Beaver to be in the school play, he climbs a tree and vows to hide "until he dies." Bad weather leads Beaver to climb down, and the situation is resolved when Beaver talks to his teacher. While everything seems to work out well in the end, it is important to note that Beaver and Wally have good reason to engage in this pattern of deception, as Beaver recalls a time when Ward did use corporal punishment on him, suggesting that the boys are well aware of the potential for violence that lurks underneath the jovial façade of the nuclear family.[33] Throughout the series, Ward periodically recalls that he does not want to repeat his father's pattern of using corporal punishment in his own family. He and June occasionally recall moments of shame from their own childhoods that make them more understanding of Beaver and Wally's foibles.

The mischief that the boys find themselves in often originates outside the Cleavers' well-ordered home, as the boys are regularly lured into bad behavior by friends from less disciplined households. The anxious mother of Beaver's best friend, Larry Mondello, is shown to be ill equipped to govern her family when Mr. Mondello is away on one of his frequent business trips, leaving Larry free to cook up fantastical plans that lead Beaver astray. Larry regularly reports on "hollering" and corporal punishment at his house. Wally's best friend, the undisciplined Eddie Haskell, regularly entices the boys into disastrous courses of behavior for which they are firmly punished, leading Eddie to refer to Ward as "the warden." While Ward and June may compare well to other families, the boys clearly worry about the threat of punishment and violence at home. Although Ward is represented as a more or less benign king of the castle, it is clear that Beaver fears his father, as he regularly engages in deception to avoid punishment. The stories work because everyone, including the audience, understands the potential for violence in the traditional nuclear family. Child viewers are being socialized into deception along with Beaver, while adult viewers gain tips for disciplining their children into morally upright behavior.

In a later episode, Beaver even faces the disciplinary arm of the state when he receives a ticket for driving his go-kart without a license, despite Ward's strict orders not to do so. Rather than telling Ward about his transgression, Wally tries to pass as Beaver's guardian in court. When Beaver hears others getting jail time he starts crying, and the judge sends them home because they have been "punished enough." When they decide to tell Ward, he urges them to always come to him with their troubles.[34] Regardless, the pattern of deception and punishment repeats in numerous episodes throughout much of the series.

As the boys grow older, they internalize Ward's regime of discipline. For example, when Beaver shows Larry Mondello Ward's special baseball autographed by stars such as Babe Ruth and Lou Gehrig, he convinces Beaver that they should play catch with it. Trouble ensues when the ball lands in the middle of the street and is run over by a truck. Larry and Beaver try to recreate the autographs on a new ball, making obvious errors like "Baby Ruth." A visibly enraged Ward confines Beaver to home without television for a week. When he later considers retracting the punishment, Wally urges Ward not to.[35] Wally has clearly internalized the punishment regime, as presumably Beaver will when he gets older.

Political Time

Leave It to Beaver is set in a specific political time. Ward is a veteran of World War II. Beaver and Wally are children of the Cold War period who imagine themselves working on "missiles" and as "space scientists."[36] Beaver covets an "Eskimo" sweater that was designed to commemorate Alaska becoming the forty-ninth state. *Beaver* evokes a feeling of nostalgia for a simpler time when many were thought to share a common set of moral values and national destiny. From a contemporary vantage point, we now know that that was never really the case. Not all women were full-time homemakers like June in the post–World War II period. The aptly entitled *Not June Cleaver: Women and Gender in Postwar America, 1945–1960* documents the experience of women of various races, ethnicities, sexualities, classes, and marital statuses who were working in a wide variety of unionized jobs, as activists in the peace movement, Mexican barrios, and the civil rights movement, and a variety of other positions.[37]

Complexities became more apparent in mainstream politics in the wake of President John F. Kennedy's assassination, which occurred less than three months after *Beaver* left prime time. As the era of Camelot ended, a new more turbulent era began in which public conflict over basic political values became visible in American society. This new period would be defined by mass movements focused on peace, Black civil rights, women's equality, and LGBT liberation. *Beaver* precedes this period, expressing time from a linear and singular perspective. The series begins with Beaver in elementary school and ends with him preparing to enter high school. Wally begins in junior high and is preparing to enter college by the end.

There are only a few exceptions to this linearity, revealing interesting cracks in the façade of the perfect nuclear family, each of which is destined to split wide open in the transitional period that follows. Beaver discovers photos of his father from his time in the military and wonders what his life was like then; Ward occasionally recalls punishing moments from his childhood in a manner that affects his own parenting; and June finds an old scrapbook that prompts the entire family to reminisce about key events drawn from the run of the series. For example, after hearing his principal talk about World War II, Beaver looks for Ward's war trophies, but finds only surveying equipment because Ward had the far less adventurous task of building new bases. Beaver also discovers photos that depict Ward with a full beard, leaning on an army mate in a seemingly boozy manner, wearing a grass skirt and a sleeveless mid-drift. This leads Beaver to realize that his father led a different kind of life prior to marriage and parenthood.[38] However, even in these limited examples, there is no real contestation of subjectivity. This illusion of unity limits conflicting views, decreasing the emergence of a more critical perspective.[39] However, contemporary viewers take in these episodes knowing that this illusion of unity would soon shatter. This creates the possibility of more critical openings.

Perhaps the closest the series comes to more directly revealing a crack in the ideal nuclear family occurs when Beaver learns that a friend from camp (i.e., outside Beaver's immediate community) has parents who are divorced. "Chopper" Cooper's father is in his third marriage and his mother is with "Uncle" Dave, who has dropped him off for an overnight at the Cleavers'. At first, this aberration from the traditional nuclear family appears quite desirable to Beaver. Chopper is receiving all kinds of gifts from his parents, has several half-brothers and half-sisters, and more independence than is common for a kid his age. Beaver even starts to hopefully ask Ward and June whether they might be thinking about a divorce. It is only when Chopper is forced to return home because his mother has "the weepies" that Beaver begins to understand that Chopper's parents are trying to buy his affection, and that Chopper wishes he had a "real" brother like Wally. As Chopper explains the realities of his life, including the fact that he gets the weepies too sometimes, Beaver comes to understand that alternative family forms are fraught, filled with sadness and violence, nothing that anyone would really desire after all. In the end, the episode reinforces the central lesson of the series: true happiness can be had only within the confines of the traditional nuclear family.[40]

Difference and "Others"

Beaver also airbrushes out others who do not conform to the dictates of the traditional postwar nuclear family, such as people of color, the poor, single women, and/or homosexuals. In 234 episodes, only one Black character is ever shown, a maid at a wedding reception in an episode called "The Parking Attendants."[41] When others are included, they appear for one episode, so that Beaver can learn a valuable object lesson, at which point they are never heard from again. Most of the time, they are read through Ward and June's cautious and protective white, middle-class perspective, which fears difference but in the end calls for Beaver and Wally to tolerate others unlike themselves. But not always. Sometimes others are represented in a manner that reveals ignorance and prejudice, perhaps foreshadowing the explosion of disunity and conflict that arises in the post-*Beaver* era. The central point of these examples here is not to sit in judgment of the traditional assumptions of earlier times, but rather to show how pervasively the traditional nuclear family was defined by white, heterosexual, middle-class norms during this period.

For example, after overhearing Ward mumble that their bills are going to send the Cleavers to the poorhouse, Beaver wants to learn more about how poor people live. He befriends a trashman who lives next to a junkyard and has a great time visiting his two sons there. While Ward and June allow the visit, they are very skeptical, imagining that the trashman's family will be rude and dirty. When Beaver invites them to his house so they can see for themselves, it turns out that the trashman's boys are clean and polite, and in awe of the Cleavers' backyard, garage, and other elements of the household that Wally and Beaver take for granted. In the end, everyone learns the lesson that "the grass is always greener"—the title of the episode.[42]

The Cleavers' handyman, an old friend of Ward's, has a drinking problem that he and June have concealed from Wally and Beaver. While painting at their house, Andy says that he "needs a drink" and Beaver naively offers him a glass of water or fruit punch, which Andy promptly rejects. Beaver then shows him where Ward keeps his special brandy and runs off to play. Upon returning home, Ward finds Andy drunk and realizes that he and June need to teach the boys about "life's evils," which Wally refers to as "the bad junk in the world." Later, a sober Andy delivers the episode's object lesson, telling Beaver that drinking to excess leads only to unhappiness.[43]

In another episode, Beaver remembers Ward's bromide to be kinder and more considerate of others and lets Mr. Jeff, a "tramp," into the Cleaver house. Mr. Jeff washes up, eats, and takes one of Ward's good suits on his way out the door. Upon realizing that the suit is missing, the boys try to track down Mr. Jeff in town, to no avail. Beaver is disappointed that his good deed has been misused, even though Ward assures him that that is unusual. Days later, Beaver receives a thank you letter from Mr. Jeff with five dollars in it, letting him know that he was able to get a job because of Beaver's kindness, and promising to send more money each week until he has paid for the suit.[44]

At school, Beaver's new friend Chuey speaks only Spanish. Wally's friend Eddie Haskell volunteers to use his beginning-level Spanish skills to teach Beaver how to say "You're a good guy" in Spanish, but really teaches him to say, "You have a face like a pig," which makes Chuey cry. When Chuey's parents come to the Cleavers' house to investigate, Beaver offers up his line yet again, and they leave upset. After Wally figures out what Eddie has done, Ward uses an old Spanish textbook to write a letter of apology to Chuey and his family, and Chuey returns with flowers and a note from his parents asking forgiveness, leading the adults to reflect that "we learn from our children."[45]

Despite these instances of tolerance and inclusion, other episodes reveal a stunning disregard for difference across race, class, gender, and sexuality lines. For example, when Larry Mondello is left out of a new secret club in which Beaver is a member, Larry creates his own secret club called the Fiends, who wear paper bags that stand in for "velvet hoods," armbands with skulls, and a blindfolded initiation rite. This plot-line seems oblivious to the rising power of the Ku Klux Klan during this period.[46] Larry's rationale for the club is revealing: "What's the use of having a secret club if you can't keep other guys out?" While parallels to the Klan are not discussed during this episode, Ward does offer Beaver yet another bromide in response to Larry's club: "The worst reason to form a club is to keep people out."[47] Nonetheless, just two episodes later, after watching a movie called *The Mad Hypnotist*, Beaver tries out his own hypnotic power on squirrels. Seeing Beaver do this, Wally's friend Eddie Haskell pretends to be under Beaver's power, calling him "master" and saying things like "Slave kill for master, Slave steal for master." This rather cavalier language ends when Wally chases Eddie straight into a pile of mud.[48]

After June complains to Ward that she is tired from cleaning the house all the time, the Cleavers hire a maid, a clear mark of their class status. The maid is already overscheduled, so she sends her daughter. Following the traditional pattern of young men sexually using the women in their family's employ, Wally becomes attracted to the maid and starts hanging around her to "help" her. Rather than considering the undue pressure this puts on the young maid, Ward and June become concerned that Wally's grades are falling. June speaks to the young woman's mother, who dismisses her daughter and is thus forced to do all the work herself, employing the traditional "solution" to the Cleavers' problem.[49]

As we saw earlier, Beaver was not punished when he punched a kid who called him a "sissy." That sort of language is hardly surprising, as the *New York Times*, the national paper of record, regularly used such language to refer to homosexuals and those who did not conform to gender norms.[50] The show provides no explanation for Beaver's odd, never-married Aunt Martha, who clearly does not understand gender norms, or for elderly neighborhood spinster Miss Cooper, who Beaver thinks is a witch.[51]

Beaver and his viewers are taught again and again that the traditional white, middle-class heterosexual nuclear family is central to social stability and personal happiness. These norms affected the shape of public policy at that time. The nuclear family was the first line of defense against communism and treason, central threats to the American way of life. As Stephanie Coontz has noted, "Anti-communists linked deviant family or sexual behavior to sedition."[52] Traditional gender norms such as women raising children were followed, as in *Beaver*, but women were warned not to create too strong an attachment, especially with boys, as overbearing mothers were thought to be a primary cause of psychological pathology, which could lead to the development of homosexuality.[53] To the extent that gays and lesbians were visible to mainstream society at all, they were seen as outsiders who threatened to undermine the traditional moral foundations of the nuclear family and the state. As such, it was virtually impossible for most Americans to imagine homosexuals in mainstream politics and society, let alone as respectable married couples who might productively contribute to society or perhaps raise children of their own.

Beaver offers little critical distance or reflexivity on the traditional values that the family was transmitting at that time, making a more critical stance on homosexuality and the family nearly impossible. By contrast, *thirtysomething* offers an abundance—some have said an overabundance—of reflection on the nuclear family's politics of gender, economy, discipline and punishment, and difference, opening space for views that challenge the givenness of that family form. However, traditional values also persist in *thirtysomething* alongside newer alternative views, as is common during transitional periods.

Thirtysomething and the Transition from the Traditional to the Alternative Family

In the following sections, I focus on the hour-long weekly drama *thirtysomething*, which ran for four seasons and eighty-five episodes from 1987 to 1991. Initially dismissed by many as self-indulgent yuppie whining, *thirtysomething* built a fiercely loyal viewership and became critically acclaimed, reflecting and shaping its times, becoming "an ingrained part of late 20th century popular culture."[54] It was used by family therapists to get new parents talking about mixed feelings regarding marriage, parenting, sex, work/life balance, and a host of other topics, leading the American Psychological Association to give the show an award for promoting "the notion of inner thinking."[55] When a number of its scripts were compiled into a book in 1991, Robert Thompson noted that "the writing on *thirtysomething* achieved a new apex of artistic legitimacy for prime-time television."[56] Thirty years later, a podcast focusing on the show ran for three years, and an oral history of the show was published, affirming the *New York Times'* judgment that *thirtysomething* was a "zeitgeist-defining" series that foreshadowed a new golden age of television to come in the late 1990s.[57] As late as 2020, ABC had planned to reprise the original series, with the original writers and six members of the original cast returning, but the COVID-19 pandemic put its development on hold.[58]

Thirtysomething is a drama focused on the relationships and inner lives of seven adults, rather than the outward antics of kids, as was the case in *Beaver*. Its central characters are baby boomers who rebelled against their nuclear families of origin during the turbulent 1960s. They are the children of Ward and June, Beaver in his thirties. They are often disdainful of the nuclear family even as they nostalgically yearn for many of its purportedly simple pleasures. They worry (a lot) about becoming like their parents as they age.

It is clear that the traditional family no longer works in the seamless way that it did for the Cleavers. Gender norms are no longer accepted as given. Economic stability seems to be a thing of the past. The discipline and restraint that monogamy requires are regularly questioned. Narratives are perspectival and multiple, allowing for more critical reflections in and through political time. Characters with identities that were more or less invisible in the previous era are represented here, at least as minor figures. Even though these new characters are rendered as ultimately unfulfilled or even tragic figures, their presence opens up new narratives that portend more critical possibilities on the horizon, beyond the transitional period. In sum, *thirtysomething* provides an anxiety-ridden transition from the nuclear family into an uncertain future.

Plot and Characters

Thirtysomething explores the interactions between a central heterosexual couple, Michael and Hope Steadman, and their core group of five friends: Michael's business partner Elliot Weston and his wife, Nancy, Hope's best friend, Ellyn Warren, Michael's best friend, Gary Shepherd, and Michael's cousin Melissa Steadman. Together they constitute an alternative to the traditional nuclear family, a family constituted (mostly) by choice rather than by blood. The show is primarily dramatic, with light comic relief coming for the most part from Melissa's banter and Ellyn's foibles (those wacky single gals!), as well as creative flashbacks and parodies featuring all cast members. As the series progresses, this family of friends both yearns for and upends the traditional nuclear family. Traditional family norms and practices that were unselfconsciously accepted in the *Beaver* era are found to be largely unworkable in this new era, but what lies beyond such norms remains largely unclear.

Hope and Michael live in a traditional Arts and Crafts home in the suburbs of Philadelphia. The façade of their house is beautiful, but its interiors are visibly in need of work, and are regularly torn apart to their bones and then reconstructed, a metaphor for the family itself. While the Steadmans appear to be the best "hope" for the traditional nuclear family as the series opens, by the end of the series their future together is uncertain at best. As a Princeton graduate, Hope had a promising career in her twenties as a magazine writer investigating corporate abuse and environmental degradation, only to give it up in her thirties to stay at home and raise Janey and Leo. In the very first episode she jokingly calls Michael "Ward" when he comes home from work, an obvious reference to Ward Cleaver, an indication that she knows she is following the traditional path of stay-at-home moms like June Cleaver. After Michael's father dies later in the show, they visit his childhood home and Hope exclaims, "Oh my god, it's *Leave It to Beaver!*"[59] The humorous way that she acknowledges this also suggests a measure of critical distance and challenge to those older ways.

As the show develops, full-time homemaking proves somewhat unfulfilling, so Hope returns to work, only to worry that she is much less effective at her job than she used to be, and an inadequate parent to boot. Michael fulfills the traditional male role as the main breadwinner throughout the series, whether Hope works or not. He recently left a large, impersonal advertising firm to start up a small, self-owned business with his friend Elliot Weston, intent on creating a smaller, more creative, and humane workplace devoid of the corporate culture that forced them to compromise their core values. While they are much happier running their business, they struggle to adequately support their families in an increasingly austere and amoral environment that rewards a cutthroat, bottom-line approach. Ultimately their business fails, and they must submit to increasingly dominant neoliberal business norms.

In the first episode, Elliot reveals to an astonished Michael that he cheated on his wife, Nancy, establishing a pattern that contrasts Michael's discipline with Elliot's indulgence. Nancy and Elliot's marriage seems far less stable than Hope and Michael's. Like Hope, Nancy was a professional, a painter, but she has been at home raising two children for some time. When Elliot leaves her, their traditional family is destroyed and then reconstructed into an alternative form. She reconnects with her own personal and professional desires. She starts dating, rediscovers her artistic talent, and begins a career writing children's books and teaching at the local art school. Over time, Elliot grows up, at least somewhat, once he realizes that Nancy can get along just fine without him. He admits that he kept Nancy down when they were together, badly betraying and hurting his family.

Ellyn Warren has been Hope's best friend since high school. She is single, an ambitious city administrator in Philadelphia who supervises twenty-seven employees. She and Hope were both once young career women on the rise, but they have struggled to maintain a close relationship since Hope took on the more traditional stay-at-home mom role. Hope thinks that Ellyn cannot possibly understand how difficult it is to raise a child, while Ellyn believes that Hope has forgotten how hard it is to fulfill the dictates of a demanding job while also finding a good man. Ellyn dates often but cannot commit to anyone who is seriously interested in her, and they cannot commit to her if she is seriously interested in them.

Gary Shepherd has been Michael's best friend since college. He is a prime example of a man undomesticated by the responsibilities of the nuclear family: promiscuous, conventionally attractive, sexist, and single. In the first episode, he and Michael are at an outdoor gear store. Gary is ogling a woman, following her around in the aisles, and asking Michael how sex is now that he and Hope have a baby. When Michael (untruthfully) responds, "Same as ever," Gary concludes, "At least she's beautiful. She'll lose the weight." Gary's reluctance to accept the limits and compromises of committed relationships dooms his on-again, off-again relationship with Michael's cousin Melissa Steadman and makes it impossible for him to gain tenure at Penn, where he is an assistant professor of medieval literature.

Melissa Steadman is a single woman and a successful, if often insecure, photographer. She is rather bohemian (compared to the others) and thus somewhat of a challenge to traditional family norms. Regardless, she also yearns to find a man and settle down and start a family. From the very start, this is a driving desire of hers, as indicated when she is holding Janey and tells Hope, "I want this baby. Can I have her? I know, I know, how am I going to have a baby when I'm dating babies." Melissa has great love for Gary and feels very burned by his lack of commitment, though they maintain something of a friendship.

Gender

Much of the series focuses on the gender differences between men and women. Reflecting the transitional nature of this period, the central characters of *thirtysomething* either enact or yearn for the nuclear family, while also insisting on more fulfilling lives at home and at work, challenging the rigid sex and gender roles of the traditional family. For example, Michael and Elliot often revel in having traditional wives: "We're really lucky, we have wives who want to stay home with the kids and all that stuff," says Elliot. Michael agrees, saying, "Hope seems really into it." But the reality for Hope and Nancy is much more complex. Talking with Hope, Nancy notes, "Motherhood is like a lost art. We're dinosaurs."[60] At times, the nuclear family is distanced in a much more disdainful manner, such as when career woman Ellyn refers to Hope's staying home to raise children as "like it's 1956 again."[61] They all know that the days of June Cleaver are gone, but they are not sure what's next.

Rather than supporting the family as in *Leave It to Beaver*, traditional gender differences threaten to tear the family apart in *thirtysomething*. Hope regularly questions the wisdom of being a stay-at-home mom, even though she regards it as a choice that she and Michael have made. She is often conflicted about finding the right home/work balance and resentful that Michael does not seem to feel the same. She wants to be taken seriously as a thoughtful adult whose talents are not limited to childcare. Out at a business dinner with Michael, she cannot get a word in edgewise, so she fantasizes a slow-motion segment in which she says, "Am I invisible here or what?" as the men continue to converse uninterrupted. After she makes an ill-received comment about the environmental impact of disposable diapers, she excuses herself to call the babysitter, and lactates when she hears Janey crying, forcing her to return to the table with a large milk stain on her fancy blouse, a gender marker if there ever was one. When Hope decides to return to her former job part-time, they want her back full-time. She does not understand the new computers, her work product is mediocre, and she worries that she is neglecting Janey. Michael is supposed to help with childcare, but he comes home from work exhausted, complaining about not having sex and wondering aloud why Hope can soothe Janey but not him. He finally concedes that he liked having Hope at home all day rather than working.

Hope understands that her marriage fulfills traditional sex and gender norms. She occasionally flashes back to her college days in women's studies classes at Princeton, recalling a professor who warned her to guide her energies into her own creative work, lest she waste her life subordinating herself to a man. When Hope fantasizes the professor asking her in real time what she plans to do with her life, she does not have a ready answer. She knows that traditional sex and gender roles are problematic, but she cannot identify a suitable alternative. Instead she blames her professor (her figurative mother) for leading her to a dead end: "You were teaching us to be rigid and insane, like the men we despised."[62]

Despite Michael and Hope's persistent problems, their friends think of them as a model couple. When Nancy and Elliot enter couples therapy to try to save their failing marriage, Nancy overtly compares their sniping to Michael and Hope's public sweetness.[63] Divorce is a real option for them, rather than a one-time object lesson that happens in "other" families, as was the case in *Beaver*. That said, the nuclear family dies hard. Its rosy façade makes it difficult to imagine viable alternatives. Nancy believes that her world will fall apart when Elliot leaves her. Yet, as they near the brink of divorce, she rediscovers her artistic career, builds her self-confidence, starts dating again, and finds that single motherhood is not only workable, but desirable. She writes and illustrates a book with her son, Ethan, empowering him to master the nightmares he has been having in the traumatic wake of Elliot's sudden departure.[64] She embraces new gender norms, learning how to balance the demands of home and work more effectively, and how to set boundaries with Elliot as well as with her own more traditional, protective mother.[65]

Like many men, Elliot has learned about male masculinity from his father. Although his father initially presents as jovial on the surface, the reality beneath the traditional façade is more complex, as is often the case during transitional periods. He is a serious drinker who only sporadically follows through on promises. He abandoned his family around the time that Elliot was the age of his own son, Ethan. Nonetheless, Elliot is eager to impress him and gain his affection. Elliot's sister, on the other hand, remains angry that their father abandoned them. She urges Elliot to avoid their father's manipulative ways and think about the future rather than the past, also common during transitional periods. Regardless, Elliot creates a sophisticated multimedia sales presentation, making his father look current in front of his clients. While out celebrating with two women his father hired for the evening, they unexpectedly run into Nancy, who is furious that Elliot has left Ethan with a stranger at his father's hotel. Elliot's dad subsequently shames him for allowing Nancy to publicly embarrass him, and then demonstrates a traditional tactic for dominating her by buying Ethan a toy rocket that she had said was not age-appropriate. When the rocket explodes and risks blindness for Ethan, he still wants Elliot to go out of town with him to the next presentation. When Elliot opts to stay home with his son, his father chastises him by referencing traditional sex and gender roles, saying, "Be a man." Elliot gets angry at him for the first time in the episode, realizing that the old ways were not all that they were cracked up to be: "What's that, Dad, someone who walks out and lives in hotel rooms? That's not what I want." His father responds with a slur commonly levelled against "emasculating" women like Nancy, cleaned up somewhat for television: "She's really got you whipped." For the first time, Elliot understands that he has been selfish toward his family, and realizes that like his father, he too needs to grow up.[66]

Improbably, Nancy and Elliot not only reconcile, but do so in a manner that allows them both to be fulfilled at work and at home, resetting the terms of their no longer traditional family. Nancy develops a more complex understanding of her marriage and family that is not singularly romantic. When Hope worries aloud that Nancy's decision to get back together with Elliot is mistaken, Nancy responds, "It's not so easy. Someday Michael will tell you something that rocks you to your very soul, and you'll have to figure out what to do with that."[67] She concludes, "I could start again, but there's something about Elliot, the way his mind works. We all kid ourselves when we love someone. We have to." When Michael asks Elliot whether he would ever cheat again, his views have also clearly shifted: "No. I see my family for the first time as us."[68]

However, the future of this less gendered family is uncertain, befitting the transitional period. Just as they begin to experience happiness at work and home, Nancy learns that she has ovarian cancer, becoming a tragic rather than a redeemed character.[69] As it turns out, the most tragic figure of this story is Gary, arguably the most transformed of all when it comes to sex and gender norms. He begins the series as a good-looking, sexist guy who deeply fears commitment. He is not able to stay with quirky Melissa or with a more conventionally beautiful and accomplished "perfect" woman.[70] He would rather play the field on his own terms than commit to a nuclear family. And yet, by the end of the show, he has become a stay-at-home dad in a monogamous relationship that challenges the gendered structure of the traditional family form.

Unlike other women, Susannah is not instantly taken in by Gary's charms. She is not interested in domesticating any man. She is more devoted to her work in an anti-poverty agency, a distinct deviation from traditional female femininity, as well as the other single women in the show. While Melissa and Ellyn are also professionally accomplished, they are driven to find a man, settle down, and have a family. Once Susannah starts seeing Gary, she challenges his traditional sexist assumptions, warning him not to protect her in some "big, strong masculine" way.[71] The central *thirtysomething* characters never accept her into the chosen family they have constructed, finding her to be a "judgmental bitch."[72] When Susannah unexpectedly becomes pregnant, she considers having an abortion independent of Gary's input. In the end, they talk through their fears of intimacy and decide to raise the baby together, creating a family arrangement well outside the bounds of the traditional nuclear family.[73]

Having recently been denied tenure at Penn, a professional emasculation of sorts, Gary becomes a stay-at-home dad to newborn Emma.[74] We
see him in the park with other moms and baby strollers, while Susannah remains busy at work, a direct reversal of traditional gender norms.
Naturally, Gary's more conventional male friends give him grief; for example, Michael tells him, "It's good your father's not alive to see you
disgracing yourself." When Gary's mom comes to help with the newborn, she says, "It's a shame your [deceased] father isn't here to see her."
Thanks to Michael, Gary knows just how to respond: "He'd be critical.
He would buy me an apron." Gary argues that it is far harder for him to
stay at home than for a woman, because he has to challenge entrenched
gender norms, while women only need to fold into traditional female
femininity: "Women have to do it. For me to be home feels unnatural,
like the whole world is passing me by." When Gary confesses that he is
afraid he will dominate his family the way his father did, his intuitive
mother perceives that he is somewhat ambivalent and counsels him in
a way that underscores that men in the transitional period can choose
(or reject) parenthood: "Only if you want to do it. I'm not sure you do."[75]
    Gary subsequently decides to work both in and outside the home. He
joins the emerging gig economy as a part-time instructor at a city college, quite a few steps down from his tenure-track line at Penn. Susannah, the dominant partner, gives in to hyphenating Emma's last name
and they (finally) find time to have sex, solving a problem that continues to plague more traditional Hope and Michael throughout the series.
When conditions deteriorate at work and breadwinner Susannah is offered a job in New York, Gary pledges to support her decision to take it.
But he becomes ambivalent when they visit the city, where he sees crime
and economic instability. When he tells Susannah that he'd rather stay
in Philadelphia, rather than folding to his wishes, as a more traditional
woman might, she refuses. Adding yet another alternative aspect to their
relationship, they decide to live at a distance during the week and be
together on the weekends, noting that the family form is shifting: "We
wouldn't be the only couple doing it." In another sign of gender reversal,

it is Gary who wants a more visible sign of their commitment to each other: "I wish we had something more solid than luck."[76] Against all odds, they get married, Susannah leaves for New York immediately after with the baby, and Gary is left to tear up as the train leaves the station.

After all these challenges to traditional gender roles, Gary suddenly dies in a car accident, just as the friends are celebrating Nancy's cancer remission. Hope underscores that this runs against the natural order of things: "It's not supposed to happen like this. We have old parents." Nancy adds, "It wasn't supposed to be Gary. But I got better."[77] Old girlfriend Melissa notes how much Gary had changed, saying that he loved Susannah more than anything. When Susannah responds, "He changed everything in my life," Melissa underscores the co-equality of their relationship, saying, "You changed him."[78] In the end, Susannah and Gary's unconventional relationship is *thirtysomething*'s most creative alternative to the traditional nuclear family, opening up a world of possibilities beyond the nuclear family, while also foreshadowing an uncertain future.

Economy

Even though Ward Cleaver occasionally complained that household spending was going to lead the family to "the poorhouse," he never had to worry about job security. *Thirtysomething* is rife with economic and political anxieties. The series premiered in September 1987, just weeks before a major stock market crash on October 9, now known as Black Monday. On that day, markets across the world fell, more than 20 percent in the United States and 45 percent in Hong Kong. The series ended in May 1991, just a few months after the close of combat in Operation Desert Storm of the First Gulf War, in which the United States and a multinational force fostered a new world order after the fall of the Berlin Wall. A few months after that, the Soviet Union collapsed, George H. W. Bush lost his bid for reelection, and Bill Clinton became the first US president drawn from the baby boomer generation.

Most episodes of *thirtysomething* feature stressful interpersonal conflict between some subset of the primary ensemble of characters that is ultimately resolved for togetherness: love, family, and/or friendship. But what cannot be negotiated are the new norms of the emerging neoliberal economy, which strain families and workplaces to the breaking point. Expenses are not met and businesses fail, undermining the household economies that supported the traditional nuclear family.

Michael cannot escape these anxieties no matter where he works. After graduating from Princeton, he wanted to be a writer, but he took a position in an advertising firm, compromising his ideals for economic stability. There he met Elliot, who was unhappy from the very start. Less willing to get along to get ahead, Elliot was fired. After Michael became disillusioned and quit, they started the "Michael and Elliot Company," a small, more creative advertising business that struggles to make ends meet. Elliot highlights the connection between the viability of their business and maintaining their nuclear families, saying, "We need this account. We have two wives, four kids, two cars, two mortgages. We are the breadwinners now." Unlike Ward Cleaver, they cannot rely on a stable economy and lifelong position in one company to provide material well-being for their families. Both the economy and their families are in transition, making it increasingly difficult for even these white, middle-class, privileged Ivy League graduates to maintain a nuclear family and a healthy home/work balance.

When the company fails, they have trouble finding work. Hope underscores how unlikely their predicament would have been in an earlier time: "This is just not the way it was supposed to happen. Not for us. And I'm frightened."[79] Michael tries to retool by taking a night class in creative writing at a local college, but it turns out that he is awful at it. He gives up writing again and gets a temporary job at DAA, a cutting-edge advertising agency, even though he dislikes the company head, Miles Drentell, who is creative but lacks integrity. Drentell's inhumanity is on full display right away, as he sends Michael on a last-minute trip despite the fact that Hope has just miscarried, saying, "Remember, you came to me." Michael explains to a very unhappy Hope that he has to go, using the gendered language of the traditional nuclear family as well as neoliberal individual choice jargon: "I'm the provider here. We could've chose different, it could've been you, but we chose differently. I have responsibilities."[80]

If Michael is most caught up in the system, his best friend, Gary, is the least committed to it. Unlike Michael, Gary is an idealist who believes that no one should ever compromise, and he is willing to pay a high price for his conviction. He knows that he will never be able to afford a house, but he is committed to avoiding bourgeois life, telling Michael that he and Susannah are "different." Michael just laughs, but Hope worries aloud, "Are we as totally compromised as Gary and Susannah think?" Michael responds glibly, "Of course we are, we're working on a family," adding that Gary and Susannah "are just doers, but life is not just about doing, but who you do it for."[81]

As Michael get pulled deeper into the machinations of big advertising, he becomes more committed to neoliberal economics and his troubles with Hope grow. She is disgusted when Drentell attends a dinner party at their home and his girlfriend tells a "joke" about a homeless man. After everyone leaves, Hope and Michael fight about it, revealing the growing gap in their core values. Michael worries that her visible disdain is making it harder for him to "protect the family," while Hope counters that "the world is dying" and calls Michael a hypocrite.[82]

Hope subsequently volunteers at a homeless shelter in the city that is under pressure due to Reaganist cuts in social service funding. Though her Ivy League sensibilities are taken aback by the smell, dirt, and chaos of the shelter, she keeps returning, providing childcare while parents look for work. She meets a woman of color named Mary Kennedy who lost her job as a file clerk at a law firm because she had become visibly pregnant and subject to domestic violence. Earnest Hope instantly responds, "That's illegal!"[83] She asks Michael to hire Mary at DAA, but in the end, that proves to be impossible. While Mary is understanding (it likely happens to her all the time), Hope is indignant. Later in the evening, after dining at a very posh downtown restaurant, Michael and Hope encounter a panhandler. Hope forces Michael to give him some money, and they fight about it afterward. Michael tells Hope that she can afford to volunteer at the shelter only because his work is paying for her time there. Meanwhile, Hope discovers that Mary has left the shelter, due to a thirty-day occupancy limit. Hope is distraught and fights with Michael again. He tells her that he is "not the enemy," but she is not so sure, wondering, "Then who are they? Who decides who will and won't have a chance in life?" Michael responds, "I love you and your growl at the world." But she is not amused, asking, "How can I enjoy my life when so many have nothing?"

Meanwhile, Michael's deepening reliance on Drentell forces him to confront his own ambition, a trait that he has worked hard to deny most of his life. He is promoted to creative director (number two on the organizational chart) after harshly disciplining former peers and friends, including Elliot, who refuses to make compromises that would allow him to succeed in an increasingly hierarchical and austere workplace. This comes to a head when Elliot botches an important commercial shoot, wasting resources and annoying everyone involved.[84] Although the commercial comes out well in the end, Drentell humiliates Elliot in front of coworkers and Michael is forced to fire him (although he secretly keeps Elliot on health insurance, showing that he still has humane sensibilities, particularly since Nancy is still undergoing chemotherapy). Drentell pushes Michael even further, forcing him to break up long-standing creative teams to see "who is the engine and who is the baggage." When Michael objects, saying, "They're people," Drentell responds with the bottom-line ethic of the new era: "They're dross, excess."[85]

Michael carries out the orders, but for him this is the last straw. Unbeknownst to Drentell, Michael plans to use cutthroat neoliberal tactics to topple him, organizing a hostile takeover of DAA by its biggest client, Minnesota Brands. Furthermore, he lets Elliot in on his secret plan, telling him that the workplace is about to change for the better, providing what they always wanted. Alas, all businesses in this brave new world are ruthless, even if they are based in friendly, midwestern Minnesota. The bottom line is all that matters for the head of Minnesota Brands. In any case, Michael is unable to get the final board vote he needs to secure the takeover. Drentell finds out, but instead of firing Michael, he is in awe of his bravado. As a condition of staying, Michael forces Drentell to take Elliot back. Michael stays with Drentell even after he asks Michael's cousin Melissa out "to see her portfolio," and then tries to force her to have sex against her will.[86] Shortly thereafter, Drentell asks Michael to meet him at his downtown club to discuss a new venture. When Michael notes a conspicuous absence of women, Drentell laughingly responds, "They pop out of a cake occasionally."

It is not just workers who are at risk in this neoliberal order. Even an agency like DAA is not secure in this era of austerity. As Drentell himself notes, "The Gilded Age has concluded. The new era is one of loss."[87] The more Michael succeeds at work, the worse he feels, and the more his family is destabilized. He develops heartburn, insomnia, and chest pain. As Michael seems to be nearing a breaking point, Drentell offers him his own job as head of DAA, as Drentell plans to head a new global venture. Ever manipulative, Drentell entices Michael to the new job by saying he could "make it humane." Taking the bait, Michael tells Hope and she shakes her head and asks, "Will you sleep even less?"

The conflict between Michael's personal values and work comes to a head when a spokesperson for DAA's new campaign is spotted in an anti–Gulf War protest on the nightly news. When the client wants Michael to fire the actor and produce new patriotic spots featuring servicepeople, flags, and Desert Storm, Michael asks Hope, "Am I selling a new order?" Drentell promptly rejects his new commercial that forefronts peace, stating the obvious: "We're using the war to sell. . . . This is the ad world. I thought you understood that." At that point Michael decides to completely divest from DAA, selling his stock and resigning his position. When Drentell shows up at Michael's house to convince him to stay, Michael does not bite, enunciating his own bottom line: "Sometimes you have to do something that's yours. And honest." Miles calls him a fool and tells him he has destroyed himself. Underscoring the uncertainty that is common to the transitional period, Michael immediately asks Hope, "What have I done?"[88]

Time

Leave It to Beaver was largely unselfconscious about its setting, giving the impression that the nuclear family is a given that exists outside time and space. By contrast, the main characters of *thirtysomething* regularly reflect on time, using artistic devices that were seldom used in television then, including flashback, fantasy, parody, and other forms of reflexivity. They are keenly aware of the difference between their parents' era, their own formative years in high school and college during the 1960s, and the late 1980s/early 1990s in which *thirtysomething* is set. This sensibility allows the characters to challenge the givenness of the nuclear family and to consider a wide range of alternatives to it. While the nuclear family remains an option in this transitional period, it is considered a choice, rather than a given. Because they fear that they will become just like their parents, the main characters often distance themselves from their more traditional time. Yet, at other times, they yearn for its supposed simplicity.

Hope's mother is very critical of her, leading Hope to worry that she is overly judgmental with her own children. For his part, Michael occasionally "sees" Hope's mother in the mirror when he is looking at Hope.[89] Nonetheless, they still occasionally identify with the previous generation, as when Hope finds an old diary in a trunk in her basement written by Sally, the previous resident of the Steadmans' house, who miscarried while her husband was away fighting in World War II, just as Hope miscarried while Michael was away due to work. Hope travels back in time and meets Sally, learning that she later became pregnant again, just as Hope will too. The episode closes with Sally leaving the house to Hope, saying, "It is yours now, take care of it," followed by Hope and Michael having sex in the backyard, presumably conceiving their second child.[90]

In an episode entitled "The Mike Van Dyke Show," Michael has a recurrent dream sequence about *The Dick Van Dyke Show*, a popular television series that ran from 1961 to 1966, focusing on the traditional family and work life of Rob Petrie. Michael is cast as Rob, and Hope as his wife, Laura, suggesting an identification of the two eras. Yet the two shows are distinct from each other in ways that opens critical space. For example, "Mike Van Dyke" is a situation comedy rendered in black and white and includes a laugh track, while *thirtysomething* is a color drama that features New Age musical interludes between scenes. Although Michael and Hope begin this episode fighting about whether to follow Jewish or Christian holiday traditions, Hope and Janey are later in a serious car accident, a potentially tragic situation. "Van Dyke" provides a window into the absurdity of the traditional nuclear family (from the perspective of a viewer in the 1990s), while also allowing him to realize how precious his (somewhat traditional, somewhat alternative) family is to him. In the end, they discover that the accident was caused by Hope's fatigue and dizziness because she is pregnant again, probably from the backyard sex of two episodes ago.[91]

Shared experiences are remembered through multiple, conflicting subjectivities, suggesting that the simple, unified narratives of the past are largely impossible, and often self-serving. For example, as Nancy and Elliot's marriage begins to unravel, they arrange a double date night with Hope and Michael. A series of flashbacks reveals that everyone came away with a radically different understanding of what went wrong that night. Did Elliot flirt with the hostess at the restaurant? Was he unsupportive of Nancy's idea to write a children's book? These conflicting narratives lead Hope and Michael to fight about what "really" happened, breaking open the placid façade that seems to shield their own marriage from scrutiny. It ends with Michael unselfconsciously telling Hope, "Don't walk away from me," the same line that Elliot seems to have said to Nancy while they were fighting, suggesting that there is much more conflict about marriage and family than typically meets the eye.[92]

Less prolonged reflections on time occur throughout the series. For example, dressed in a boxy women's business suit, city planner Ellyn meets Hope and her baby for lunch in a downtown park, noting, "It's weird to be in a park without tear gas," highlighting their rebellion from the previous generation and the distance that both they and society have come since the turbulent 1960s. Sometimes the reflections on time are more drawn out, presented through artistic devices like fantasies. In an episode focused on her worry that she will become too old to have a child, Melissa fantasizes that she is a contestant on a game show called *Beat the (Biological) Clock*, an obvious parody of the old *Beat the Clock* television show. When she worries that her friends will find her boyfriend Lee too young for her, she fantasizes him acting immaturely at a dinner party, telling fart jokes, wearing a bib, and eating off a baby's plate.[93]

At times, these reflections and fantasies persist throughout an entire episode. In one episode, Hope and Michael are having persistent troubles in bed, while their high school–age babysitter and her boyfriend (played by a very young Brad Pitt) are having no problems whatsoever. Michael tells Hope that "there is no right moment with you," while she argues, "You're just not here with me. This is not the kind of life I thought we'd have. You're obsessed with your job." There is no winning as Michael retorts, "What about your attention, sexual attention? To make me want you. It's not automatic anymore." Meanwhile, their babysitter is having sex on their couch in the middle of the night. In this context Hope fantasizes about her high school years and what it would have been like to be with Michael as a younger guy, while Michael flashes back to a New Year's Eve party when he was just starting to see Hope and everything in their relationship was new and exciting. These devices suggest that there are distinct times within a marriage, rather than the single straight line that appears to run through relationships such as the Cleavers' in the traditional period. She underscores the different time within their marriage, asking and asserting, "It's not the same anymore, is it?" and he responds flatly, "No."[94] By the end of the episode, Michael confesses that he is afraid to fail at his job, while Hope worries aloud that he is having an affair.

Even more serious reflections occur during Nancy's bout with cancer and following Gary's death. These events raise issues of mortality for the group, rupturing any thought of stability, disrupting the idea that the family is a safe haven from a heartless world. Seeing their peers directly face death leads to the grim realization that their time is short, and that their generation will eventually pass, just as their parents' did, intensifying the urgency of the choices they make about their increasingly alternative families.

Discipline

"Discipline" here refers to behavioral restraint, as it did in *Leave It to Beaver*. However, in *thirtysomething* it is largely refigured as sexual restraint. Monogamy is a standard norm of the traditional nuclear family that persists into the transitional family period. But unlike Ward and June, each central *thirtysomething* character fantasizes about and has various opportunities to have affairs. Some do and some do not, opening new parameters for marriage and the family during this transitional period.

As the series opens, Elliot has already cheated on Nancy, establishing himself as one of the least disciplined of the main characters.[95] Although Michael is amazed by Elliot's pronouncement, before long he is presented with an opportunity to have sex outside his own marriage, when an unconsummated love from college comes to town, staying with Michael and Hope in their house. When she visits Michael at work, Elliot (now separated from Nancy) asks her out and Michael is clearly jealous and distressed when she returns to the Steadmans' home late that evening. As she continues to flirt with Michael, Hope accuses him of wanting to sleep with her. Their houseguest comes home the following night with Gary, easily the most promiscuous character in the show. Waiting up again until she returns, Michael tells her to go to a hotel.

After days of agonizing, he finally goes to her hotel room, shares the last page of an intimate poem they wrote together back in college, passionately kisses her, and then immediately disciplines himself, saying, "This can't happen. There are other people involved who I love," and returns home to Hope, who is there waiting for him.[96]

Hope's opportunity arises with her boss, John, who works primarily in Washington, DC. Michael is gaining power and making more money at work, but he is increasingly distant with Hope, who is visibly pregnant. After making a lunch date with John, she sees his face while kissing Michael. Hope subsequently floats the idea of working in DC to Michael, but he wants her home in Philadelphia. Later, Hope awakens with a start from a dream about the "infidelity train" (presumably a commuter to Washington) with known cheaters Elliot and Ellyn on board. Still later, she meets John in DC, where they share an intimate dinner, a slow dance, and then go back to Hope's hotel room. She asks him, "Did I come for the job or you?" and he responds, "I wish you weren't married," as Hope talks at length about the demands of Michael's job and her wish for a life of her own. John kisses her passionately, but then leaves, imposing external discipline. Hope calls Michael to say that she is staying an extra day, only to spend her time visiting tourist attractions rather than pursuing John any further. Upon returning home, she informs Michael that they have to work harder at their relationship.[97]

In the very next episode, John (improbably) stays at the Steadmans' house while he is in town for business and they are away in Arizona for Hope's parents' fiftieth anniversary. He is occupying not only their home, but also Hope's thoughts. Meanwhile, Hope and Michael fight to the point of separation while in Arizona. Michael is openly jealous of John and confronts Hope. Hope responds that Michael is too angry, and he counters that she is too judgmental. The episode ends with Hope admitting that she sometimes hates him, and both concede that they are scared. She asks whether he is going to leave her for work, implying that he is having an affair of a different sort. By the end of the episode, they both experience some relief as Michael tells her that he loves her.[98]

Gary, a well-known philanderer in the group, has by now become fully domesticated into marriage and family. Once he commits to Susannah and their new baby, he remains monogamous, even when she is away for weeks in New York. He does regularly flirt with and fantasize about a young checker at a local grocery store who also has a small child. But unlike the Gary of old, he never acts on it. He seems to have successfully internalized sexual discipline, even though his alternative family diverges from the nuclear family in so many other ways.[99] But he is still willing to use his old cheating persona to punk his straitlaced friends, together with Ellyn, another known cheater who has become his close, but platonic friend in Susannah's absence. Together, they stage a series of events that purposefully lead the others to believe that they are having an affair. In the end, once their friends are totally convinced, Ellyn announces that she is going away for a weekend with her new flame, Billy Sidell. The joke is on the traditional married folks, who apparently are so traditional that they cannot even imagine an adult woman and man having a nonsexual friendship.

Ellyn openly stepped out on her previous boyfriend and boss, Steve Woodman, while they were living together. But when she met Billy the stakes changed, as they both seemed ready to commit to a long-term monogamous relationship. Shortly after a romantic weekend that appeared to seal their commitment, Ellyn learns that Billy cheated on her, sleeping with his (girl)friend with benefits Madison. Worse still, this news emerges while all three of them are staying at Ellyn's place while Madison is in town for a visit. Billy pledges that it will never happen again, but Ellyn kicks him out, and insists that they both get tested for AIDS. Madison tells Ellyn that Billy slept with her only because he was afraid of being so in love with Ellyn. When Billy goes back to Ellyn's apartment to retrieve his sketch pad, they get stuck in the elevator together and she eventually gives in after he proposes, presumably joining the ranks of the married couples who fantasize about cheating, but don't pull the trigger.[100]

Others

Unlike *Beaver, thirtysomething* offered recurring if somewhat periph-
eral roles to people of color and gay men. African American Mark
Harriton is an account manager who is Michael and Elliot's boss when
they start working for Drentell, but before long Michael surpasses him,
becoming creative director, the second most powerful position in the
agency. Mark appears in a few episodes in the office, on the basket-
ball court, and at social engagements with his wife, including a party
at the Steadmans', but he is never given more than a line or two and as
such his character remains almost entirely undeveloped. There is also
a recurring discussion of Michael's Jewish background in distinction
from Hope's Christian upbringing, especially during the December
holidays. While it adds a fair amount of conflict to their marriage at
these times, it always resolves in a compromise arrangement, as both
a menorah and a Christmas tree adorn the Steadman living room.[101]
Despite these sensibilities, *thirtysomething* also participates in bigotry
that was rampant at that time, as for example when Elliot and Gary
share some big laughs about Geraldo Rivera doing a show on "the new
transvestites."[102]

The most developed "others" in the show are Russell Weller and Peter
Montefiore, two gay men who would have been entirely illegible on
Beaver. Gay-adjacent Melissa, a perpetually single bohemian woman,
meets Russell at an art opening and they are hitting it off until he leaves
suddenly, having received word that a friend of his has been diagnosed
HIV-positive. While a serious gay character in a mainstream television
series is an important development, it bears noting that nearly all subsequent story lines tie Russell's character directly to the AIDS crisis. Melissa and Russell's concerns about dating and mating are presented as
parallel, but he is concerned about maintaining sexual intimacy in the
life-and-death context of AIDS, while she is obsessing about whether
she will find a man in time to have a baby.

Both Melissa and Russell present viable alternatives to the traditional family. However, consistent with the ambiguity that is common during the transitional period, neither alternative works out. Melissa considers asking Gary to father her child, whom she will then raise as a single woman. Even gay Russell is suspicious of her plan, underscoring the challenge it presents to the mainstream: "It's big stuff. You want to tear down the structure of society as we know it." She responds, "No, just move the wall a little," suggesting that it is more aligned with transitional reform rather than a revolutionary dismantling of the traditional family. Nuclear family exemplar Michael cautions Gary against doing it because "it takes commitment." In the end, Melissa abandons the idea, telling Gary that they have already brought up two kids (themselves), and now it is time to let them go. Gary becomes a big brother for a young Black man who is never seen again after this episode, perhaps a further sign of Gary's inability to commit.[103]

For Russell's part, he just wants to have sex without risking his life. He meets Peter at DAA, where he works with Michael. Their brief affair is the minor plot in an episode entitled "Strangers," which focuses largely on Melissa's relationship with new boyfriend Lee. The episode opens with Melissa and Lee having sex in a fairly explicit manner, given network standards at that time. Their relationship is also alternative: Lee is only twenty-three and Melissa is more than ten years older than him. Later, Peter and Russell are also shown in bed in a much more modest shot, smoking a postcoital cigarette and talking about when they came out and how many of their friends have died from AIDS, as gay people often did at that time after having had sex with someone for the first time.[104] Unlike Melissa and Lee, they were not allowed to touch. A more demonstrative scene was cut when key advertisers balked. Even the scaled-back version lost over $1.5 million in advertising revenue, leading the episode to be run only once. Be that as it may, the men were shown together in bed, shirts off, clearly after having had sex, a huge step forward for network television at that time.

Neither of these alternative relationships works out in the end. Melissa and Lee cannot overcome the problems born of their age difference. Peter never calls Russell back. When Melissa asks Russell what happened, he simply says, "It's not a time to be making attachments," presumably referring to AIDS.[105] Russell is stunned when they do meet again in the following season, at a New Year's Eve party at Hope and Michael's. When Melissa jokes that "at least you're not the token fag," he chastises her, saying, "Don't say that word." There is no happy ending for Peter and Russell, even in this transitional period. They do not wind up together again then or anytime thereafter.[106]

The next we hear is that Peter has contracted AIDS, a presumptive death sentence at this time. When Drentell becomes angry about Peter's approach to an important account and tells him that work on the campaign should be more like a team sport, Peter accuses him of calling him a fag and asks to be fired. Michael tells Drentell that they should keep Peter because "he's a good man" who needs health insurance. Drentell counters, "Let's do something pro bono on the subject," and that is the end of the gay story line on *thirtysomething*.[107] Melissa, who is alternative but straight, does wind up with Lee in the end, at least according to Gary's ghost, who visits Michael during this episode, in part to tell him not to worry about her.

Conclusion

Thirtysomething offers various alternatives to the traditional nuclear family model. While these new models are not always completely viable, it is clear that the old way of organizing family life does not work anymore. Gender roles are shifting, the economy is unstable, time is being reflected on rather than accepted as a given, sexual discipline is not as strict as it once was, and "other" perspectives are being integrated into mainstream narratives. Hope's discomfort with the uncertainty that characterizes transition is clear from her assessment of the constant work being done on her traditional home: "If we ever finished the house and made it perfect, I don't know if we could live here."[108] It makes sense that she and Michael, as the most traditional couple of the series, would be most uncomfortable with the changes in the family form that lie ahead. By the end of the series, change has come not only to the Steadmans' traditional home, but also to the world around it, as the post–World War II order crumbles and the United States launches the First Gulf War. Already far from the stability and singular perspective of *Beaver*, *thirtysomething* characters are sad and anxious. They cheat, or at least fantasize about it. They get sick and die. Businesses go under. "Others" become visible and offer new perspectives that challenge traditional ideas about family and friends.

Amidst these transitions, the viability of Michael and Hope's largely traditional marriage is unclear. They have been teetering on the brink of separation for some time. Their conflict comes to a head in the final episode, when Michael is offered a job in Los Angeles and Hope is offered one in DC. Ellyn emphasizes the importance of this traditional couple for all of the friends, saying, "You can't split up!" while Hope notes the slow pace of change that is common to protracted conflict during transitional periods: "It's not about a fight. It's suddenly very cold, like covers off, and there you are." In Hope's view, Michael has already decided to take the job in Los Angeles (the way a traditional patriarch would). But she refuses to join him, rejecting her role as a traditional wife: "I love you, and want best for you, but I can't be there as wife anymore. . . . It's about me. I haven't felt something I want to do. I haven't felt that way since we decided to get married." Michael responds with the same traditional understanding of family that he has adhered to throughout the series: "We're a family. I want us to stay one. I'm only me because of you." As he begs her not to leave him, she folds and hugs him. It remains unclear whether they will go to California or DC, or perhaps stay in Philadelphia, underscoring the tentative status of family, traditional and alternative, heading into the future.

Concluding Period: *The Americans* Blows the Nuclear Family's Cover

The Americans is a dramatic series that lays bare the relationship between family and state, with disastrous consequences for the nuclear family. The series was broadcast for six seasons over seventy-five episodes on the FX Network between 2013 and 2018. In the concluding period, viewership is more varied, unlike during the *Beaver* and *thirtysomething* eras, when most people watched series on three major networks. *The Americans* has been called "the best show on television" and "among the defining shows of this decade," during a period that has come to be known as the "platinum age" of television.[109]

The Americans focuses on both adults (à la *thirtysomething*) and children (à la *Beaver*) in the Jennings family: husband Philip (Matthew Rhys), wife Elizabeth (Keri Russell), and their two children, Paige (Holly Taylor) and Henry (Keidrich Sellati). The series loosely parallels historical events such as the FBI's investigation of Directorate S during the Reagan years. In both the series and real life, the KGB placed sleeper agents, known as "illegals," in the United States, where they posed as ordinary Americans to infiltrate key intelligence agencies and military installations. Show creator Joe Weisberg has said that *The Americans* is more about marriage and family than it is about espionage, suggesting that the spy story is the façade of the show, much in the way that the northern Virginia suburbs provide cover for the true (Soviet) identities of Philip and Elizabeth Jennings. The series focuses on whether the Jennings family can successfully further the state goals of upending American democracy while also socializing the next generation into key Soviet norms and values.

Despite their secret spy gig, the Jenningses appear to be a typical family, the same as any other in their suburban subdivision. They own and manage a successful DuPont Circle travel agency and are raising two seemingly ordinary kids. On the face of it, the Jenningses seem as normal as the nuclear family across the street, FBI counterintelligence agent

Stan Beeman (Noah Emmerich), his stay-at-home wife, Sandra (Susan Misner), and their son, Matthew (Daniel Flaherty), who is roughly the same age as Paige. Stan and Philip become best friends. Despite their close, even homoerotic relationship, they are suspicious of each other, leading Stan to break into the Jennings garage on more than one occasion to check for evidence of spying. He repeatedly tells his wife that there is "something off" about Philip. She teases him about being suspicious of everyone, a habit that he is trying to kick from years spent infiltrating a white supremacist group earlier on in his FBI career.

Right from the start, the Jennings family challenges the purportedly natural origins of the nuclear family. Since Philip and Elizabeth were strangers when the KGB introduced them, their story of origin is based not in the nuclear family's ideology of love and companionship, but rather in a communist ideology that prioritizes state desires over individual desire. Theirs is not a marriage of love, but a partnership that aims to subvert American institutions, the nuclear family included.

In contrast with the nuclear families in *Beaver* and to some degree *thirtysomething*, the Jennings family is anything but politically neutral. Neutrality and political disinterest are merely the mantle they must take on to successfully pretend to be a typical American nuclear family. For them, the deepest expression of love is not romantic love, but rather solidarity with comrades, directed in part by the state. In the end, when they are presented with a choice between the state and their "natural" family, they choose the former, remaining true to their communist roots, even as they lay bare the strong but ultimately destructive pull of the American nuclear family as we know it.

Episodes revolve around Philip and Elizabeth's work as Soviet spies. They engage in a wide range of instrumental, perhaps even sociopathic behavior, including sexual affairs, polygamy, sadomasochism, threesomes, cheating, lying, stealing, fraud, and all manner of violence, including the murder of innocent bystanders. Sex, love, and even children are regularly manipulated to further the state's goals, typically with implied or actual violence readily apparent. While they clearly care about their own children, they often neglect them, leaving them alone at night or even for days to conduct operations. Family plans are frequently interrupted at the last minute when the KGB calls, as the state must always be prioritized over family.

The genius of the show is that it compels us to identify with and root for Philip and Elizabeth as they risk their lives each week, violently furthering the goals of their mother country, much in the way we sympathize with anxious Tony Soprano as he furthers the goals of his mob, murdering and cheating while maintaining an ostensibly traditional home and family in suburban New Jersey. We root for these cold-blooded killers. They break the bones of a murdered double agent to fit them into an easily disposable suitcase, saw off the head and hands of a comrade killed by the FBI to prevent identification, stage a hanging of an innocent young IT technician to save an operation from going sour, and so on. There are few, if any, limits on what they will do to further their mission.

In the course of their work, they offer various alternatives to the traditional nuclear family that make same-sex marriage look tame by comparison. Their own marriage is arranged, a sham designed by and for the convenience of the state. Philip's most frequently used disguise is "Clark Westerfeld," which leads him to engage in bigamy by marrying lonely Martha Hanson (Alison Wright), secretary of the director of counterintelligence at the FBI. Despite using the marriage to gain access to sensitive information from Martha, Philip appears to truly care for her, at one point removing his disguise to show her what he really looks like, a KGB taboo.[110] That aside, when it becomes clear that the FBI is on to Martha, he turns her in to the KGB, which promptly sends her against her will to the Soviet Union, where she will live out an even lonelier life. That said, Philip's intercession on Martha's behalf undoubtedly saved her from simply being killed by the KGB.[111] But in the end, both of his marriages have been constructed by and are first and foremost for the benefit of the state.

Another long-run disguise of Philip's, "Jimmy," cultivates alienated teen Kimmy, whose father heads the CIA's intelligence unit on the Soviet Union. In order to bug her father's briefcase and gain crucial intelligence information, Jimmy exploits Kimmy's vulnerability and need for attention. Because Kimmy is roughly the same age as Philip's own daughter, Paige, these interactions raise the question of whether there are any limits, incest taboo included, on his use of sex for his country. However reluctantly, he does sleep with Kimmy for information. Disgusted with himself, Philip realizes that he cannot continue down that path. He breaks up with her on the phone, saying, "You need someone your own age. I care about you. I have to move on." He then provides a closing tip that will allow her to avoid being assassinated by the KGB during an upcoming vacation to Greece: "If someone asks you to go to a communist country when you're in Greece, don't!"[112]

These revelations open space for more critical thinking about the nuclear family's purported origins, as well as its gendered, economic, and violent roots. If we can see these alternatives in the Jennings family and still root for them, we become better positioned to adopt a critical stance toward the nuclear family, perhaps accepting alternative families that other neighbors have constructed, such as same-sex marriages.

Political Time

Like *thirtysomething, The Americans* includes various flashbacks that produce critical reflection. In a sense, the entire series is a contemporary reflection on the Reagan era's Cold War rivalry between the United States and the Soviet Union. Episodes are set in 1980s culture, using its fashions, décor, fads, and music to induce viewer nostalgia as well as a critical distance from that time. It is somewhat unusual for a mainstream television series to integrate places like Poland, Afghanistan, and Nicaragua into plotlines, and even more uncommon to center a critical Marxist view of US domestic and foreign policy. The political time created in *The Americans* allows us to critically reconsider the political practices of the 1980s through the lens of an alternative ideology, knowing full well how the story will end: neoliberalism will consolidate globally, the Soviet Union will fall, a Black man will be elected and reelected president, and LGBT families will become legally protected in mainstream US politics.

The first episode of the series uses flashbacks to present Philip and Elizabeth's individual stories of origin as KGB spies, as well as the story of their initial entry into the United States as a married couple. Like the origin stories of most nation-states, their stories of origin are rooted in violence and repudiation of the past.[113] Their mission this episode, set in 1981, is to capture a defecting KGB officer and send him to the Soviet Union for punishment, suggesting that there is no way to escape the hold of one's home state. When the mission is botched, they take the defector home with them, bound and gagged in the trunk of the family car, parked in the attached garage of their subdivision home, a metaphor for the often-hidden violence of the family and state if there ever was one. In a flashback to the Soviet Union in 1960, we see the defector, then Captain (now Colonel) Timoshev, raping Elizabeth, a perk of the job for him, but for her a lesson in how to depersonalize sex, avoid vulnerability, and exact revenge, no matter how long it may take. Following the flashback, we see Elizabeth back in 1981 northern Virginia opening the trunk, saying, "Remember me, Captain?" and then beating him to a pulp. That steely ruthlessness stems from his "training," after which she vowed never to be afraid again.

As Philip comes to understand that Timoshev raped Elizabeth, he kills him, a violent mark of his loyalty to her. Together they decompose the body with chemicals, dispose of it in the port, and have sex afterward in the car, the violence an apparent turn-on. Later, Elizabeth reveals her true story of origin to Philip, telling him her Russian name (Nadezhda) and her birthplace (Smolensk) and saying that her father died heroically fighting Nazis in Stalingrad when she was two (a myth about her founding father that later proves false). Like most regimes, Philip and Elizabeth believe that their violence is necessary and rooted in self-defense. In a 1962 flashback, Philip learns that he will have to leave his Soviet girlfriend Irina behind forever to come to America, and we see him tearing up her picture right before being taken to meet Elizabeth. An earlier flashback to Philip's youth shows him bludgeoning another boy to death with a rock after the boy repeatedly stole scraps of food that Philip scavenged for his starving parents.[114]

Philip and Elizabeth's story of origin as an American couple appears in yet another flashback, to the summer of 1965 in a Washington motel room. They have just entered the country and it is blistering hot outside, but their motel room has an air conditioning unit. Elizabeth is astonished, having never seen such a thing before, while Philip is pleasantly surprised to experience something he had only read about. He touches Elizabeth's hair and advances toward her to have sex, but she says that she is not ready. He continues, reminding her that their mission depends on the façade of family, noting, "We're supposed to be married, we're expected to have children."[115] But she firmly declines, beginning an off-again, on-again exchange between them that will continue clear through to the end of the series.

During one of their many periods of marital conflict, Philip sleeps with his old girlfriend from the Soviet Union, Irina, who is on a brief operation in New York City. Afterwards, she tells him that he has a grown son, and asks him to defect to Canada with her. But he declines, an early indication of his devotion to Elizabeth. Meanwhile, Elizabeth realizes that she has missed him and wants a "real" marriage, "where they can say what's true."[116] But in a turn that will happen again and again, once one of them commits even a bit, the other one betrays the relationship. When she asks him whether he slept with Irina, he lies, saying, "Nothing happened. It's only been you. It's always been you." In no time Elizabeth finds out that he slept with Irina, and is furious with him for betraying her, and with herself for being vulnerable. He apologizes profusely and begs her for another chance, telling her he loves her. She responds flatly, "Love. Huh," and then distances herself, closing down all vulnerability: "We can do our jobs, fulfill our mission, the reason we were sent to America. But we can't do this. We will never do this." They are both severely damaged people for whom love and companionship are dicey propositions at best, making their devotion to the state all the more fierce.

After all, they are both spies who are trained not to trust anyone, while deceiving others into thinking that they are entirely trustworthy, often using sex to that end. Although they have sex with marks regularly to gain information, before long Philip again sleeps with someone else unrelated to a work matter, and Elizabeth reverts to a strictly business-only partnership with him, despite all his efforts to explain his infidelity. As her KGB handler Claudia warns Elizabeth, "If you start thinking of your marriage as real, it doesn't work. You are of no use to us. The men don't think of them that way. It was an arrangement. Do you understand that?"[117] Philip was trained at an early age to be able to sleep with any-one regardless of age, sexuality, or kink while appearing to "make it real." Elizabeth has been through the same training. In the very first episode she performs oral sex on a mark to gain access to key intelligence infor-mation, as the 1980s hit "Harden My Heart" plays in the background: "I'm gonna harden my heart / I'm gonna swallow my tears."[118] They must depersonalize sex to avoid connecting meaningfully with anyone. The problem is that they also lose the ability to do so with each other. They never develop the trust necessary for a "real" romantic partnership, though they do remain work partners throughout the show, disciplined and committed to the end when it comes to the state.

Even Elizabeth's substitute father, General Zhukov, the leader of Di-rectorate S training, cannot break through her hard shell. In a series of flashbacks, Zhukov intuits that she is unhappy about Philip. Trying to teach her about love, he talks to her about his connection to his dog Malish, asking a simple question: "Do you know what love is, Eliza-beth?" As always, when it comes to vulnerability, she offers a flat answer, possibly learned from a book: "It's a feeling." Zhukov elaborates, "A most profound feeling. Fate brought us together. Malish is not smart or pretty, but I love him because I take care of him every day, as he does me in his own way. If you care for something, Elizabeth, you find that you love this creature, and your life will be empty without it."[119] Later, while she is pregnant and considering an abortion, Zhukov cautions her against it: "We all die alone. Before that, we make choices. I lived for my work, the Party, and now I miss what I never had." Still later, after she has been with Philip for eleven years, Zhukov notes that she is loyal and intelligent, but that she fears surrender more than anything. When a CIA operative kills Zhukov, Elizabeth's sole instinct is to avenge him. Despite Zhukov's lessons, love still amounts to violence and retribution for her, and this will continue to be the case throughout the series.

Gender

While *Beaver* reproduces traditional sex and gender norms in the nuclear family and *thirtysomething* begins to challenge them, *The Americans* completely upends them. Elizabeth is hardly a stay-at-home mom. For her, traditional American sex and gender norms are hopelessly regressive, a product of a politically backward, capitalist system. She and Philip are co-equal partners in the family travel agency and in their undercover work as spies. If anything, Philip behaves in ways that are more aligned with traditional female femininity than Elizabeth. His moral sensibilities sometimes lead him to care for others and deprioritize state desires. Elizabeth is much more aligned with the all-business-all-the-time aggressiveness traditionally associated with male masculinity. Soft power be damned, unless it is instrumentally useful for an operation.

In contrast, FBI agent Stan and stay-at-home mom Sandra Beemans' much more traditional marriage ends in divorce, suggesting that the nuclear family just does not work anymore. Stan is too protective of his wife, a behavior that aligns with traditional sex and gender norms as well as his role as an FBI agent. (Not once in the entire series do we see a female FBI agent.) "I never asked for protection," says Sandra. But for Stan, traditional male masculinity is natural: "But that's what you do, if you want to have a family." Traditional norms notwithstanding, Stan has a long affair with a Russian double agent, becoming even more distant until Sandra leaves him for another more sensitive, less traditional man she met in EST (Erhard Seminars Training, a self-help group popular in the 1970s and 1980s that encouraged people to get in touch with their feelings and shed traditional roles, to reclaim their authentic selves).

Philip and Elizabeth's gender reversal is clear right from the start. Over Elizabeth's objections ("the mission comes first"), Philip insists on dropping off a wounded comrade outside a hospital during a botched operation, making them late to transport a failed defector back to the Soviet Union.[120] He even calls the hospital later to check on their comrade, only to find out that he died almost immediately, despite the extraordinary risk Philip took to save his life. Much later in the series Phillip reveals his softer, more romantic side when he arranges for them to be married by a Russian Orthodox priest in their spy network, formalizing their partnership beyond their work for the state. (True to form, they become cold and distant toward each other shortly thereafter.)

While he remains ruthless in his work, over time Philip becomes quite remorseful about his violent behavior afterwards. For example, after quickly dispensing with a student who unexpectedly shows up in a lab while Philip is stealing the plans for the ARPANET (a precursor of the Internet), he regrets having killed him "for some x's and o's on a 'virtual highway.' I don't even know what that means. Do you know how many people I've killed? Have you looked into their eyes, watched them die?"[121] Meanwhile, Elizabeth cannot repress her eye-rolling dismissal when Philip starts to regularly attend EST. Through EST, Philip comes to believe that his childhood violence set him up for KGB recruitment. Elizabeth, on the other hand, believes that the state's end justifies violent means, an instrumental mindset traditionally associated with male masculinity. Philip decides to quit spying altogether—at least until he is pulled back in, first by democratic forces that have propelled Gorbachev to power and then by Elizabeth when she needs his help completing one last job. In the end, he cannot say no to the state or Elizabeth.

Despite this, Phillip occasionally takes on traditional male masculinity, asserting "king of the castle" type dominance, suggesting that sex and gender norms in the concluding period may be fluid rather than rigidly set by nature or choice. When he approaches Elizabeth in a manner suggesting sexual ownership, saying, "You're my wife," she responds, "Is that right?" and pulls a butcher knife on him, compelling him to back off immediately.[122]

Philip again exhibits more traditionally protective behavior when he sees welts on Elizabeth's back, the result of a violent sexual encounter with a source she is working for information. As he angrily announces, "I'm gonna deal with it," Elizabeth repels his purportedly chivalrous behavior, responding that she could have dealt with it if she wanted to. Philip tries to justify retaliating by reverting to traditional sex and gender roles: "Somebody beat the shit out of my wife." Elizabeth corrects him, saying, "You are not my daddy." He persists even further, saying, "No, I'm not your daddy, I'm your husband. What do you think husbands do?" Elizabeth responds with a disarming "I wouldn't know," directly questioning the legitimacy of their state-constructed marriage.[123] Their "marriage" breaks down the rigidity of traditional sex and gender norms, while never resulting in a complete reversal of those norms or a stable conclusion to the struggle. Neither of them wins or loses all the time, suggesting that sex and gender norms in a contemporary family are a perpetual struggle.

Political Economy

The stability of the economy was assumed in *Beaver*. While Ward occasionally fretted about "going to the poorhouse," there was never any question about the continuity of his job or the merits of a capitalist economy. Major economic dislocations are central plotlines in *thirtysomething*. Michael and Elliot's advertising agency goes bankrupt, Gary is forced to join the emerging gig economy after losing his job at Penn, and Hope volunteers at a homeless shelter that is bursting at the seams with needy families. Despite these major economic dislocations, there is no discussion of alternatives to market capitalism.

The Jenningses have two family businesses, a travel agency in DuPont Circle and an undercover spy operation, both of which ultimately fail. These events are thought of as battles in the Cold War between capitalism and socialism. When the travel agency prospered at first, Philip expanded and remodeled the travel agency offices, hired more agents, and bought new desktop computers, investing in the very technology that would bring the business down. As the business fails, Philip becomes more openly critical of basic tenets of capitalism such as growth, complaining to FBI agent and best friend Stan that there is always "pressure in business to grow. What's so bad about staying the same?" He also admits to Elizabeth, "It's bad, it's not adding up. Maybe I moved too fast. I don't see how cutting back will fix it."[124]

Capitalism's unrelenting drive for profit is shown to displace workers and destroy entire sectors of the economy, including travel agencies. The Jenningses can no longer afford the tuition at their son Henry's upscale New England prep school, even with hockey and academic scholarships. Philip uses his manipulative spy skills to persuade the reluctant headmaster at the boarding school to restructure tuition payments, if only to buy time. Meanwhile, Philip is forced to fire several employees, including two who have been with him from the start. After one of them, Stavros, slams the office door after being fired, Philip visits him at his apartment unannounced several weeks later out of guilt. Stavros remains livid but does let Philip know that he is aware that there was funny business going on behind the scenes at the agency. He assures Philip that he will not tell, suggesting that in the end, the worker is truer to the owner than the owner is to him.

The possibility of defecting entices Philip throughout the series. Whatever its faults, capitalism provides creature comforts like air conditioning, sports cars, tailored suits, and spacious housing—all things that he and Elizabeth had never experienced before coming to the United States. Elizabeth cynically responds that if he defects, he could use the money to "buy a diamond-plated coffin" (implying that the KGB would kill him).[125] After buying a fancy new sports car, much to the delight of his very American son, he asks a disdainful Elizabeth, "Don't you enjoy any of this sometimes?" She responds, "It's easier here. It's not better."[126] Finding out that she has reported his petit bourgeois tendencies to the KGB, he responds, "I fit in, I liked it. So what?"[127] Even as the travel agency continues to fail, Philip buys yet another luxury car and several tailored suits. Elizabeth, on the other hand, subscribes to the Marxist teaching that capitalism creates imaginary appetites that feed an unquenchable desire for additional material goods. When a new operative in training, a white graduate student from South Africa, asks Elizabeth whether she likes his new stonewashed jeans, she recites Marx chapter and verse: "The production of too many useless things results in too many useless people."[128] In one of the rare lighter, yet still critical moments of the series, one of the Jenningses' KGB handlers points out the absurdity of capitalist freedom while ordering food in a diner: "Fourteen kinds of omelets, twenty kinds of hamburgers. How does one choose?"[129]

Part of Elizabeth's persistent distrust of Philip stems from his ongoing attachment to material things. To her this signifies his lack of commitment to the state. She even reports Philip's material desires to the Center from time to time, leading the KGB at one point to kidnap and torture them, as it suspected that Philip had become a mole. He had not, but he did get badly beaten and waterboarded to within an inch of his life. Afterwards, their KGB handler Claudia foregrounds Elizabeth's devotion to socialism: "I know you'd throw yourself on a fire for the Motherland. Him? I'm not so sure."[130]

But who has ownership of the children? Their parents? The church? The state? No one but themselves? When Philip points out to Elizabeth that their American-born and -bred children share values with their friends more than with their parents, she tersely responds, "I'm not done with them yet." Nonetheless, she soon gives up on converting Henry to socialism. He is a dyed-in-the-wool, all-American boy who excels at school and in sports and is learning hetero dating norms, complete with a stash of erotica in his bedroom floor, including a photo of his neighbor

Mrs. Beeman in a bikini. After winning a scholarship to attend a board-ing school in New Hampshire, he is largely absent, presumably prepar-ing to live out a comfortable life in America.

But Paige is a different story. Much to the horror of her parents, she begins dating Matthew Beeman, son of the FBI agent across the street. She also becomes a born-again Christian. Although Philip and Elizabeth forbid both, like most kids her age she rebels and continues to deepen her involvement. However, the KGB has other plans for Paige, and it is not prepared to take no for an answer. It wants her to become a second-generation Directorate S agent who will eventually work at the Depart-ment of Defense or State. As she slowly comes to understand who her parents really are, she gives up the FBI agent's son and her Christianity, adopting violence and secrecy as part of her training.

Others

While *Leave It to Beaver* largely excluded "others" and *thirtysomething* included them in minor roles, "others" are front and center in *The Amer-icans*. As Soviet spies, Philip and Elizabeth are others. Centralizing their perspective creates critical distance right from the start, disrupting the otherwise apparent givenness of established norms. We take on their perspective and root for them to succeed, reversing the mainstream way of seeing things, much the way we do when purported homosexual Paul Child suffers persecution at the hands of the FBI in *Julie and Julia*, dur-ing a period when gay people were thought to constitute a mortal threat to American democracy (see introduction). These reversals open space for new ways to consider assumed villains and their alternative families.

In the 1980s Cold War context, Soviets were seen as the ultimate oth-ers of Americans, much like homosexuals were seen as the ultimate others of heterosexuals. Homosexuality is not a moral issue for Philip and Elizabeth. Blackmailing closeted intelligence personnel is but one of many sexual tools that can be used to extract valuable information to further the desires of the state. Just as homosexuals had to learn the ways of heterosexuals to survive, so too do Philip and Elizabeth learn the ways of Americans to save their country from the mortal threat posed to it by Reaganism. For them, the "others" are capitalists and constitutional democrats who are hopelessly impervious to blatant inequality and deeply ingrained bigotry.

Unlike *thirtysomething*, which revolves around sustaining meaningful intimate relationships and friendships, *The Americans* features few genuine relationships. With few exceptions, there are only others whom Elizabeth and Philip manipulate to forward their work. For them, friendship and love are illusory at best.

People of color play significant, developed roles in *The Americans*. Elizabeth's one true love (besides the state) and her one true friend are both people of color. Her lover is radical Black activist Gregory, whom she recruited to the party at a SNCC event in the heyday of the civil rights movement. As one television critic has noted, the character of Gregory "illuminate[s] the predicament of the politically aware African American in ways that American television rarely attempts," acknowledging their status as "strangers in their own country."[131] Gregory and Elizabeth bond over a shared commitment to radical equality and a willingness to sacrifice everything—even their lives—for the cause. Their biracial, extramarital, anti-capitalist relationship is transgressive of mainstream family norms, performing the kind of coalition building that was common in the Communist Party and Black radicalism at that time.[132]

Gregory and Elizabeth's relationship imperils her decision to make her marriage with Philip "real," not just one of convenience, for the Soviet state. When they rendezvous at a public chess game, Gregory offers Elizabeth a cigarette and a kiss, but she rejects both, saying, "We can't do this anymore. Us." When he reminds her that Philip is just her cover, she reverts to traditional familial roles: "No, he's my husband." Gregory responds by challenging the traditional family: "Marriage ain't real, domestic shit ain't real, Elizabeth. I know you." All business, Elizabeth needs him for a job, concluding, "Just get your guys together."[133]

Although Gregory believes that marriage and domestic life are not real, he is nonetheless a true romantic. While working an operation together, he asks Philip, "Do you love her, really love her? It's a simple question." Like Elizabeth, Philip uses traditional family to distance Gregory: "You don't have a family, do you, Gregory?" Gregory challenges him, revealing that Elizabeth openly disdained "playing house" with Philip just before Paige was born: "She came to me [and said], I can't go back and raise this child, live this lie." Like Elizabeth, Gregory is in love with the cause, and this binds them together: "She needed something greater than her, greater than you or me. When she told me who she was, it was like I already knew." The nuclear family is only a façade, necessary for the real work to proceed. Thus Gregory implores Philip, "Let her have a little piece of something real."[134]

Meanwhile, Philip is furious with Elizabeth: "You lied to me for fifteen years and shared your deepest feelings about us with him." She shrugs it off, saying only, "I told him it was over, and he just wants to hurt you." Phillip responds incredulously, "That's all you have to say?" Elizabeth later reminds Philip that she was only seventeen when they met, had never had a boyfriend, had been raped by her KGB trainer, and had found herself living in a "strange house and country, with a strange man." In a rare moment of vulnerability, Elizabeth explains the great need she felt: "I met Gregory and he was passionate about the cause, about everything, about me. I recruited him, and he didn't want anything, just believed, like me. He was the first person I could talk to. I needed that. It just happened." Drawing Philip into the story, she notes, "It never really happened that way for us, did it?" When he softly concedes the point, she responds, "I'm so sorry, I wish that it had," as she holds his hand. "But I feel like it's happening now."[135] As always, this newfound emotional intimacy is not sustained for long.

As for Gregory, he meets the tragic fate of many "others" represented in American television and mainstream American society. Toward the end of the first season his cover is blown, leading the KGB to order his exfiltration to the Soviet Union, but he resists, having never even visited there. True to the cause as always, Gregory and Elizabeth are both re-signed to his fate. "We always knew this day would come," says Gregory, and Elizabeth responds, "The world is a shitty place."[136] Ever the ro-mantic, Gregory asks Elizabeth to live with him underground in Los Angeles. When she tells him that this is impossible, he replies, "I just wanted to live for something, and I've done that. Now I'm done." Urging her to leave Philip, he says, "Don't take him back. Find somebody else. He's gonna soften you all up." They sleep together for the last time and Gregory leaves the safe house in the morning, is spotted on the street, and shoots several police officers before they kill him in a barrage of gunfire.

Another "other," Young-Hee Seong, a Korean immigrant, is Elizabeth's only friend besides Gregory. They appear in about the same number of episodes, eight for Gregory and six for Young-Hee. She is a successful Mary Kay consultant ostensibly training "Patty," one of Elizabeth's many personas. As they become friends, Young-Hee invites single Patty into her raucous, multigenerational, humorous family, introducing an ele-ment that is sorely missing in Elizabeth's life. They discuss serious mat-ters as well, such as how difficult it is to bring up children in a capitalist culture, foregrounding the critical possibilities that arise from the per-spective of "others." Despite this genuine connection, for Elizabeth the state always comes first. She drugs Young-Hee's husband, Don, makes him think that they've had sex and that she's become pregnant, so her angry "family" can confront him as the cause of Patty's subsequent sui-cide, blackmailing him and obtaining the secret codes that will aid the development of Soviet chemical weapons. Meanwhile, Young-Hee leaves increasingly desperate phone messages for Patty, wondering where she is and why she is not returning her calls.[137] Afterwards, Elizabeth cries at home with Philip, a virtually unheard-of level of vulnerability for her.[138] Ironically, all of this has been done in vain, as they are never able to access the codes, an early foreshadowing of the Jenningses' eventual re-alization that all their violence and sacrifice have ultimately been for naught, as it slowly becomes clear that the Soviet regime is failing. By the end of the series, they will have destroyed many families, including their own, for no clear end.

Philip and Elizabeth's only other friends are two KGB agents, Leanne and Emmett Connors, who are also Soviet spies posing as Americans while raising two children who have no idea who they really are. "Nothing prepares you for them growing up here," Leanne tells Elizabeth.[139] Wanting to "see" each other's children, they arrange to be at the same carnival and view each other's families from afar. But state business comes first, as always. Emmett cajoles Philip into receiving secret information from a third party. When Philip and Elizabeth go to drop it off at the Connorses' hotel room, they find that Leanne, Emmett, and their daughter, Amelia, have all been slaughtered. Just as they leave the scene, they see the Connorses' son, Jared, going back to the room from the pool and hear his tortured cries. Philip and Elizabeth have lost their only real friends, and are now also worried that the same people who killed the Connorses will also kill them, leaving their own kids behind to fend for themselves.

In a turn of events surprising even to an agent as hardened as Elizabeth, it turns out that young Jared killed his whole family because his parents did not want him to become a second-generation Directorate S spy. In the way of most teenagers, he explains that his parents did not understand him: "My parents didn't love me. My family was a lie. My whole life was a lie." In the end, Jared's throat is slit by a homosexual Navy officer turned informant whom the Connorses had been blackmailing. As Jared dies in Elizabeth's arms, he remains true to the state to the bitter end, using words that Elizabeth has used many times to justify her own violent acts: "What we do, we do for something greater than ourselves."[140]

And now the KGB wants to train Paige as a second-generation spy. Philip and Elizabeth have just seen the results of such training and it is not pretty. The KGB thinks that it can reform the second-generation program by ordering their parents to comply. As Philip and Elizabeth's handler Claudia puts it, "She's not just yours. She belongs to the cause, as we all do. You haven't forgotten that, have you?"[141] She concludes by ordering them to tell Paige who they really are and begin her training.

Discipline and Violence

The Americans makes it abundantly clear that family life is governed in no small part by discipline and violence. The Jennings family's entire reason for being is to forward the interests of the Soviet state and wreak violence on the American system. They kill strangers as well as accomplices in the blink of an eye and dispose of them like garbage, while destroying their families. They threaten to kill a child of a mark who threatens to turn them in, cold-bloodedly taking his picture out of the guy's wallet: "Danny, right?" And sometimes they kill parents in cold blood, in one instance leaving their five-year-old child to find them murdered.[142] Philip and Elizabeth have also done a severe violence to their own children. Henry and Paige could not be told about their parents' violence, let alone its roots in the Soviet state, leaving them in the dark about who their parents really are and who they can become as adults. The state has disciplined Philip and Elizabeth so well that they are willing to sacrifice just about anything—including their own children—to further the cause.

There is no question that violence is the family business. But will it be transmitted to the second generation, and subsequent generations going forward? This is certainly the KGB's plan for Paige. It believes that Paige belongs to the state and to the global movement for socialism. Like many parents, Philip and Elizabeth frame the question as if it is really about what Paige wants. But they both have strong views about what she should do. Following his more individualist inclinations, Philip thinks that Paige belongs to her parents for now, but what she does with her life is ultimately her choice. Having become miserable doing the state's bidding, he does not want Paige to follow in his footsteps. He even goes so far as to tell the KGB that he and Elizabeth will quit if it recruits Paige without their permission. Devoted to the state as always, Elizabeth says that Paige should decide, but is entirely confident that, under her tute-lage, Paige will opt to join the KGB. For Elizabeth, it is unthinkable to re-sist the state, recalling that when she joined the KGB, her mother "didn't blink. She told me to go and serve my country. When I was called, my mother didn't hesitate."[143] In yet another gender reversal, Elizabeth uni-laterally decides that Paige will join the KGB, telling Philip, "It is hap-pening. It is just happening. I am doing it, with or without you."[144]

Looking for meaning, Paige had earlier joined a church youth group inspired by Jesus because he "sacrificed himself for the greater good." Elizabeth sets about telling her about "the real heroes, the people sacri-ficing themselves for this world, not some stupid children's story about heaven," and begins to train Paige by telling her a founding myth of her own, one that counters the brutal reality of the American founding myth. Elizabeth's narrative begins with the story of America's long his-tory of racial injustice.[145] It features Gregory, but instead of portraying him as her lover, Elizabeth says that she, Philip, and Gregory were radi-cal activists working together in the civil rights movement. She knows that this will appeal to Paige because she is appalled by South African apartheid. Priming Paige for illegal activity, Elizabeth notes, "We didn't just sing songs and march. We fought in other ways. It wasn't always legal. It was right. . . . Sometimes doing good is harder than going to ral-lies and signing petitions."[146] After hearing Elizabeth tell these stories, Philip wonders, "Am I going to come home one day and Paige will just tell me that she knows who we are?" In her usual matter-of-fact way, Elizabeth simply responds, "I honestly don't know."[147]

Both Philip and Elizabeth prime her for recruitment further by ex-plaining how they are working to foil an American plan to destroy So-viet wheat by developing a destructive new insect. As a kid with a sense of social justice, Paige is appalled. However, this story turns out to be entirely wrong. The insects turn out to be part of a project designed to combat hunger globally. Philip and Elizabeth allow Paige to think that their work for the Soviet Union thwarted an evil project, even though it is becoming increasingly clear to them that they have sacrificed their lives to a failing state that cannot even feed its own people. The most that Elizabeth can concede is, "We have our problems, but everyone is in it together," a convincing conclusion for Paige, who is now reading Marx.[148]

Paige is horrified when she finds out the truth that her parents are Soviet spies, which she tells the only trusted adult she knows, Pastor Tim. Elizabeth is furious when she finds out, yelling at Paige, "You were supposed to put this family first," even though Elizabeth always puts the state first. Paige responds in a manner that distinguishes herself from her parents: "I'm not a liar."[149] Meanwhile, Pastor Tim is horrified at the violence that Philip and Elizabeth are doing to Paige, noting in his diary, "I've seen sexual abuse, but nothing compares to what PJ [Paige Jennings] has been through. There is psychic injury. I fear the damage is already done. How can she trust anyone ever again? How can she ever know what the truth is? She doesn't even know how much she is suffering."[150]

To some degree, this violence encapsulates the moment of truth all children must come to terms with when they realize that their parents are not exactly who they have said they are, hiding the whole truth "for their own good." This maturation process parallels a more advanced stage of political socialization: fully adult citizens must reckon with the brutalities of their founders and abandon childish myths in order to construct an adult narrative that blends idealism and realism, patriotism and critical dissent.

Despite her breach of trust, Paige is trained. She learns to fight, appreciate Russian culture, lie, and manipulate friends. She is taken on missions where she witnesses killing. And she continues to find out more and more about who her parents really are. She knows that her parents use sex to work sources, notwithstanding Elizabeth's repeated denials and warnings not to sleep with anyone unless she cares for them. "There's a lot of bullshit out there, Paige."[151] But Paige has been trained by the best to ferret out truth and Elizabeth has slipped. "Why would I sleep with them if I didn't like them?" she asks.[152]

In a foreshadowing of the tragic conclusion of the series, Paige warns Elizabeth that she will never speak to her again if Elizabeth keeps lying to her. Spy-in-training Paige "works her sources" and finds out that Elizabeth has been having sex with one of Paige's fellow students at Georgetown who is interning at Senator Sam Nunn's office, all to gain access to crucial intelligence about an upcoming arms summit. For Paige, this is the last straw: "I've known all my life—every lie, every time—and I know you're lying now." Elizabeth explains that sex does not matter, either for her or for Philip. "I had to fight. Always. For everything. People were killed. They died all around me. If I had to give everything so that my country would survive, so it would never happen again, I would do it gladly. We were proud to do whatever we could."[153] Unconvinced, Paige responds, "No wonder Dad can't stand to be in the same room with you. I should've done what Henry did and get as far away as possible as soon as I knew."

Paige has experimented with American individualism, religious communitarianism, and Soviet socialism. Her world will never be the same, knowing what she knows now. She has been enculturated into a form of individualism that will become even more neoliberal. The evangelical religion that she was so enamored of will sell itself out to the Republican Party. The Soviet Union will fail. And most of all, she and her family will prove to be violent and deceptive beyond all imagining.

Conclusion

Once their cover is blown (by the Russian Orthodox priest who married them), Elizabeth and Philip quickly prepare to return to Moscow before the FBI can arrest them. Their family does not remain intact. They leave their son, Henry, behind, in the hope that their neighbor, FBI agent Stan, will take care of him in their absence. Paige joins them as they head for the Canadian border. Seated in three different places on a train so that they are not easily identifiable, they cross from the United States to Canada. Breathing a sigh of relief, both Elizabeth and Philip are mortified to see Paige standing on the train platform. In an unexpected reversal of enormous proportions, Paige outplays these professional spies, declaring her independence from her parents once and for all, as they remain on the train and cross over into Canada.

Elizabeth and Philip do escape the law, but they lose their family in the process and face likely death in Moscow at the hands of the very same people that they gave their whole life to, the KGB, which appears to have betrayed the ideals of the Revolution to maintain its own power. The children are left behind, "just another element of a now-discarded alias. Finally stripped of their American cover and free to be themselves, they do not know where to begin. They stand together, but oddly apart, staring out at Moscow, a city that seems at once foreign and home."[154]

What will happen to Paige? Unlike Henry, she is implicated. Back at the DC apartment where she learned to love Russian culture under the guidance of her mom and handler, Paige downs a shot of vodka. Why did she stay? Was it that she could not leave Henry? Or maybe she was lying in wait all along for her chance to escape. Her reasons for leaving her parents are as unclear as her future. But there is little doubt that she will have to reckon further with her parents' lies and violence, if only to save her own skin and make a life of her own moving forward. While their moment of truth may not be as dramatic as this television rendering, anyone who survives childhood must come to terms with their parents' past in order to be able to define their own lives and create the next chapter of their story, no matter what values their parents instilled in them.

The Jenningses' story suggests that family is neither natural nor performative at its core. Paige is bound to her parents by blood. Yet that biological bond, widely regarded by many as natural, does not hold the family together in the end. They have been performing the nuclear family for years, yet somehow, at the crucial moment, that is not determinative. Despite that, Philip and Elizabeth are truly devastated when their daughter decides to leave them and stay behind in the United States. Even these ruthless killers agonize over the destruction of their family.

This kind of pop culture contradiction reveals a great deal about how transformation occurs in US politics, slowly and often in contradictory fashion.

LGBT people and their families have come to be tolerated in mainstream American politics. Challenges remain, but this is the now-dominant narrative. But is it enough to be satisfied with equalizing the conditions of LGBT populations with straight people? That will make life better for some, maybe, but many will still be left out because of persistent power dynamics that underlie US institutions. Although the Stonewall Rebellion has been widely lauded for founding the modern LGBT movement, the interests of its instigators—mostly people of color, drag queens, homeless street youth, and hustlers—have largely remained marginalized, rendering them somewhat illegible, particularly in mainstream law and politics. These exclusions betray the radical potential of the LGBT movement that was part and parcel of Stonewall.

The Americans suggests that the nuclear family has always been a construction, a façade that hides the more vicious underbelly of family life. This new understanding of family opens plenty of space for the public to embrace alternative family forms, including same-sex marriage. Pop culture redefines the family and questions the natural basis of traditional values that it socializes into its children. But what lies beyond the nuclear family now that the mainstream has come to better understand its exclusions and violence? And how might this future square with the radicality of the early LGBTQ movement, a diverse group of folks who aimed to undo the social and political institutions that were brutally oppressing them: the church, the state, and their supporting institutions, such as the nuclear family?

Machiavelli once said that all nations are founded on violence. This chapter suggests that this is also true of families. There is a violence to the act of deceiving children about who their parents really are, often leading grown-ups to idealize their parents or become entirely cynical once they find out the truth. In a similar way, many of us are taught to idealize our political founders until violent realism and exclusion make it impossible to continue to do so. Perhaps such founding myths are necessary for the nation and its citizens at a certain time of political development. But what happens when children develop into adults, and citizens develop into critical thinkers who need to make crucial decisions about what direction to take moving forward? What happens when our parents and the country's founding fathers are revealed in all their violent, self-deceptive, self-justifying complexity? Do we go with them, or leave them at the station, reimagining our political origins? To explore these questions further, I explore two recent visions of political (re)foundings in pop culture: the musical *Hamilton* and the Netflix original television series *Sense8*.

Conclusion

Foundings, Popular Imagination, and the Future of American Politics

Who would have thought that a movement built on the slogan "Smash the Church, Smash the State" would gain mainstream public acceptance in just fifty years? Now that the mainstream public has come to accept LGBT rights, and the limitations of traditional ideas and practices have been revealed, where might popular imagination be headed in the future? What lies beyond the right to privacy, inclusion in the military, and marriage equality? Can the LGBT movement continue to cultivate a radical political imagination while also remaining legible in mainstream political culture? What would a shared non-reproductive sexual ethic look like? How should toxic masculinity's deadly violence be addressed? Now that the nuclear family has been exposed, what new family forms will emerge? This conclusion addresses these questions by exploring the most fundamental political transformation of all: political foundings. The basic terms of politics are reimagined during foundings: Who counts as a political subject? In what political direction should we head? How should our basic institutions be structured? Foundings are world-building. Below I offer a critical interpretation of two recent examples of foundings represented in pop culture: the enormously popular musical *Hamilton* and the niche Netflix series *Sense8*. *Hamilton* focuses on racial representation at the founding and *Sense8* on trans and intersectional representation. Both open up significant questions about political subjectivity, masculinity and violence, sexual ethics, and family forms, offering distinct visions of the future of US politics.

Hamilton's Founding

In this section I discuss the musical *Hamilton*, a reimagining of the American founding. By casting men of color to play American founders, this musical offers an alternative to white dominance during the revolutionary period. As important as this representational reversal is, *Hamilton* avoids directly addressing key issues pertaining to white dominance at that time—most prominently, slavery. Its plot remains largely within the traditional framework of heroic male masculinity. While its racial reversals prompt the public to imagine what a multiracial democracy might look like, *Hamilton* nonetheless whitewashes significant power dynamics, encountering a persistent problem of representation in pop culture: How do you represent an excluded group without replicating historical patterns of oppression that have shaped its identity?

Hamilton is one of the most influential pieces of pop culture of recent times. Called "a turning point in American theater history," it was nominated for a record number of Tony Awards and has also won a Grammy and a Pulitzer Prize.[1] It has spawned productions in Chicago, San Francisco, and London, as well as a number of travelling companies in smaller cities throughout the United States. An art exhibition designed for circulation to other venues opened in Chicago in April 2019 before the pandemic, showing a variety of *Hamilton*-related art and history exhibits, at a cost of forty dollars per person.[2] Huge numbers of "Hamilfans" carrying "Hamiltomes" lined up at a lakeshore venue at 5:00 a.m. (five hours before the opening), no small matter in Chicago, where the winter winds blow well into April.[3] Free cast recordings of *Hamilton* have been made available on Spotify and elsewhere, and a low-cost *Hamilton* mixtape featuring covers of the original songs debuted at number one on the Billboard Top 200.[4] Since the emergence of *Hamilton* there has also been an increased interest in books and exhibits about the US founding, especially those that include information about Hamilton. This is just a small taste of the many ways that the musical's ideas and imaginings are circulating throughout US (and English) culture, even among those who have not been able to attend the show itself.[5]

Hamilton challenges status quo mainstream politics most visibly by reversing the race of the original founders, all of whom were played by men of color in the original cast. In this way *Hamilton* foregrounds race at the founding in a manner that is inclusive and reflective of the racial and ethnic profile of contemporary America. Seeing people of color as protagonists and heroes of any sort (let alone as founders of the nation) has been as uncommon on Broadway as it has been in many other forms of pop culture. Many attendees, even those who enter the theater skeptical, report leaving powerfully moved, even transformed by the performance. For example, after taking 120 students to the show, teacher Seth Andrew of the Democracy Prep Public Schools reported, "It was unquestionably the most profound impact I've ever seen on a student body."[6] This is undoubtedly owing to the powerful feelings engendered by the novel experience of seeing men of color playing founding fathers, using a contemporary Black cultural form, rap, to centralize race in a manner that is associated with revolution.

Cultural studies scholars have long noted that identity reversals are an important if often limited intervention in dominant pop culture.[7] This suggests that "Black" occupation of "white" founding roles could transform Blackness in the popular imagination by disrupting the almost automatic linkage of power and legitimacy with whiteness. It explains why even the first glimpse of a person of color (Lin-Manuel Miranda in the original cast) using rap to introduce himself as Hamilton regularly produces spontaneous cheering from the audience. Seeing people of color integrating rap and traditional Broadway stylings into the founding story entertains and excites audiences. If only for a few hours, this reversal allows audience members to imagine a story of the American founding that is no longer plagued by white power. Other moments of spontaneous applause also suggest great joy in resisting the traditional narrative of white dominance. A well-known example occurs when the musical portrays immigrants as positive contributors to the burgeoning nation and economy, as Hamilton (originally from the West Indies) and Lafayette (originally from France) proclaim, "Immigrants! We get the job done!" Response to this line became even more rousing following the 2016 electoral victory of President Donald J. Trump, who relied on anti-immigrant nativism to rally voters throughout his campaign. In this way, *Hamilton* allows audiences to participate nightly in imagining a multiracial government that challenges white dominance, generating greater desire for such a community beyond the confines of the theater.

Miranda's take on the founding period wistfully harkens back to the revolutionary excitement of that era, devoid of its racial exclusions and brutalities. It reminds us of a time when the American revolutionary character was evident. It reverses the racial violence of that era and sets the stage for multiracial democracy in the present and beyond. It asks us to imagine an idealized version of New York City and America, in which people of many racial and ethnic backgrounds dance, socialize, fight wars, revolt, and create new political institutions together. It makes sense that many people have been moved by these representations. But as queer theorist Jack Halberstam has pointed out, "Role reversal never simply replicates the terms of an equation."[8] For all its many virtues, *Hamilton* also constricts political reimagination of the American founding in many ways, as perhaps any idealist representation would.

Even though the brutal reality of slavery would have been unavoidably present to the actual founders, *Hamilton* includes no such representations. This is perhaps understandable given that it is often difficult to make visible those who have been excluded from representation without replicating the very real historical patterns of domination to which they have been subject. Persistent stereotyping suggests that oppressed people are incapable of successfully occupying positions of political, societal, and cultural power. Mainstream representations of African Americans have often been grounded in stereotypes of laziness, below-average intelligence, lasciviousness, and criminality. Similarly, women have traditionally been portrayed as weak and passive, judged by their sexual attractiveness to men, and thought to be naturally good at being wives and mothers. Gay men are often represented as swishy and comic, or lascivious and shady. These stereotypic representations make the exclusion of Blacks, women, and gays from power appear to be natural or based in "common sense."[9] One solution to this problem is to offer a more complete representation of people of color, women, and LGBT people.

Hamilton's representation of the founding is, of course, fantastical. Black people were present during the revolutionary period, and they would have been present in many of the historical scenes enacted in *Hamilton*, largely as property of white people. Enslaved people were held in 40 percent of the households in New York City at that time, placing the reality of slavery front and center in most people's daily lives.[10] The issue of slavery was central to constitutional and political debates during this period. Black people could have been written into the musical as enslaved people whose freedom was taken from them, as soldiers who fought in the Revolutionary War, and as active organizers of revolts that challenged slavery in the United States and in the Caribbean, an area that is referenced in Hamilton's story.

Historians have noted that Hamilton was not as strong an abolitionist as he is portrayed to be in the musical.[11] To be clear, while this is a very important line of inquiry, I am not primarily concerned here about whether the musical gets the historical facts about Hamilton "right" or "wrong." I am more interested in how the musical's omissions and representations, however fantastical, constrict and/or expand political imagination about the US founding.

Hamilton promises transformation without disrupting the fundamental story lines of the national narrative, offering an idealized story while providing the comfort of the predictable and the familiar. Although the Hamiltome is entitled *Hamilton: The Revolution*, its creator, Lin-Manuel Miranda, has said that the musical is "a story of America then, told by America now" that uses "traditional speeches" to "renew American character, not reinvent it."[12] An author's understanding of their own text is, of course, not necessarily determinative of its meaning. Audiences have a significant role to play in that regard. However, the original understanding typically holds considerable sway in establishing the meaning of any text. This may be especially the case as regards *Hamilton*, due at least in part to the fan fervor that the charismatic Miranda generated among the Hamfam, even before the musical had been staged.[13]

While no one should expect the same kind of analysis of political power and interests from a musical that one would find in an academic tract, the combination of racial reversals with the omission of slavery from *Hamilton* merits further discussion. Miranda chose to deal with the problem of racial representation in the context of the founding by decentralizing the debate about slavery, removing the one scene that was slated to engage it, "Cabinet Battle #3." This has led historian Leslie Harris to deem *Hamilton* "racially mischievous but not transformative."[14]

If people of color had been America's founders, it is likely that they would have discussed slavery and refused to constitutionalize it. Empowered people of color would have forwarded their own interest in freedom over white property owners' economic interest in maintaining slavery. A real-life example of this kind of transformation occurred in 1791 in Saint-Domingue, around the same time that the US founders were writing slavery into the new nation's higher law. There, a successful slave revolt resulted in the founding of Haiti in 1804.[15]

As Derrick Bell's theory of "racial realism" has suggested, it is also quite likely that the white US founders would again choose to forward their interests in pursuing economic gain and uniting the country by constitutionalizing slavery, if given the opportunity to reconsider that decision in light of contemporary historical knowledge and moral standards.[16] The opening story of Bell's fantastical *And We Are Not Saved: The Elusive Quest for Racial Justice* features former civil rights activist Geneva Crenshaw time travelling back to the Constitutional Convention of 1787 to try to convince the founders not to constitutionalize slavery.

Time travel narratives are an important part of popular culture. They typically focus on whether people in contemporary life can intervene into the past and change it for the better, confounding the boundaries of linear time. Bell's story imagines what might have happened if the founders had had to confront powerful arguments against slavery from a contemporary Black woman—a person who would have been directly affected by their decision, and who would have knowledge about its disastrous long-term effects. As often happens in time travel, the past proves to be quite sticky. Crenshaw fails to change the founders' minds, in no small part because they were unwilling to see or fully understand the contradiction between their ideals on rights and equality on the one hand, and the constitutionalizing of slavery on the other. Bell argues that this "constitutional contradiction" has plagued the country ever since. He chronicles additional stories about voting rights, affirmative action, reparations, and a host of other reforms, suggesting that inclusion is tenuous at best, often subject to serious conditions and significant costs.

Historian Lyra Monteiro addresses the problematic nature of *Hamilton*'s racial reversals in this way: "Is it necessarily a good thing [for people of color] to feel ownership over a celebratory, white narrative of the American past?"[17] Following Monteiro, we might also ask whether it is a good thing for white people, who are the majority of theatergoers, to be encouraged to imagine that relatively easy racial reversals of the sort offered in *Hamilton* provide a transformative solution to the persistent problems of racial inequalities and power disparities that have plagued the United States since its founding.

The representation of gender is also problematic in *Hamilton*. While male founders are typically represented as public heroes in an epic tale of political conquest and creation, women are largely pining after the men who are busy shaping the big world. Women scheme about how to get the most desirable man (in this case, Hamilton) to notice them, and then remain at home to raise children or provide other acts of care in the private sphere. Rather than reversing these tired sex and gender norms, *Hamilton* follows the traditional Broadway form, representing the male hero as the protagonist who is striving for greatness with undying support from traditionally feminine females. This is consistent with the classic way to imagine and represent male masculinity and nation building as an epic story of adventure and development through male bonding. For example, George Washington is regularly portrayed as a great American icon, the father of the country, while lesser but still great men such as Hamilton are seated at the right hand of the father.[18]

Hamilton does diverge from the classic form somewhat by refusing to idealize the founders completely. They are often represented as fallible men who are profane, petty, egotistical, cheating bros who revel in drinking to excess and chasing women. It is also far less self-serious than most treatments of the founders, as it frequently exhibits a broad sense of humor. Nonetheless, at its core it is a traditional story of heroic men coming into their own, bending the world to their will, building a new country, and creating a radically new form of government. The musical centralizes Hamilton's role in these events, following the Great Man template of history.[19]

Male companionship and competition are highlighted throughout the musical in the rivalry between Hamilton and Aaron Burr, which culminated in a dramatic duel to determine who was most dominant. This ritual form of problem solving was common among male elites at that time, and it included several practices that allowed duelists to back away from the challenge midstream. Hamilton's inability to do so is portrayed as foolish in the musical. The duel has tragic consequences not only for Hamilton, who is killed, but also for his wife, who, yet again, is left to pick up the pieces in the wake of his reckless behavior.

As historians have noted, the Revolution's radical potential for women was being discussed at that time, perhaps most famously by Abigail Adams's "remember the ladies" plea, written to her influential husband, John. Abigail Adams was not alone in thinking that the Revolution might lead to greater freedom for women. As Catherine Allgor notes, "Coverture is an idea and cultural reality as crucial to understanding our revolutionary origins as terms such as 'liberty,' 'independence,' and 'democracy.' Unlike those terms, however, it is largely unknown to the American public."[20]

Like the founders, the writers of *Hamilton* had ample opportunity to address women's subjection as part of the revolt but chose not to do so. This is hinted at as soon as the Schuyler sisters are introduced: Angelica (whom Miranda has called "the smartest character"), Eliza (who becomes Hamilton's wife), and Peggy. Angelica yearns to be a central player in the unfolding story as she sings "Look around, look around, the revolution's happening in New York," and coaxes her sisters to ignore "Daddy's" dictates to be home by sundown and avoid downtown. She notes that she has been reading Thomas Paine's *Common Sense*, recites the opening lines of the Declaration of Independence, and announces that she is going to compel Thomas Jefferson (another rival of Hamilton's) to include women in the sequel, even though she is well aware that men will call her "intense or insane." Her call for a "sequel" Declaration 2.0 regularly produces spontaneous cheers from the audience. But rather than accepting this moment as an opportunity to offer a broader understanding of who counts as a political subject, Miranda reinforces traditional sex and gender norms. Aaron Burr (Hamilton's archrival) hits on Angelica, while her sisters and the rest of the company repeatedly tell her how lucky she is just to be alive and in New York at this exciting time. There is no further mention of including women in the Revolution, or any recognition of women's oppression through coverture. Instead, in the next scene featuring women, the Schuyler sisters find themselves at a "winter's ball," a fairytale-like setting where women are rendered "helpless" by Hamilton's charms, even as they cattily position themselves to be the sole object of his affection. Rather than opening our political imagination to multi-gendered democracy, *Hamilton* falls back on traditional representations of women that have long been central to the mainstream account of the founding, complementing the story of male power, virility, and conquest, sexual and political.[21]

Regarding sexuality, the original cast included several gay actors, and the musical is chock-full of homosocial bonding. Although John Laurens is included in the musical, *Hamilton* omits any discussion of Laurens's correspondence with Hamilton, which has been described as "intense and romantic" to a degree that suggests a same-sex relationship.[22] Instead, Laurens is portrayed as just another one of the founding bros, presumably interested in heterosexual conquest. Such conquest need not be read as definitive evidence of heterosexual desire. As early queer theorists pointed out some time ago, intense homosocial bonding does not necessarily map onto a specific sexual identity—it can open a range of possibilities.[23] This is a story line that begs for further development.

It is also worth noting that Hamilton is the central founder associated with the development of modern capitalism in the United States. He was also among the least democratic of the founders, persistently seeking to adapt older British forms of aristocracy and monarchy into the American political environment. As the first secretary of the treasury, he wrote the influential "Report on Manufactures." This paper outlined a plan for the development of an early form of global capitalism in the United States, which Hamilton believed was key to securing independence and freedom for the fledgling nation. In that sense, it is perhaps fitting that *Hamilton* has become an extraordinarily commodified product that creates seemingly endless demand for both cheap and expensive products that many are eager to consume, over and over. While the success of *Hamilton* has hinged in no small part on elites for whom the exorbitant ticket prices are not prohibitive, it has also relied on the desires of those who might fantasize about moving in elite circles in the future, a capitalist aspiration if there ever was one. Attending the musical has become something of a status marker: Have you seen *Hamilton*? How many times? In New York? With the original cast? And so forth. Those who are not able to afford the several hundreds, if not thousands of dollars for one night's entertainment can always hope that lightning will strike and they will win the daily (ticket) lottery. Pre-COVID-19, this ingenious device served the purpose of keeping *Hamilton* front and center in the minds of Hamilfans, while also replicating an American Dream–like promise that anyone can succeed if they persistently work hard enough (in this case, to get a much-desired ticket for the popular musical).

In many ways, *Hamilton* provides a useful circulation of basic information about the founding, as well as a much-needed infusion of men and women of color into both Broadway and the story of the founding. These representations have undoubtedly expanded the public imagination about who constitutes the nation. However, *Hamilton*'s omissions and misrepresentations create a fantasy that suggests that reversing white male dominance will be easy and fun. As we have seen, slavery, coverture, sexuality, and class have largely been airbrushed out of *Hamilton*, despite ample opportunities to address these topics. As such, the end product largely reinforces status quo power relations, resulting in what Allgor has called a "failure of imagination."[24]

What is missing in *Hamilton* is a more self-conscious, critical take on the ideology and power behind the traditional founding narrative as well as its many exclusions and violences. The musical's final number is sung by Hamilton's wife, Eliza. "Who Lives, Who Dies, Who Tells Your Story" suggests that stories matter and that who tells them may matter even more. Hamilton's wife outlived him, as well as many of the other major characters. As a result, she became pivotal in telling Hamilton's story. She compiled his papers, raised funds for the Washington Monument, and established the first private orphanage in New York City. In doing so, she stood by her man to the end and beyond, despite his many infidelities and ego-driven schemes, including the duel that ended his life. She also continued to fulfill the traditional women's role of raising children in and beyond her own family. Although she has the last word in this musical, that word unfortunately appears to make her complicit in her own oppression, something that Miranda seems to have overlooked. In his marginalia in the Hamiltome, he notes that "the line that made him cry hardest" occurs at Eliza's sister Angelica's burial, which, he says, puts her "near Alexander, but not with him for all eternity."[25] Here Miranda continues to highlight a heterosexual affair that Hamilton purportedly had with his wife's sister. However, this affair is as unsubstantiated as his affair with John Laurens, which is not mentioned once in the entire musical. Angelica is left to pine for a possibly unrequited love in perpetuity, while Laurens remains in the closet for all eternity.

Queering Foundings: Consent, Dissent, and Violence

So what to make of the American founding, and the founding of the LGBT movement, both of which have recently been represented in pop culture in a manner that reproduces status quo ideology? As discussed throughout this book, pop culture frequently offers narratives that represent both elite and popular interests. These contradictions can create a vantage point that provides a richer understanding of how power works, as well as how it might be transformed. To that end, cultural theory scholars have long counseled that pop culture narratives can be read "against the grain" to reveal more complex story lines that challenge the persistent stickiness of status quo political imagination.

The story of the founding of the modern LGBT movement during a riot in New York City's Stonewall Inn in 1969, by now well known, has many elements in common with the story of the American founding. In a retrospective report on the twenty-fifth anniversary of the uprising, the *New York Times* linked the two, calling Stonewall "the raid heard around the world," an obvious play on Ralph Waldo Emerson's line "the shot heard 'round the world," which refers to the beginning of the American Revolution at the Battles of Lexington and Concord. Seemingly insurmountable state power prevented the rights of the participants in both uprisings from being recognized. England was the strongest imperial power in the West at the time of the American Revolution, and the divine right of kings was the central founding story that legitimated monarchy, the dominant form of government. The idea that an undisciplined, ill-resourced, ragtag group of colonists might be able to overcome the mighty forces of King George III and establish a new form of government based on the ideas of political equality and the consent of the governed seemed rather unlikely, to say the least. Who would have thought that the nation founded by these upstart colonists would one day supplant England and become the most dominant imperial power in the world?[26]

Similarly, it seemed improbable that an unorganized, multi-gender, and racially diverse group of drag queens, homeless street youth, and hustlers would be able to successfully take on the New York City police force over three nights at the Stonewall Inn. However, like the colonists, they were fed up with being treated like second-class citizens by status quo power, being served watered-down yet expensive drinks in a mob-controlled bar where they were regularly subject to arrest that could lead to loss of family, employment, and faith communities, as well as institutionalization and shock therapy. At the time of the revolt, their resistance to state power merited a few paragraphs in the back pages of the city section of the *New York Times*.[27]

We have seen the ways that *Hamilton* both expands and constricts political imagination about the founding of the United States. What is the parallel story about the LGBT movement? Perhaps a classic civil rights narrative that suggests that LGBT people can be easily integrated into mainstream politics, without any major disruptions, other than that first revolutionary outburst at Stonewall. Recent representations of Stonewall that have written key people and issues out of the story have proven to be quite popular. For example, the 2015 feature-length film *Stonewall* centralized a white, masculine, cisgender young man from Indiana who comes to New York City to attend Columbia University. This film suggested that he threw the "first brick" in the rebellion, decentralizing the trans people and people of color who were at its forefront, a problem of representation that has been replicated in the movement as it developed after Stonewall.[28] Popular Internet examples that make similar representational choices include the short video *Stonewall: Profiles of Pride, Veterans from the Stonewall Riots of '69.*[29]

Perhaps a queered understanding of foundings might help. Foundings are not simply about new beginnings; they also entail a repudiation of a previous political regime.[30] In other words, foundings (or stories of origin) contain elements of both dissent and consent. They repudiate dominant state power and its norms, clearing space for the community to generate new principles of justice that can serve as the basis for new laws and institutions. The American founding includes a direct rejection of British monarchical authority over the colonies and dissent from the idea that kingship is a legitimate form of government, as well as a new concept of justice based on political equality and consent of the governed, as detailed in the Declaration of Independence. This founding created new political subjects, practices, and institutions, eventuating in formal constitutions in the Articles of Confederation and then the Constitution of 1787, which bound the former colonists into a people and a nation, the United States of America.

Since dissent and consent are present at the emergence of new political communities, it is reasonable to think that "normal" politics outside revolutionary periods would also contain elements of dissent and consent. Just as tension between consonance and dissonance produces movement in music, the dynamic relationship between the politics of consent and dissent sparks political transformation, as the numerous examples mentioned at the beginning of this book attest, including nearly universal suffrage, the abolition of slavery, minimum wage and maximum hours laws, birth control, and marriage equality. These transformations result from the intersection of mainstream and radical politics. Contrary to much popular and scholarly belief, radical politics has been present throughout American political development. It becomes more visible in mainstream politics during specific political times, typically during periods of significant social dislocation. During such times, the basic terms of politics are often reconsidered.

Foundings are also grounded in violence, as political theorist Niccolò Machiavelli noted at the dawn of modern political formation in the West. This is certainly true of the American founding as exemplified by the US government's forcible removal of Native Americans from their lands and the intentional destruction of their tribes and cultures. Prior to European contact, diverse indigeneous cultures had developed in what is now North America, with a combined population estimated at as many as seven million people in more than six hundred tribes with differing cultures, languages and dialects, diets, beliefs, and customs. These governments were the oldest in North America at that time, recognized as sovereign by their people for far longer than the United States has existed, and well before European colonization began on the continent in the sixteenth century.[31]

Further, it is well established that such violence extends beyond the birth of new political communities, becoming a fact of life in everyday law and politics. In a piece that has been especially influential in academic communities that study the relationship between law and society, legal theorist Robert Cover argued, "Legal interpretative acts signal and occasion the imposition of violence upon others. A judge articulates her understanding of a text, and as a result, somebody loses his freedom, his property, his children, even his life. Interpretations in law also constitute justifications for violence which has already occurred, or which is about to occur. . . . Neither legal interpretation nor the violence it occasions may be properly understood apart from one another."[32]

While the violence of the state is regularly accepted as legitimate, fantastical violence that emerges in pop culture is often subject to closer scrutiny. Political science has long taken for granted that the state holds a monopoly on the legitimate use of force within a given territory. Influential theorists such as Max Weber believed this to be the defining characteristic of the modern state. Pop culture is grounded in representation, which allows it to be imaginative and often fantastical. Yet it can be quite powerful.

Adapting Benedict Anderson's conception of the nation as an "imagined community," Jack Halberstam has called pop culture narratives that offer fantastical revenge "imagined violence." Following Anderson's insight that communities should be understood by the style in which they are imagined, rather than by their genuineness, Halberstam argues that pop culture representations should be similarly evaluated.[33] Resisting the widely accepted moral imperative to avoid fighting violence with violence, Halberstam suggests that real violence may be productively fought with the imagined and fantastical violence of pop culture. They argue that fantastical violence can produce a fear of retaliation in violent rapists, homophobes, white supremacists, police, and others who engage in brutality against vulnerable populations. Halberstam explains that "the power of fantasy is not to represent [the real], but to destabilize the real."[34] For example, a pop culture tour de force such as *Thelma and Louise* may not prevent rape, "but it might make a man think twice about whether a woman is going to blow him away."[35] Its power is less about advocating violence than it is about complicating "an assumed relationship between women and passivity." In this way, it can disrupt the default understanding of gender, "challenge white heterosexual masculinity and create a cultural coalition of postmodern terror."[36] More recent mainstream examples of "imagined violence" enacting similar disruptions include Quentin Tarantino's *Inglorious Basterds*, *Django Unchained*, and *Kill Bill*.

The Reimagined Founding of *Sense8*

Hamilton's racial reversals produce a powerful reimagining of the American founding that expands contemporary understandings of political community. As often is the case with pop culture, *Hamilton* also contradicts itself by offering representations of race, gender, class, and sexuality that reinforce status quo or even regressive politics, constricting political imagination and reinforcing unjust exclusions from full participation in the political community. These contradictions invite a more critical interpretation that moves beyond mere reversal toward greater destabilization of status quo race, gender, class, and sex norms. They prompt us to read the narrative of *Hamilton* and the founding against the grain, to identify more imaginative queer alternatives to a largely straight mainstream narrative.

In *Hamilton* King George III upholds status quo politics, but he is the queerest character in the show. His signature song, "You'll Be Back," is a fan favorite. However, it is one of the few songs in the show that does not incorporate a Black musical style. The king does not rap. Played by Adam Groff, His Majesty was the only white person cast in the original production of *Hamilton*. He sings in standard Broadway form while representing the patriarchal and monarchical status quo. He affirms the dominant understanding of just government at that time, the divine right of kings, which asserted that his rule (and the rule of other monarchs) stemmed back to the grant of dominion over the Earth that God gave to Adam in the biblical story of human origin contained in Genesis. In King George's time it was commonly believed that it was God's will for subjects to be obedient to monarchical rule (and thus heretical for them to dissent). God also was believed to have given Adam dominion over Eve, creating a natural order of patriarchal gender dominance that compelled the subjection of women to men.

From the perspective of both monarchy and patriarchy, "You'll Be Back" can be read as a breakup song of sorts that threatens violent mass murder of the colonists if they continue to reject the divine order. The threat is grounded in the king's purported love for his subjects and his knowledge of what is truly best for them. He implores the colonists to come to their senses by denouncing independence and returning to the English fold, suggesting that he does not really want to wield power violently, but that he will, if forced to do so (by disorderly subjects). Despite the king's claim of love, his admission suggests that scholars like Cover are right to assert that violence always lies beneath the orderly veneer of everyday politics. Further, the king's evocation of the mortal danger that women typically face when they reject the private rule of abusive men suggests that some are more subject to this violence than others. The colonists' declaration of independence is similarly risky, moving beyond the boundaries of ordinary politics into regime-level discord, which the king openly concedes is fraught with violence. Here the king unites public and private authoritarianism, patterning himself after abusive men who commonly proclaim their love for their partners even as they threaten or perpetrate actual violence against them.

But *Hamilton*'s king is not only a representative of the status quo. He is also an "other," a flaming (if not fully acknowledged) queer. He sings these lines to the colonists in as arch a manner as can be imagined:

You say

The price of my love's not a price that you're willing to pay

. . .

You'll be back

Soon you'll see

You'll remember you belong to me

Oceans rise

Empires fall

We have seen each other through it all

And when push

Comes to shove

I will send a fully armed battalion to remind you of my love.

. . .

When you're gone

I'll go mad

So don't throw away this thing we had

'Cuz when push

comes to shove

I will kill your friends and family to remind you of my love.

"You'll Be Back" opens up so many possibilities. It falls to queer King George to highlight the violence that is part and parcel of political foundings. This simultaneously sympathetic and humorous, repulsive and violent, pathetic and mad character introduces the idea that violence is always lurking beneath the pleasant façade of dominion, threatening to emerge at any time if subjects do not remain passive and loyal. Perhaps more than any other character in *Hamilton*, he deeply understands the dirty little secret of the violence and power that are necessary to maintain order. This truth appears to be so commonplace that audiences typically laugh at the king's performance in a knowing and entertained way: Violence is required not only to establish but also to maintain public and private power.

Hamilton also suggests that violence is required to become a man. Lin-Manuel Miranda's own notebooks in which he recorded his early imaginings about *Hamilton* closely tie male masculinity to violence. In large capital letters that take up an entire page in a notebook that otherwise crams as many words as possible on each page, Miranda writes in boldface lettering,

I WISH
THERE WAS
A
WAR.
—Alexander Hamilton,
Age 14

This yearning for war is repeated at least three times during the musical. However, the connection between violence, Hamilton's personal growth, and the fledgling country's development is left unquestioned. *Hamilton* simply assumes that violence is necessary for men to develop the power of male masculinity and the state. A queerer sensibility is needed to better understand the importance of "I wish there was a war," as well as Miranda's fascination with it. The revolutionary spirit of the founding and contemporary pop culture needs to be mashed up in a manner that destabilizes a constitutive component of the dominant order, white male masculinity. Perhaps Hamilton's would-be lover John Laurens would have a role to play if such a mash-up of his character was rewritten to make him as compelling as queer King George.

To this end, I draw on the original Netflix television series *Sense8*, demonstrating how a self-consciously queer political imagination could expand our understanding of political foundings and, to put it in the words of Victoria Hattam and Joseph Lowndes, "what we want from politics."[37] *Sense8* critically reflects on disproportionate power relations, offering an interesting new take on what it means to be human in contemporary global society. Created by the Wachowskis (twin trans women who also directed the *Matrix* films, *Bound*, and *V for Vendetta*), *Sense8* consists of twenty-four episodes over two seasons. Running from 2015 to 2018, the series won two Emmy Awards and has been critically acclaimed for its representation of LGBTQ characters and themes, as well as for transgressing status quo political representations of sex, gender, sexuality, race, and nationality.

Sense8 is a science fiction story of origin, a queer founding. Often referred to as speculative fiction, science fiction is a genre that typically features imaginative alternative world-building, often with a futuristic focus that allows viewers to escape from an often-dystopic present.[38] Sometimes using imagined violence, this founding story repudiates contemporary mainstream understandings of the political subject, individual autonomy, sex and gender, and family, offering a new concept of justice. *Sense8* features eight individual characters (called "sensates") of varying races, genders, gender identities, and sexualities, who are emotionally and mentally linked despite physically living in different global capitals. Each character slowly comes to understand the "we"-ness of their connection to the other seven and the extraordinary power this connection produces. They create a new political subject that is both individual and collective all at once; they come out, and then instigate broader social and political transformation, paralleling the way that the LGBT movement was built through and after Stonewall.

Many of the plotlines in *Sense8* resonate with queer history, providing new ways to think more expansively about the problems born of LGBT inclusion in mainstream politics that are discussed throughout this book: the dominance of individual autonomy as the mainspring of political and moral action (chapter 1), persistent and toxic violence expressed through male masculinity (chapter 2), and the lack of interesting alternatives to the nuclear family as a primary form of social organization (chapter 3). The series helps us to imagine how to extend the radical spirit of the LGBT movement's founding beyond popular acceptance of LGBT civil rights.

The tagline of *Sense8*, "I AM WE," highlights the new political subject at the core of the series. Born at the same time on the same day, the eight sensates central to the series form one of many "clusters," called "Homo sensorium," a more highly evolved form of human life that has branched off from Homo sapiens. Even though the sensates are thousands of miles apart, they can feel the same feelings, think the same thoughts, and draw on each other's skills, particularly when they need help. This extraordinary ability allows them to overcome the rigid barrier between I and we, producing a new political subject that is both an I and a we at the same time, a collective of autonomous individuals.

The cluster has a political imagination that is not yet fully legible in mainstream politics. As a result, mainstream power regularly disciplines the cluster's expanded vision of individual and communal life, sex and gender norms, and family. They are called "crazy," and in several instances threatened with imprisonment, lobotomy, and/or death. For example, Nomi (pronounced "Know me") Marks, a white trans woman hacktivist who was rejected by her biological family of origin, narrowly escapes having a lobotomy performed against her will to correct her "brain disorder." Reflecting on this with her Black lesbian non-sensate girlfriend, Amanita Caplan (a bookseller at City Lights in San Francisco), they realize that just as it seems impossible in contemporary times for people to imagine I and we as one embodied being, it was also difficult for most people to see and accept queer people like them in earlier times. That is, *Sense8* reminds us that what society considers "crazy" or unthinkable has radically changed over time. This realization makes it easier to imagine that a new, more evolved form of mainstream politics could emerge in the future that experiences I and we simultaneously, transforms sex and gender, and creates new family forms.

The new "sensate" political subject transcends the isolating and amoral implications of atomistic individualism, without succumbing to the problematic moralizing of traditional community standards. Chapter 1's analysis of the move from community moral standards to individual ethical calculations contributed to greater public acceptance of the decriminalization of sodomy. However, viewers of the film *Brothers* were left with a severely socially dislocated white straight male subject whose violence nearly destroys himself and his family. Rather than opting for either the I or the we, the typical choice offered in mainstream US politics, *Sense8* repudiates both the atomistic individualism and traditional communitarian standards that lie at the core of the liberal political order, imagining a critical new political subject that brings the I and the we together: the sensate. This new political subject offers a new, sometimes orgiastic form of group sexuality that has nothing whatsoever to do with reproduction.

As we saw in chapter 2, shifts in sex and gender norms in the James Bond film series paved the way for greater popular acceptance of LGBT people in the armed forces. Yet greater inclusion emerged side by side with greater acceptance of the same violent nationalism that has often been used to buttress regimes that have oppressed LGBT people, people of color, and women. James Bond's over-the-top violence parallels well-known tactics undertaken by MI6 and the CIA. That violence leads to Bond's own demise, as his prototypical (if shifting) version of white male masculinity can no longer avoid the consequences of its own excesses. *Sense8* repudiates nation-state loyalties, rigid sex and gender identities, and disciplined sexuality. Sensate clusters embody identities that transcend rigid sex and gender identity, and embrace the unruliness of sex, sometimes against the backdrop of fantastical violence leveled against traditional oppressors.

Chapter 3 tracked the repudiation of the nuclear family and its foundational political commitments, including its capitalist political economy, gender norms, and violence. These shifts opened the way for greater public acceptance of same-sex marriage, while also revealing the violence that underlies and undermines the traditional family form. *Sense8* clusters constitute a new social form that critically acknowledges the violence of the traditional family and transcends it. This new form of social bonding is neither blood-based nor chosen, and its sexual expression is expansive, rather than restricted to traditional monogamous couplings.

Entitled "What Is Human?," episode 10 in season 1 provides an extended example of imagined violence, showing what it might look like to queer violence through a central gay character, a critical component missing in the founding narrative of *Hamilton*. This episode focuses on their own personal foundings, as the sensate cluster relive their births into their mainstream families in all their bloody messiness. Beginning at the Garden of Exile at the Jewish Museum, an actual place in Berlin that officially opened on 9/11, the episode includes themes that are central to foundings, including a sustained meditation on the bonds that brings humans together into society and the violence that tears them apart. The Garden contains several large columns that are designed to destabilize visitors as they walk through, to promote deep reflection on the questions that the Holocaust raises about human nature and violence. The sensates are seen there together (transcending geographic space), reflecting on the following quotation that is inscribed there in German: "Is the Holocaust an aberration, or a reflection of ourselves?"

The I and we sensates are represented as one political subject, one consciousness, by camera shots that move back and forth between them, as exemplified by the visual movement between Wolfgang Bogdanow, a white straight male living in Berlin, and Lito Rodriguez, a cis gay male living in Mexico City. An actor and a closeted gay man, Lito is particularly skilled at pretending to be someone else. Wolfgang, a safecracker, is excellent at wielding violence to protect his own interests as well as those of his friends. In one scene, an organized crime boss named Steiner threatens to kill Wolfgang for stealing a large cache of diamonds with his gangly childhood friend Felix, whom Steiner has already beaten to a pulp. Steiner has pinned Wolfgang to the ground with a gun to his head and is repeatedly calling Felix a cocksucker. Wolfgang needs to gain access to the gun planted under his car tire to defend himself, but he is uncharacteristically stymied by fear because Steiner reminds him of his abusive father.

Meanwhile, over in Mexico City, Lito's fear has stymied him too. He lacks the courage to come out as a gay man, fearing that he would lose his career and the considerable material comfort that goes along with it. Wolfgang's call for help brings Lito instantly to Berlin, "with" Wolfgang, the I and the We embodied together, using Lito's skill at dialogue and acting to distract Steiner long enough for Wolfgang to retrieve his gun, shoot all of Steiner's henchmen, and then blow up Steiner's getaway car with a rocket launcher stashed in Wolfgang's trunk.

Steiner receives his comeuppance as Lito, a Mexican gay man, activates this "imagined violence" that destabilizes straight white male masculinity, à la Halberstam's suggestion. Rather than following the traditional practice of heroically wielding violence against "others," straight white men are the villains in this scene. Lito destabilizes the power of men who slur and bully gay men, perhaps causing perpetrators in real life to think twice about using such tactics in the future. This scene transforms Lito from a gay victim into a queer hero whose actions disrupt the toxic violence of white straight male masculinity. In this imagined society, queers are powerful agents who transform the violence of patriarchal society. They also can transform straight white men like Wolfgang who have been stymied by the violence of their fathers, left to yearn for wars like Hamilton, or as the opening scene of the episode in Berlin reminds us, genocidal violence.

Wolfgang's entire life has been tainted by patriarchal violence in two of its most virulent forms. Domestic violence and incest destroyed his traditional family of origin. His father repeatedly beat him and raped his older (step)sister (who later is revealed to have been Wolfgang's biological mother). Exemplifying the narrow mindset that fuels patriarchal violence, Wolfgang's father taught his son that "there are only five things important in life: eating, drinking, shitting, having sex, and fighting for more." Young Wolfgang strangled his father to death to prevent him from killing his sister, a violent conclusion that fantastically ended his father's patriarchal reign over his family. Empowered by Lito, Wolfgang has now also violently destroyed Steiner, a homophobic, amoral, self-aggrandizing leader of a criminal gang, the embodiment of the lifestyle that Wolfgang's father touted.

As Wolfgang thanks Lito at the close of the scene, closeted Lito responds that "lying is easy. It's what I do." In the wake of reconstituting the violence that underlies homophobic power, Lito feels free to come out, reunite with his boyfriend, and restore love to his life in this new imagined society (perhaps in the way that John Laurens longed to during the American Revolution). But first he must return to Mexico City to help his "beard," Daniela Velázquez, escape from a violent heterosexual relationship. Wolfgang "arrives" to help Lito, again using imagined violence to vanquish yet another perpetrator of patriarchal violence, saying, "Fighting is easy. It's what *I* do." Having righted his relationship with Dani, Lito tells her, "Come on, let's go home," and they head to his boyfriend Hernando's apartment, where Lito pledges to come out publicly. The scene ends with the establishment of a decidedly non-nuclear family. Lito subsequently comes out to the world, standing "alongside" the other sensates in his cluster, giving a public speech at the annual Pride Celebration in Rio as the huge queer crowd cheers him on.

Conclusion

Imagined violence can destabilize status quo male masculinity, blowing it to bits, just as the newly constituted queer tours de force of Lito and Wolfgang have done, and perhaps John Laurens and Alexander Hamilton could have done also. Lito and Wolfgang's I and we political subjectivity provides an alternative to Hamilton's violence and undermines traditional toxic male masculinity, offering a new form in its place. The ability to wield imagined violence subversively is not limited to male characters in *Sense8*. To provide one of many possible examples, Sun Bak, a powerful financier based in Seoul who has been wrongfully accused of killing her father, uses her kickboxing skills to escape from prison along with an older woman who killed her husband to defend herself from his repeated attacks. These queer uses of imagined violence repudiate traditional society, destabilize its key supporting practices and institutions, and clear narrative space for a new society that includes expanded political subjects, practices, and institutions.

As we have seen, the sort of expansive political imagination exemplified by *Sense8* is particularly important in the midst of fear. Fear and a will to power have been particularly legible in US politics at least since the election of Donald J. Trump in 2016. Such fear seeks to constrict political imagination, limit possibilities, and make us believe that nothing is possible short of what is right before us, making politics a grim slog to seemingly inevitable peril and tragedy. Trumpist white male supremacy has been playing on a seemingly incessant loop for the past several years, propping up increasingly authoritarian rule. Its endemic violence became more legible in mainstream politics on January 6, 2021, when Trump's followers stormed the Capitol in a failed attempt to restore him and his brand of straight white male masculinity to power.

In place of fear, *Sense8* offers a vision of social and political transformation, but not in an idealistic or naïve way that disregards the persistence of power, and not in a realist way that cynically resigns us to be subject to power. *Sense8* certainly has many dystopic plotlines, as is common in speculative fiction. One entails the Biologic Preservation Organization (BPO) hunting down clusters across the world, to perpetuate capitalist power and wealth, obstructing the transformation of the old society and the founding of a new one. The BPO uses any and all means to maintain power, no matter how totalizing its effects may be. Over the course of the series, the sensates ultimately vanquish these older forces of greed and hate—at least for now—but not without enormous costs and significant losses. That said, the I and the we sensates survive and live on to fight another day, continuing to make the new society more legible and accepted in mainstream politics.

Sense8 suggests not only that such victories are possible, but that they should be celebrated, even if they remain incomplete. It teaches that yearning for finality and stability is misplaced. Having faced down the old ways, the queer sensates persist, deeply aware of power and its many misuses and dangers. The sensates know that traditional power crushed many of their queer forebears. They understand the gravity of the basic question posed at the Jewish Museum in Berlin about human nature. And yet they are still capable of great joy. Their expansive political imaginations intact, they stand ready to continue the work of building a new society. Thus, the series ends, for now, in a fabulously queer celebration of the wedding of Nomi and Amanita, foregrounding the multi-gendered, multiracial democracy that is straining to come into being as the old authoritarian world falls away. They celebrate with their radical, non-nuclear sensate cluster social unit, but also with Nomi's conventional family of origin, who are slow to learn and often recalcitrant, performing the way that radical and mainstream politics can intersect and transform us and our political desires.

Sense8 is hardly the only site where compelling alternative visions are playing out in contemporary pop culture. While television viewership has become undeniably fragmented in this age of growing access to various forms of social media, this is not cause to lament the lack of a shared community. Rather, emerging platforms offer a multitude of politically expansive representations that can circulate globally. Of course, other platforms propagate authoritarian and totalizing visions. In the way of most pop culture, most offer representations of both at the same time. This is to be expected. It need not lead to resignation.

Expansive political imagination opens us up to new possibilities, helping us to anticipate the future bravely, knowing all the while that we may be seen as crazy for doing so, especially at the very moment when we seem most stuck and in need of a broader vision. Even when political imagination embraces the past, it can recall the radical imagination that propelled some of us forward out of the brutally limited oppression that was taken for granted during the political times of the American and LGBTQ movement foundings. Our ideas and practices have evolved, creating political changes and demands that were once impossible for most to see or even imagine. This remembering can circulate through popular culture, providing us with the hope and examples we need to transform the LGBTQ movement and liberal democracy into new political forms that we cannot yet fully imagine.

Pop culture can help us to envision unknown futures that lead beyond what we think we know about and desire from contemporary politics. Reflecting on these representations can spark us to claim a more just and radical future—even as they remain legible enough to the mainstream, even as we continue to operate in the social dislocation of its visibly decaying institutions. Rather than allowing our political imaginations to be stuck at whatever is in front of us at any given political time, we can commit to expanding our imaginations to see, accept, and produce more just, more inclusive, and more democratic futures—especially those that may seem entirely improbable in our current political time. If we are fortunate, history will repeat, and what was once unthinkable will come to be seen as not so radical after all, as what we expect out of mainstream politics, what we desire, is transformed before our very eyes.

ACKNOWLEDGMENTS

People may attribute a book to the person who wrote it, and there is, of course, something to that. But the truth is that all good work takes place in communities. A book like this one sees the light of day only because creative people working together have challenged orthodoxies for years, making ideas that once seemed heretical more visible, more known, and eventually more accepted.

As an academic discipline, political science has long been very slow to change, and many of us bear the scars that prove that. I have been very fortunate to find pockets of joy and creativity in several cutting-edge disciplinary and interdisciplinary communities that value the kind of work I do and the kind of person I am. I'm grateful to the folks I've worked with in the Western Political Science Association (the best conference in political science, in my opinion), especially the regular attendees of the Feminist Theory Workshop at the Western, which the amazing Shane Phalen first organized over thirty years ago. I probably wouldn't have lasted in the profession without the advice and support of colleagues in the Feminist Theory group, so many of whom have become wonderful friends, including my mentor Mary Hawkesworth, Heath Davis, Cristina Beltrán, Anna Sampaio, Angie Wilson, and so many others.

The legal studies scholars in the Law and Studies Association also warmly welcomed my work, especially Michael McCann, Jeff Dudas, Jinee Lokaneeta, Renee Cramer, Paul Passavant, and many others. I'm also very thankful for my friends fighting the good fight in the Law and Courts Section in the American Political Science Association, especially Julie Novkov, Mark Graber, Christine Harrington, Leslie Goldstein, Carol Nackenoff, Keith Bybee, Rogers Smith, Howard Gillman, and Cornell Clayton. These folks helped me develop my ideas and made the profession a hospitable place to be, while having a lot of fun along the way.

It is exciting to see what has become of the Sexuality and Politics Section since Angie Wilson and I organized it way back when, making it only the thirty-eighth organized research section in the over hundred-year history of the American Political Science Association. Folks working on LGBTQ politics, including Erin Mayo-Adam, Zein Murib, and Ed Kammerer, are just a few of many fabulous scholars who have taken the baton and run with it.

To have two great chairs in two different departments is perhaps more than one could hope for in political science. Yet that's what I've been given. Thanks so much to Nukhet Sandal at Ohio University and Scott Hibbard at DePaul for supporting my work and offering kindness and friendship all the while.

Ilene Kalish is an amazing editor, a great reader, and a direct communicator. I so appreciate being able to work with her and all the top-notch folks at New York University Press and am so happy for this book to be a part of the excellent work that they consistently put out into the world.

I have been so fortunate to have dear friends in communities in Athens and Chicago, who have made the rest of life enjoyable while I was finishing this book, even during the toughest of times. Thanks to Melissa Sterne, Josie Raymond, Karen Sheley, Marissa Fillipo, Julie Schraith, Alicia Burns, Kelly Luchtman, Deborah Marks, and Melissa Taylor for providing friendship and meals during a particularly stressful period. Special thanks to my very dear friends Helena Silverstein, Andrea Bunch, Deb Thompson, Daniel Moak, Kirstine Taylor, Marina Baldisera Pachetti, Yoichi Ishida, Laura Black, and Ted Welser. Extra thanks to animal friends Frankie and Huck, for providing the very best models of how to live a well-balanced life.

My favorite community is always the home I've made with Kate Leeman, the best life partner ever, hands down. Let's make it rain!

NOTES

INTRODUCTION

1 I use "LGBT" when referring to the movement, and "gay," "lesbian," "bisexual," and "transgender" when referring to the specific groups that constitute it. As Zein Murib has shown, each group has its own history and interest. There is nothing natural or given about the LGBT formulation. Originally formulated as GLBT, these groups formed a working coalition in the late 1990s/early 2000s to combat growing challenges coming from the political right. See Murib, "Rethinking GLBT as a Political Category in US Politics," in *LGBTQ Politics: A Critical Reader*, ed. Marla Brettschneider, Susan Burgess, and Christine Keating (New York: New York University Press, 2017), 14–33. Since that time, it has become conventional to use the LGBTQ acronym as a shorthand when referring to the movement for the rights of these groups. While the *B* and the *T* are included in the acronym, they are often not given full consideration in either the movement or popular culture, reinforcing the lack of visibility of both groups in mainstream politics and popular culture. See B. Lee Aultman and Paisley Currah, "Politics outside the Law: Transgender Lives and the Challenge of Legibility," and Charles Anthony Smith, Shawn Schulenberg, and Eric A. Baldwin, "The 'B' Isn't Silent: Bisexual Communities and Political Activism," both in Brettschneider, Burgess, and Keating, *LGBTQ Politics*, 34–53 and 89–109. Bisexuals and trans people have often folded into the acronym, typically with little consideration. Radical political and cultural frameworks have given greater, if still often incomplete, consideration to these groups. When I discuss these more radical elements, I use the term "queer" or the acronym LGBTQ. This book aims to engage the problem of (il)legibility by exploring the intersection of mainstream and more radical political and cultural expressions, arguing that the intersection of the two has produced significant change in political order, bringing previously illegible groups and political issues into the mainstream political imagination.

2 Susan Burgess, *The Founding Fathers, Pop Culture, and Constitutional Law: Who's Your Daddy?* (New York: Ashgate, 2009), 116, n.9.

3 See, e.g., the work of political scientists Gary Mucciaroni, *Same Sex, Different Politics: Success and Failure in the Struggle over Gay Rights* (Chicago: University of Chicago Press, 2008); and Stephen Engel, *Fragmented Citizens: The Changing Landscape of Gay and Lesbian Lives* (New York: New York University Press, 2016) explored the rights and liberties that have been part and parcel of this shift,

explaining which were likely to be recognized and which were not. Legal studies scholars such as Michael Klarman have similarly discussed the doctrinal basis of LGBT rights as they were gaining recognition, cautioning that rapid change might produce backlash. See Klarman, *From the Closet to the Altar: Courts, Backlash, and the Struggle for Same-Sex Marriage* (New York: Oxford University Press, 2014).

4   Linda Hirshman, *Victory: The Triumphant Gay Revolution* (New York: Harper Collins, 2012).

5   Gary Mucciaroni, "Whither the LGBTQ Movement in a Post–Civil Rights Era," in Brettschneider, Burgess, and Keating, *LGBTQ Politics*, 525.

6   "LGBT Rights," Gallup, 2022, https://news.gallup.com.

7   Anne Norton, *95 Theses on Politics, Culture, and Method* (New Haven: Yale University Press, 2004).

8   Robert C. Lieberman, "Ideas, Institutions, and Political Order: Explaining Political Change," *American Political Science Review* 96, no. 4 (2002): 697.

9   For an excellent discussion of this problem, see Jeremiah J. Garretson, *The Path to Gay Rights: How Activism and Coming Out Changed Public Opinion* (New York: New York University Press, 2017).

10 Scholars have long posited that growing public support for LGBT rights is the result of increased numbers of people in the LGBT community coming out to their friends, families, and coworkers. See, e.g., Gershen Kaufman and Lev Raphael, *Coming Out of Shame: Transforming Gay and Lesbian Lives* (New York: Doubleday, 1996). This is a story that resonates with the queer community, as coming out has also been a central narrative of the LGBT movement at least since the Stonewall Riots. Anna Wilson, "Death and the Mainstream: Lesbian Detective Fiction and the Killing of the Coming-Out Story," *Feminist Studies* 22 (1996): 251–78.

11 Michael J. Shapiro, *Cinematic Political Thought: Narrating Race, Nation, and Gender* (New York: New York University Press, 1999), 23.

12 As David Kamp describes Paul Child's position, "essentially he was to serve as a benign propagandist for the Marshall Plan." See his fascinating book about the rise of food culture, *The United States of Arugula: The Sun-Dried, Cold-Pressed, Dark-Roasted, Extra Virgin Story of the American Food Revolution* (New York: Random House, 2006), 51.

13 In her posthumously published autobiography, Julia Child notes that the investigation of Paul came out of the USIA's Office of Security, run by a protégé of J. Edgar Hoover's named McLeod. She notes that not only did Paul laugh when asked whether he was a homosexual, but that "when they asked him to 'drop his pants,' he refused on principle. He had nothing to hide and said so. The investigators eventually gave up on him." Calling "the whole episode shockingly weird, amateurish, and unfair," she reports that Paul felt he "had proved himself a monument of innocence." Julia Child, *My Life in France* (New York: Random House, 2007).

14 Stephanie Coontz, *The Way We Never Were: American Families and the Nostalgia Trap* (New York: Basic Books, 2016), 35–36.

15 David K. Johnson, *The Lavender Scare: The Cold War Persecution of Gays and Lesbians in the Federal Government* (Chicago: University of Chicago Press, 2004), 2. This has been true not only of academic books, but also of trade books that address the issue, even those that clearly have a gay sensibility. David Kamp's history of the emergence of foodie culture mentions only that Paul was "smeared as a suspected Communist during the McCarthy era," while adding that Julia Child sometimes offered "indiscreet, eye-rolling references to the 'fairies' of the food world." Kamp notes that while such talk was not appreciated by many of the popular chefs at the time who were homosexual (such as renowned master chef James Beard and *New York Times* columnist Craig Claiborne), it did not lead Child's contemporaries to mistake "an ultraliberal" like her for a bigot. Kamp, *United States of Arugula*, 108. Indeed, it was accepted practice in the 1950s to unselfconsciously refer to gay people as fairies, perverts, and security risks, even in the national paper of record, the *New York Times*. See Susan Burgess, *The New York Times on Gay and Lesbian Issues* (Washington, DC: SAGE/CQ Press, 2011).

16 Johnson, *Lavender Scare*, 155.

17 See, e.g., Stephen Skowronek, *Building a New American State: The Expansion of National Administrative Capacities, 1877–1920* (Cambridge: Cambridge University Press, 1982); Rogers Smith, "Political Jurisprudence, 'The New Institutionalism,' and the Future of Public Law," *American Political Science Review* 82, no. 1 (1992): 89–108; Karen Orren and Stephen Skowronek, *The Search for American Political Development* (Cambridge: Cambridge University Press, 2004).

18 Lieberman, "Ideas, Institutions, and Political Order," 709.

19 See Susan Burgess and Kate Leeman, *Radical Politics in the United States* (Thousand Oaks, CA: SAGE/CQ Press, 2017); and Howard Zinn, *A People's History of the United States* (New York: Harper Collins, 1980).

20 Rogers Smith, "Ideas and the Spiral of Politics: The Place of American Political Thought in American Political Development," *American Political Thought: A Journal of Ideas, Institutions, and Culture* 3, no. 1 (2014): 130.

21 Radicals on both the political left and right are often an exception to this rule, as they have historically been more able to imagine a wider horizon of political possibilities outside the mainstream order, despite considerable state discipline compelling them not to do so. For specific examples, see, e.g., Burgess and Leeman, *Radical Politics in the United States*; and Zinn, *People's History of the United States*.

22 Outside the US context, see, e.g., *The Burning Wall: Dissent and Opposition behind the Berlin Wall* (Hava Kohav Beller, director, 2002). This fascinating documentary shows East German bureaucrats shifting from insisting that the Berlin Wall would never fall, to suggesting equally forcefully that they knew all along that the wall

would fall (but that it did not happen the way they had planned for in their role-playing exercises).

23 Lieberman, "Ideas, Institutions, and Political Order," 698.

24 For an excellent account of these developments, see, e.g., Megan Ming Francis, *Civil Rights and the Making of the Modern American State* (New York: Cambridge University Press, 2014).

25 Derrick Bell, *And We Are Not Saved: The Elusive Quest for Racial Justice* (New York: Basic Books, 1984); *Faces at the Bottom of the Well: The Permanence of Racism* (New York: Basic Books, 1992); *Gospel Choirs: Psalms of Survival in an Alien Land Called Home* (New York: Basic Books, 1997).

26 Richard Iton, *In Search of the Black Fantastic: Politics and Popular Culture in the Post–Civil Rights Era* (New York: Oxford University Press, 2008), 82.

27 For an accessible intellectual history of this debate in the early formations of critical theory and cultural studies, see Stuart Jeffries, *Grand Hotel Abyss: The Lives of the Frankfurt School* (London: Verso, 2017).

28 John Fiske, *Understanding Popular Culture* (London: Routledge, 1989), 4.

29 Paul Passavant, "'Interpretation' and the 'Empirical': Similarities between Theoretical and Empirical Political Science," *Contemporary Political Theory* 14, no. 3 (2015): 269, 264.

30 Victoria Hattam and Joseph Lowndes, "The Ground beneath Our Feet: Language, Culture, and Political Change," in *Formative Acts: American Politics in the Making*, ed. Stephen Skowronek and Matthew Glassman (Philadelphia: University of Pennsylvania Press, 2007), 204. Also see Vivien A. Schmidt, "Taking Ideas and Discourse Seriously: Explaining Change through Discursive Institutionalism as the Fourth 'New Institutionalism,'" *European Political Science Review* 2, no. 1 (2010): 1–25.

31 Judith Halberstam, as interviewed by Carolyn Dinshaw in "Theorizing Queer Temporalities: A Roundtable Discussion," *GLQ* 13, no. 2 (2007): 194.

32 Judith Butler, *Giving an Account of Oneself: A Critique of Ethical Violence* (Amsterdam: Royal Van Gorsum, 2003), 22.

33 Halberstam, in Dinshaw, "Theorizing Queer Temporalities," 194.

34 Halberstam, in Dinshaw, "Theorizing Queer Temporalities," 182.

35 Dinshaw, "Theorizing Queer Temporalities," 178.

36 Ta-Nehisi Coates, *Between the World and Me* (New York: Spiegel and Grau, 2015), 43.

37 Harry M. Benshoff and Sean Griffin, *America on Film: Representing Race, Class, and Gender at the Movies*, 2nd ed. (Oxford: Blackwell, 2009), 23.

38 Carlo Rovelli, *The Order of Time* (New York: Penguin, 2018), 73.

CHAPTER 1. FROM CRIMINAL PERVERTS TO RIGHTS-BEARING CITIZENS

1 See, e.g., Mucciaroni, *Same Sex, Different Politics*.

2 For more detailed histories of these developments, see, e.g., David A. J. Richards, *The Sodomy Cases: Bowers v. Hardwick and Lawrence v. Texas* (Lawrence:

University Press of Kansas, 2009); and Dale Carpenter, *Flagrant Conduct: The Story of Lawrence v. Texas* (New York: Norton, 2012).

3 There were surely other instances of LGBT people angrily rising up during this period, such as challenges to the arrests of both gay and straight people who were openly associating at the Ball to Benefit the Council on Homosexuality and Religion in San Francisco in 1965, and the 1966 Compton Cafeteria riots, led by transgendered people who were refused service and harassed by the police in Los Angeles. But Stonewall continues to be thought of as the genesis of the modern LGBT movement in no small part because it spawned numerous gay political groups and organized efforts such as Pride parades that increased the visibility of the LGBT community, over time creating new, more vociferous demands for equal rights and liberties regardless of gender identity and sexuality.

4 381 U.S. 479 (1965).

5 *Eisenstadt v. Baird*, 405 U.S. 438 (1972); *Roe v. Wade*, 410 U.S. 113 (1973).

6 *Carey v. Population Services*, 431 U.S. 678 (1977).

7 *Doe v. Commonwealth's Attorney of Richmond*, 424 U.S. 901 (1976).

8 478 U.S. 186 (1986).

9 Joyce Murdoch and Deb Price, *Gay Men and Lesbians v. the Supreme Court* (New York: Basic Books, 2002), 340.

10 For example, it is number two on the American Film Institute's list of the Best One Hundred Films, just behind *Citizen Kane*.

11 This is perhaps reinforced when Rick offers up *Casablanca*'s famous closing line as he and Renault walk off together into the fog, with the suggestion that they will join the Free French contingent: "I think this could be the beginning of a beautiful friendship."

12 "Top Grossing Movies of 1982," *Numbers*, n.d., www.the-numbers.com (accessed April 5, 2022).

13 As is often the case with films focused on military training, the sergeant in charge regularly berates those being trained in a variety of ways, including questioning the masculinity and sexuality of the male trainees, calling them pussies, pansies, faggots, queers, and so forth. Perhaps this toughness is compensatory for the love that drill sergeants almost inevitably seem to reveal for their favorite charges.

14 Michael Warner, *Publics and Counterpublics* (New York: Zone Books, 2005), 31.

15 Lori Marso's excellent study of gender, *Politics with Beauvoir: Freedom in the Encounter* (Durham: Duke University Press, 2017), 62–63, suggests that interdependence and community are necessary for the development of freedom.

CHAPTER 2. FROM ENEMIES OF THE STATE TO HEROES FIGHTING ON ITS BEHALF

1 See, e.g., Gary Lehring, *Officially Gay: The Political Construction of Sexuality by the US Military* (Philadelphia: Temple University Press, 2003); Mucciaroni, *Same*

Sex, Different Politics; and Carl Stychin, *Law's Desire: Sexuality and the Limits of Justice* (New York: Routledge, 1995).

2 Some of the historical material in this section is adapted from my earlier work, Burgess, *New York Times on Gay and Lesbian Issues.*

3 For more details, see, e.g., Nathaniel Frank, *Unfriendly Fire: How the Gay Ban Undermines the Military and Weakens America* (New York: Thomas Dunne, 2009).

4 See, e.g., Allan Bérubé, *Coming Out under Fire: The History of Gay Men and Women in World War II* (Chapel Hill: University of North Carolina Press, 2010).

5 See Margot Canaday, *The Straight State: Sexuality and Citizenship in Twentieth-Century America* (Princeton: Princeton University Press, 2009), 145, 150.

6 For a detailed account, see, e.g., Johnson, *Lavender Scare.*

7 For a detailed account of these transitional developments, see, e.g., Marc Wolinsky and Kenneth Sherrill, eds., *Gays and the Military: Joseph Steffan versus the United States* (Princeton: Princeton University Press, 1994).

8 *Watkins v. U.S. Army*, 875 F. 2d 699 (1989).

9 See, e.g., Margaret Marshment, "The Picture Is Political: Representation of Women in Contemporary Popular Culture," in *Introducing Women's Studies: Feminist Theory and Practice*, ed. Diane Richardson and Victoria Robinson (London: Palgrave, 1997), 125–51.

10 Jennifer M. Wood, "10 Highest-Grossing Movies of All Time," *Mental Floss*, March 18, 2019, www.mentalfloss.com. Bond follows the Marvel, Star Wars, and Harry Potter film series.

11 James Chapman, "The James Bond Film Series: Conditions of Production," in *The James Bond Phenomenon: A Critical Reader*, 2nd ed., ed. Christoph Lindner (New York: Palgrave Macmillan, 2009), 91.

12 Chapman, "James Bond Film Series," 65.

13 Ian Fleming created and developed the Bond character in twelve novels and two short story collections, beginning with *Casino Royale* in 1953. All twelve were later adapted into highly successful feature-length films.

14 Christopher Lawton, "Shaken, Not Stirred, but No Longer Smirnoff: James Bond Has Switched His Favorite Brand of Vodka," *Wall Street Journal*, September 18, 2002.

15 Craig N. Owens, "The Bond Market," in *Ian Fleming and the Cultural Politics of James Bond*, ed. Edward P. Comentale, Stephen Wall, and Skip William (Bloomington: Indiana University Press, 2005), 107.

16 Simon Winder, *The Man Who Saved Britain: A Journey into the Disturbing World of James Bond* (New York: Farrar, Straus and Giroux, 2006); Benjamin Svetkey, "50 Years of Bond," *Entertainment Weekly*, August 10, 2012, 28–31.

17 Claire Hines, "'Entertainment for Men': Uncovering the Playboy Bond," in Lindner, *James Bond Phenomenon*, 89.

18 Robert Eberwein, *Armed Forces: Gender and Sexuality in War Movies* (New Brunswick: Rutgers University Press, 2010).

19 The arguably most important critical reader on the Bond series includes only two pieces that address sexuality. Lindner, *James Bond Phenomenon.*

20 See, e.g., Judith Butler, *Gender Trouble: Feminism and the Subversion of Identity* (New York: Routledge, 1990); and Eve Sedgwick, *Epistemology of the Closet* (Berkeley: University of California Press, 1991).

21 John Cork and Bruce Scivally, *James Bond: The Legacy* (New York: Abrams, 2002).

22 Aljean Harmetz, "Sean Connery, Who Embodied James Bond and More, Dies at 90," *New York Times*, November 1, 2020.

23 See, e.g., Jeremy Black, *The Politics of James Bond: From Fleming's Novels to the Big Screen* (Lincoln, NE: Bison Books, 2005), 106.

24 Black, *Politics of James Bond*, 107.

25 Vito Russo, *The Celluloid Closet: Homosexuality in the Movies* (New York: Harper and Row, 1981). See, e.g., *Our Man in Havana* (1959), based on the Graham Greene novel of the same name.

26 In its time, *Goldfinger* was the fastest-grossing film ever. The "Making of Goldfinger" short in the special features of the DVD version claims that this is the first time a laser was used in the plot of a major motion picture.

27 Jack Halberstam references this shift in Bond briefly in their pathbreaking book *Female Masculinity* (Durham: Duke University Press, 1998), noting, "It is M who convinces us that sexism and misogyny are not necessarily part and parcel of masculinity, even though historically it has become difficult, if not impossible, to untangle masculinity from the oppression of women" (4).

28 *Casino Royale* was the first novel in Ian Fleming's James Bond series.

29 "Craig Wants Gay Bond Scene," *Contact Music*, November 29, 2006, www.contactmusic.com.

30 J. R. Jones, "The Bi Who Loved Me," *Reader*, November 15, 2012.

31 "The Bullseye," *Entertainment Weekly*, November 23, 2012.

32 A. O. Scott, "*No Time to Die* Review: His Word Is Bond," *New York Times*, September 29, 2021.

33 Anthony Lane, "One for the Road," *New Yorker*, October 18, 2021.

34 Karen McVeigh, "Pentagon Reports 3,553 Assault Complaints between October and June as Congress Considers Range of Measures to Help Victims," *Guardian*, November 7, 2013. This piece reports an increase of 46 percent over the previous year.

35 Barbara Smith, "Where's the Revolution?," *Nation*, January 1, 1998; Tommi Avicolli Mecca, ed., *Smash the Church, Smash the State: The Early Years of Gay Liberation* (San Francisco: City Lights Books, 2009).

36 See, e.g., Dean Spade, *Normal Life: Administrative Violence, Critical Trans Politics, and the Limits of Law* (Boston: South End, 2011); and Ryan Conrad, ed., *Against*

Equality: Don't Ask to Fight Their Wars (Lewiston, ME: Against Equality Collective, 2011).

37 See, e.g., Keally McBride, *Collective Dreams: Political Imagination and Community* (University Park: Pennsylvania State University Press, 2005).

CHAPTER 3. FROM DANGEROUS PEDOPHILES TO RESPECTABLE PARENTS

1 Julie Novkov and Carol Nackenoff, eds., *Stating the Family* (Lawrence: University Press of Kansas, 2020).

2 As we have seen throughout this book, popular culture embeds memories into the public imagination, sometimes in a somewhat distorted manner. For example, the last known painting of a live dodo bird was made in 1638 and the last scientifically accepted sighting took place in the late seventeenth century. Jennifer Frazer, "Pirates, Charles Darwin, and One Very Un-Extinct Dodo," *Artful Amoeba* (blog), *Scientific American*, May 22, 2013, https://blogs.scientificamerican.com. However, the dodo's extinction went largely unnoticed until 1865, when Lewis Carroll caricatured a dodo in *Alice in Wonderland*. From that point forward, the dodo became a popular reference point for both extinction and dim-wittedness. Similarly, our memory of the nuclear family is dying hard even though it is no longer the dominant model and by most accounts is certainly endangered, if not yet completely extinct. In 2014 a Pew Research Center poll found that 46 percent, or fewer than half of children, were being raised in traditional nuclear families, meaning by two parents in their first marriage. This significant decrease from 73 percent in 1960 and 61 percent in 1980 is part of a longer process of the transformation of the family that some scholars have traced back to the beginning of European settlement in North America. See, e.g., John D'Emilio, *Sexual Politics, Sexual Communities*, 2nd ed. (Chicago: University of Chicago Press, 1998); and Coontz, *The Way We Never Were*.

3 Coontz, *The Way We Never Were*, 22.

4 Irwyn Applebaum, *The World according to Beaver: The Official Leave It to Beaver Book* (New York: Harper Collins, 1998).

5 Roger Ebert, review of *Leave It to Beaver*, August 22, 1997, www.rogerebert.com.

6 Melissa and Melissa, "June Cleaver Style," n.d., www.pinterest.com/paleocon-missy/june-cleaver-style (accessed April 8, 2022); "June's Dresses in *Leave It to Beaver*," *Solid Moonlight* (blog), May 23, 2015, http://solidmoonlight.blogspot.com. On Etsy, see results for search term "June Cleaver dress," www.etsy.com (accessed April 8, 2022).

7 Michael De Sapio, "The Moral Imagination of *Leave It to Beaver*," *Imaginative Conservative*, October 12, 2017, https://theimaginativeconservative.org.

8 Deborah Werksman, ed., *I Killed June Cleaver: Modern Moms Shatter the Myth of Perfect Parenting* (Naperville, IL: Hysteria Publishing, 1999).

9 This set was later used to stage another popular television show focused on domestic life, *Desperate Housewives*, which ran from 2004 to 2012, a series with a more critical take on the promise and perils of domestic life.

10 Tony Dow (who played Wally in the series) has said, "If any line got too much of a laugh, they'd take it out. They didn't want a big laugh; they wanted chuckles." "16 Gee Whiz Facts about *Leave It to Beaver*," MeTV, December 7, 2016, www.metv.com.

11 Barbara Billingsley has said that the reason she wore pearls was that she had a "hollow" in her neck that she wanted to conceal. Barbara Billingsley, interview, July 14, 2000, Archive of American Television, https://youtu.be/E4j1dGrdo4E. The *Leave It to Beaver* feature film suggests that June believes the pearls are a turn-on for Ward.

12 Season 1, episode 3, "The Black Eye."

13 Season 1, episode 11, "Beaver's Short Pants."

14 Season 2, episode 31, "Beaver's Sweater."

15 Season 3, episode 37, "Wally's Play."

16 Season 5, episode 8, "Wally's Big Date."

17 Season 5, episode 12, "Wally's Chauffeur."

18 Season 2, episode 8, "The Shave."

19 Season 2, episode 34, "Wally's Haircomb."

20 Season 3, episode 23, "School Sweater"; season 4, episode 29, "Wally's Dream Girl"; season 5, episode 33, "Tennis Anyone?"

21 Season 3, episode 23, "School Sweater."

22 Season 3, episode 32, "Beaver and Violet."

23 Season 4, episode 24, "The Dramatic Club."

24 Season 5, episode 13, "Beaver's First Date."

25 Season 6, episode 32, "Don Juan Beaver."

26 Season 6, episode 37, "Beaver Sees America."

27 Season 1, episode 7, "Water, Anyone?"

28 Season 1, episode 12, "The Perfume Salesmen."

29 Season 4, episode 35, "Beaver's Frogs."

30 Season 4, episode 16, "Ward's Millions."

31 Season 5, episode 38, "Stocks and Bonds."

32 Season 6, episode 9, "Beaver Joins a Record Club."

33 Season 1, episode 1, "Beaver Gets 'Spelled.'"

34 Season 1, episode 24, "The State v. Beaver."

35 Season 3, episode 28, "Ward's Baseball."

36 Tison Pugh, *The Queer Fantasies of the American Family Sitcom* (New Brunswick: Rutgers University Press, 2018), 32.

37 Joanne Meyerowitz, ed., *Not June Cleaver: Women and Gender in Postwar America, 1945–1960* (Philadelphia: Temple University Press, 1984).

38 True to form, Wally and Beaver forge a letter for Beaver to share with his class that highlights made-up exploits. Ward eventually sets the record straight and says that he is happy that Beaver wants to see him as a hero, but that he did the good where he could. Season 2, episode 28, "Beaver's Hero."

39 See, e.g., Cristina Beltrán, *The Trouble with Unity: Latino Politics and the Creation of Identity* (Oxford: Oxford University Press, 2010).

40 Season 4, episode 2, "Beaver's House Guest."

41 Season 6, episode 17, "The Parking Attendants."

42 Season 2, episode 15, "The Grass Is Always Greener."

43 Season 3, episode 20, "Beaver and Andy."

44 Season 6, episode 19, "Beaver's Good Deed."

45 Season 2, episode 4, "Beaver and Chuey."

46 Burgess and Leeman, *Radical Politics*, chap. 6.

47 Season 3, episode 22, "Larry's Club."

48 Season 3, episode 24, "The Hypnotist."

49 Season 4, episode 23, "Mother's Helper."

50 Burgess, *New York Times on Gay and Lesbian Issues*, introduction.

51 Season 2, episode 23, "The Haunted House."

52 Coontz, *The Way We Never Were*, 35–36.

53 See, e.g., Burgess, *New York Times on Gay and Lesbian Issues*, chap. 3.

54 Gina Bellafante, "The Series That Shows Its Age," *New York Times*, August 20, 2009.

55 See Susan Faludi, *Backlash: The Undeclared War against American Women* (New York: Crown, 1991), 174.

56 Robert Thompson, *Television's Second Golden Age* (Syracuse: Syracuse University Press, 1997), 131.

57 Carolyn Hendler and Scott Ryan, *thirtysomething* podcast series, www.scottryan-productions.com; Scott Ryan, *Thirtysomething at Thirty: An Oral History* (Albany, GA: Bear Manor Media, 2017); Noel Murray, "6 Classic TV Series Left Out of the Streaming Boom," *New York Times*, November 19, 2019.

58 Nellie Andreeva, "*Thirtysomething*: ABC Picks Up Sequel Series Pilot with Original Cast from Marshall Herskovitz & Ed Zwick," *Deadline*, January 8, 2020, https://deadline.com. Production has been delayed due to the outbreak of COVID-19.

59 Season 1, episode 16, "Accounts Receivable."

60 Season 1, episode 8, "Weaning."

61 Season 1, episode 18, "Nancy's First Date."

62 Season 4, episode 6, "Guilty Party."

63 Season 1, episode 11, "Therapy."

64 Season 1, episode 17, "Whose Forest Is This?"

65 Season 3, episode 1, "Nancy's Mom."

66 Season 2, episode 10, "Elliot's Dad."

67 Season 2, episode 16, "Courting Nancy."

68 Season 3, episode 7, "Pilgrims."

69 Season 3, episode 12, "Another Country."

70 Season 1, episode 10, "South by Southeast."

71 Season 2, episode 17, "Best of Enemies."

72 Season 2, episode 6, "Politics."

73 Season 2, episode 9, "About Last Night."
74 Season 1, episode 20, "Tenure."
75 Season 3, episode 9, "New Parents."
76 Season 4, episode 4, "Distance."
77 Season 4, episode 14, "Second Look."
78 Season 4, episode 15, "Fighting the Cold."
79 Season 2, episode 13, "Michael Writes a Story."
80 Season 2, episode 14, "New Job."
81 Season 2, episode 17, "Best of Enemies."
82 Season 3, episode 5, "The Legacy."
83 Season 4, episode 20, "Hopeless."
84 Season 3, episode 22, "Going Limp."
85 Season 3, episode 24, "Samurai Adman."
86 Season 4, episode 3, "Control." Ellyn likens this to dating Donald Trump.
87 Season 4, episode 18, "Closing the Circle."
88 Season 4, episode 21, "A Stop at Willoughby."
89 Season 1, episode 2, "The Parents Are Coming."
90 Season 2, episode 1, "We'll Meet Again."
91 Season 2, episode 3, "The Mike Van Dyke Show."
92 Season 1, episode 4, "Couples."
93 Season 3, episode 6, "Strangers."
94 Season 2, episode 2, "Love and Sex."
95 Season 1, episode 1, "Pilot."
96 Season 1, episode 19, "Undone."
97 Season 3, episode 19, "Three Year Itch."
98 Season 3, episode 21, "Arizona."
99 Season 4, episode 8, "Never Better."
100 Season 4, episode 12, "Advanced Beginners."
101 Season 1, episode 9, "I'll Be Home for Christmas."
102 Season 2, episode 13, "Michael Writes a Story."
103 Season 2, episode 4, "Trust Me."
104 See "Did the Supreme Court Come Out in *Bush v. Gore*?," *differences* 16, no. 1 (2005): 163.
105 Season 3, episode 6, "Strangers."
106 Season 4, episode 10, "Happy New Year."
107 Season 4, episode 18, "Closing the Circle," written by well-known gay author and activist Paul Monette.
108 Season 3, episode 15, "Fathers and Mothers."
109 Matt Brennan, "How *The Americans* Became the Best Show on Television," *Paste*, March 24, 2017, www.pastemagazine.com; Daniel D'Addario and Caroline Framke, "The Best TV Shows of 2019," *Variety*, https://variety.com; David Bianculli, *The Platinum Age of Television* (New York: Anchor, 2016).

110 Season 3, episode 12, "I Am Abassin Zadran."

111 Season 4, episode 7, "Travel Agents."

112 Season 6, episode 5, "The Great Patriotic War."

113 See, e.g., Elizabeth Wingrove, *Rousseau's Republican Romance* (Princeton: Princeton University Press, 2000).

114 Season 4, episode 1, "Glanders."

115 Season 1, episode 1, "Pilot."

116 Season 1, episode 7, "Duty and Honor."

117 Season 1, episode 8, "Mutually Assured Destruction."

118 Season 1, episode 1, "Pilot."

119 Season 1, episode 11, "Covert War."

120 Season 1, episode 1, "Pilot."

121 Season 2, episode 7, "ARPANET."

122 Season 1, episode 1, "Pilot."

123 Season 1, episode 5, "Comint."

124 Season 6, episode 4, "Mr. and Mrs. Teacup."

125 Season 1, episode 1, "Pilot."

126 Season 2, episode 7, "New Car."

127 Season 1, episode 6, "Trust Me."

128 Season 3, episode 3, "Open House."

129 Season 3, episode 12, "I Am Abassin Zadran."

130 Season 1, episode 8, "Mutually Assured Destruction."

131 Matt Zoller Seitz, "*The Americans* Recap: No Future in His Sleep Tonight," *Vulture*, April 11, 2013, www.vulture.com.

132 See, e.g., Vivian Gornick, *The Romance of Communism* (New York: Verso, 2020); and Burgess and Leeman, *Radical Politics in the United States*, chap. 2.

133 Season 1, episode 3, "Gregory."

134 Season 1, episode 3, "Gregory."

135 Season 1, episode 3, "Gregory."

136 Season 1, episode 10, "Only You."

137 Season 4, episode 11, "Dinner for Seven."

138 Season 4, episode 9, "The Day After."

139 Season 2, episode 1, "Comrades."

140 Season 2, episode 13, "Echo."

141 Season 2, episode 13, "Echo."

142 Season 3, episode 2, "Baggage"; season 6, episode 4, "Mr. and Mrs. Teacup."

143 Season 3, episode 2, "Baggage."

144 Season 3, episode 4, "Dimebag."

145 Season 2, episode 12, "Operation Chronicle."

146 Season 3, episode 6, "Born Again."

147 Season 3, episode 7, "Walter Taffet."

148 Season 5, episode 6, "Crossbreed."

149 Season 4, episode 2, "Pastor Tim."
150 Season 5, episode 10, "Darkroom."
151 Season 6, episode 2, "Tchaikovsky."
152 Season 6, episode 5, "The Great Patriotic War."
153 Season 6, episode 9, "Jennings, Elizabeth."
154 Daniel D'Addario, "*The Americans* Series Finale," *Variety*, May 30, 2018, https://variety.com.

CONCLUSION

1 Renee Romano and Claire Bond Potter, eds., *Historians on Hamilton: How a Blockbuster Musical Is Restaging America's Past* (New Brunswick: Rutgers University Press, 2018), 1.
2 Michael Paulson, "A New Kind of *Hamilton* Show, This Time on Lake Michigan," *New York Times*, April 29, 2019.
3 Lin-Manuel Miranda and Jeremy McCarter, *Hamilton: The Revolution* (New York: Grand Central Publishing, 2016).
4 Romano and Potter, *Historians on Hamilton*, 5.
5 For an interesting discussion of how a specific cultural product can circulate widely, see Alisa Solomon, *A Cultural History of Fiddler on the Roof* (New York: Picador, 2013).
6 Lyra D. Monteiro, "Race-Conscious Casting and the Erasure of the Black Past in *Hamilton*," in Romano and Potter, *Historians on Hamilton*, 68.
7 See, e.g., Marshment, "The Picture Is Political."
8 Judith Halberstam, "Imagined Violence/Queer Violence: Representation, Rage, and Resistance," *Social Text* 37 (Winter 1993): 191.
9 Marshment, "The Picture Is Political," 125.
10 Leslie M. Harris, "The Greatest City in the World? Slavery in New York in the Age of Hamilton," in Romano and Potter, *Historians on Hamilton*, 80.
11 See, e.g., Harris, "Greatest City in the World?"; and Monteiro, "Race-Conscious Casting."
12 Miranda and McCarter, *Hamilton: The Revolution*, 281.
13 For a detailed discussion of this fervor, see Claire Bond Potter, "'Safe in the Nation We've Made': Staging *Hamilton* on Social Media," in Romano and Potter, *Historians on Hamilton*, 337.
14 Harris, "Greatest City in the World?," 73.
15 For more on these developments and their effects on US politics, see Burgess and Leeman, *Radical Politics in the United States*.
16 See Derrick Bell, "The Chronicle of the Constitutional Contradiction," chap. 1 in *And We Are Not Saved*.
17 Monteiro, "Race-Conscious Casting," 67.
18 See Susan Burgess, "YouTube on Masculinity and the Founding Fathers: Constitutionalism 2.0," *Political Research Quarterly* 64, no. 1 (2009): 120–31.

19 Catherine Allgor, "Remember . . . I'm Your Man: Masculinity, Marriage, and Gender in *Hamilton*," in Romano and Potter, *Historians on Hamilton*, 98.

20 Allgor, "Remember . . . I'm Your Man," 96.

21 See, e.g., Burgess, *Founding Fathers*.

22 Potter, "'Safe in the Nation We've Made,'" 345.

23 Eve Sedgwick, *Between Men: English Literature and Male Homosocial Desire* (New York: Columbia University Press, 1985).

24 Allgor, "Remember . . . I'm Your Man," 112.

25 Miranda and McCarter, *Hamilton: The Revolution*, 281.

26 Of course, the full story is more complicated than that. For example, England's archrival, France, supplied much-needed resources that ultimately enabled the Americans to successfully blockade harbors near the end of the war.

27 See, e.g., Burgess, *New York Times on Gay and Lesbian Issues*, chap. 1.

28 For a more detailed discussion of how these exclusions have played out, see, e.g., Erin Mayo-Adam, *Queer Alliances: How Power Shapes Political Movement Formation* (Stanford: Stanford University Press, 2020); and Aultman and Currah, "Politics outside the Law."

29 *Stonewall: Profiles of Pride*, YouTube, June 9, 2013, https://www.youtube.com/watch?v=2nFxpQG7nBQ&list=PLhGNG8snqou3hvaafxWeC9HFeZnPgVQto&index=2.

30 Wingrove, *Rousseau's Republican Romance*.

31 Sharon O'Brien, *American Indian Tribal Governments* (Norman: University of Oklahoma Press, 1989), 292.

32 Robert Cover, "Violence and the Word," *Yale Law Journal* 95, no. 8 (1986): 1601.

33 Halberstam, "Imagined Violence/Queer Violence," 192.

34 Halberstam, "Imagined Violence/Queer Violence," 199.

35 Halberstam, "Imagined Violence/Queer Violence," 199.

36 Halberstam, "Imagined Violence/Queer Violence," 199.

37 Hattam and Lowndes, "Ground beneath Our Feet," 204.

38 See, e.g., Victor LaValle and John Joseph Adams, eds., *A People's Future of the United States: Speculative Fiction from 25 Extraordinary Writers* (New York: Random House, 2019).

INDEX

ABOUT THE AUTHOR

Susan Burgess is Distinguished Professor Emerita of Political Science at Ohio University, a Senior Professional Lecturer at DePaul University, and author or co-editor of five other books, including *LGBTQ Politics: A Critical Reader* and *Radical Politics in the United States*.

Lightning Source UK Ltd.
Milton Keynes UK
UKHW012118190123
415643UK00001B/7